QUEERING VOCAL PEDAGOGY

QUEERING VOCAL PEDAGOGY

A Handbook for Teaching Trans and Genderqueer Singers and Fostering Gender-Affirming Spaces

William Sauerland

Rowman & Littlefield
Lanham • Boulder • New York • London

Published by Rowman & Littlefield
An imprint of The Rowman & Littlefield Publishing Group, Inc.
4501 Forbes Boulevard, Suite 200, Lanham, Maryland 20706
www.rowman.com

86-90 Paul Street, London EC2A 4NE

Copyright © 2022 by The Rowman & Littlefield Publishing Group, Inc.

All rights reserved. No part of this book may be reproduced in any form or by any electronic or mechanical means, including information storage and retrieval systems, without written permission from the publisher, except by a reviewer who may quote passages in a review.

British Library Cataloguing in Publication Information Available

Library of Congress Cataloging-in-Publication Data

Names: Sauerland, William, 1982- author.
Title: Queering vocal pedagogy : a handbook for teaching trans and genderqueer singers and fostering gender-affirming spaces / William Sauerland.
Description: Lanham : Rowman & Littlefield Publishers, 2022. | Includes bibliographical references and index.
Identifiers: LCCN 2022001219 (print) | LCCN 2022001220 (ebook) | ISBN 9781538166666 (cloth) | ISBN 9781538166673 (paperback) | ISBN 9781538166680 (epub)
Subjects: LCSH: Singing—Instruction and study. | Transgender singers.
Classification: LCC MT820 .S23 2022 (print) | LCC MT820 (ebook) | DDC 783/.0430867—dc23
LC record available at https://lccn.loc.gov/2022001219
LC ebook record available at https://lccn.loc.gov/2022001220

"Remember this, whoever you are, however you are, you are equally valid, equally justified, and equally beautiful."

—Juno Dawson,
The Gender Games: The Problems with Men and Women, From Someone Who Has Been Both

Contents

Acknowledgments	ix
List of Figures and Tables	xi
Preface	xv
1 Understanding Gender in Teaching and Learning	1
2 Shifting Perspective: Theoretical Framework and Methodology	39
3 Trans Feminine Singers	59
4 Trans Masculine Singers	101
5 Trans-Nonbinary Singers	145
6 Pedagogical Considerations for Gender-Affirming Vocal Music Education	185
7 Queering as a Teacher's Habit of Mind	227
Appendix 1 Glossary of LGBTQ+ Terms	237

Appendix 2	Short List of Songs Written for TGQ Singers or by TGQ Composers	247
Appendix 3	Musicals and Opera Featuring Gender-Expansive Characters	253
Appendix 4	Gender-Neutral Performance Attire Guidelines	259
Appendix 5	Sample Affirmation Policy Statement for Studio Teachers and Choral Directors	261
Appendix 6	Additional Resources	263
Selected Bibliography		267
Index		277
About the Author		281

Acknowledgments

Writing this manuscript has been a joyful, humbling, and deeply reflective process, supported by a large group of friends, mentors, scholars, and colleagues. I am immensely grateful to everyone who has provided feedback and guidance in the shaping and writing of *Queering Vocal Pedagogy*.

For your discussions and counsel that helped craft this book, my sincerest thanks: Dr. Harold Abeles, Brandon Adams, Dr. Cara Bernard, Dr. Jeanne Goffi-Fynn, Dr. Freya Jarman-Ivens, Dr. George Nicholson, Dr. Joshua Palkki, and Reuben Zellman.

For your incredible insight, perspective, and expertise, without which this book would not have been possible: Eli Conley, Peter Fullerton, Nicole Lumetta, Daniel Paulson, Ruth Raneiro, and Martha Rodríguez-Salazar.

For your knowledge, bravery, and incredibly influential narratives, which serve as the heart and soul of this book: B, Chrys, Emmett, Forest, Isabella, and Kelly.

For your scholarly support throughout the writing of this book: my colleagues and students at the Purdue University Fort Wayne School of Music, the Center for the Enhancement of Learning and Teaching, and from the Q Center, Jordan Sanderson and Vic Spencer.

For your enormously valuable feedback and direction throughout the granular and broader writing process: Elisabeth Eliassen and Michael Li.

For your immense support and love over many years, my biological and logical family: Tom Nelson (my husband), Rick and Peggy Sauerland (my parents), Dr. Nadia Dawisha, Dr. Nicole Hanig, Audrey Luna, Paul McCurdy, Kristen Murney, and Lynsie Stout.

List of Figures and Tables

List of Figures

Figure 1.1.	The Gender Unicorn illustrates the differences between gender identity, expression, sex assigned at birth, and physical and emotional attraction	9
Figure 1.2.	Conceptual Framework: From Theory to Studio	13
Figure 3.1.	The Main Parts of the Larynx (Supraglottis, Glottis, and Subglottis) and Other Nearby Structures	61
Figure 3.2.	Vocal ranges for traditional "female" voices	63
Figure 3.3.	Five-tone descending scale on vowels	79
Figure 3.4.	Five-tone ascending and descending scale on [jo]	79
Figure 3.5.	Descending arpeggio on [fa]	80
Figure 3.6.	Ascending octave and descending major arpeggio on "I know"	80
Figure 3.7.	(Si)ng—[i] on a three-tone scale	81

xii / List of Figures and Tables

Figure 3.8.	Five-tone descending tone with a slide on a fifth	81
Figure 3.9.	Octave arpeggio on triplets	91
Figure 3.10.	Descending thirds on [vi] and [vo] with a fast five-tone scale	92
Figure 3.11.	Measure 26 of "El Paño Moruno"	93
Figure 3.12.	Excerpt from "Voi, che sapete"	94
Figure 4.1.	Vocal ranges for traditional "male" voices	103
Figure 4.2.	Vocal slide 1 on a fifth for balanced onset and breath release	120
Figure 4.3.	Vocal slide 2 on a fourth and octave for balanced onset and breath release	120
Figure 4.4.	Exercise [ziŋa] for breath release and flexibility	121
Figure 4.5.	Exercise [nɛomi] for resonance and released jaw and tongue	122
Figure 4.6.	Stacked minor 3rds, version 1, for rounded lips and forward resonance	135
Figure 4.7.	Stacked minor 3rds, version 2, for rounded lips and forward resonance	135
Figure 4.8.	Stacked minor 3rds, version 3, for forward resonance and lifted soft palate	135
Figure 4.9.	Pentatonic scale, version 1, for range development and smooth tongue movement	136
Figure 4.10.	Pentatonic scale, version 2, for range development and breath control	137
Figure 5.1.	Two-note pairs over a tenth for stretching upper range	162
Figure 5.2.	Perfect fifth skips on half notes for stretching upper range	162
Figure 5.3.	Triad arpeggio for upper extension and balanced onset	163

Figure 5.4.	Descending fifth slides to release subglottal pressure	164
Figure 5.5.	Excerpt of "My Petersburg" from the musical *Anastasia*	165
Figure 5.6.	Rolled [r] on five-tone scale in middle-low range	177
Figure 5.7.	Octave arpeggio on different vowels for registration management	178
Figure 5.8.	Five-tone scale on [u] for upper range development	178
Figure 5.9.	Octave glide on [ŋ] in lower range for aligning lower and upper range	179
Figure 5.10.	Staccato arpeggios for balanced onset and registration alignment	179
Figure 5.11.	Descending perfect fifth glide and scale for register alignment	180
Figure 6.1.	Five considerations for gender affirming vocal music education	187
Figure 6.2.	Gender-neutral language	193
Figure 6.3.	Factors of student song selection	195

List of Tables

Table 1.1.	Important Vocabulary	4
Table 2.1.	Participant Overview	50
Table Appendix 2.	Songs Written for TGQ Singers or by TGQ Composers	247

Preface

Locating Myself

> "These walls were not meant to shut out problems. You have to face them. You have to live the life you were born to live."
>
> —Mother Abbess, *The Sound of Music*

The purpose of *Queering Vocal Pedagogy* is to explore the experiences and perspectives of trans(gender) and genderqueer singers taking one-on-one singing lessons. I examine the specific practices and pedagogies of their singing teachers to provide insight within the applied studio. Based on a multicase study representing various identities within the gender-expansive population, this book is organized around the singers. The experiences of six students and their singing teachers will provide readers an insider's view of their vocal training to understand lesson pacing, vocal exercises, repertoire, and process toward vocal development.

The application of queer theory on vocal pedagogy is to provide a framework for investigating the craft of teaching trans and genderqueer singers. Queer theory creates a greater awareness of LGBTQ+ singers and inspires an iterative practice of inquiry (*in-queer-y*) into the core of vocal pedagogy. This book will offer an alternative to the long-standing tradition of the master-apprentice teaching model, which might be effective for many vocal students but not beneficial for all. I posit that a queer application of vocal pedagogy heightens a student's agency and autonomy, whether they are LGBTQ+ or not.

As will be discussed in more detail later, queer theory (a term coined in the 1990s by Teresa de Lauretis) brings attention to minoritized and marginalized narratives in academic studies, such as the experiences of LGBTQ+ individuals. Music educator and researcher Freya Jarman-Ivens, whose writings and ongoing friendship are hugely influential on me, asserts that **queering** is an "open-ended practice"[1] of reexamining and dismantling normativity, power, and privilege. Thus, queering vocal pedagogy is a twofold action: creating space for trans and genderqueer singers within the discipline of vocal pedagogy and disentangling vocal pedagogy from normative practices and traditions that heretofore have promoted cisgender narratives.

Some of our major vocal pedagogy texts offer valuable information in the teaching of singers from a generalized perspective. Books that focus on a specific voice type provide respected information pertinent to a large swath of singers who sing in that same range or *Fach*. As a lifelong student of vocal pedagogy, I am increasingly interested in singers and voices who fall outside the normative voice categories. I am also attentive to the nature and climate of the applied studio—that is, the interactions, practices, and rapport between student and teacher that promote vocal development, artistic expression, and self-expression. *Queering Vocal Pedagogy* is the intersection of this curiosity, in which we will explore the experiences of specific singers to expand our notions of voices through an investigatory lens from within the applied studio.

I hope *Queering Vocal Pedagogy* will be of value to singers and vocal music educators who are interested in learning about gender-expansive musicians. The experiences and perspectives within this book, provided by the research participants, are not generalizable to all trans and genderqueer individuals. I do not intend to provide a summation of teaching "the trans voice." Instead, I explore vocal pedagogy as germane to the individual perspectives of the singer participants and their teachers. This book aims to continue the pedagogical discourse on teaching gender-diverse singers and to reconsider vocal pedagogy through queer theory, not only for trans and genderqueer singers but for all students, singing in various styles and genres.

As central to the framing of this book, one's sense of self is the intersection of their identity, history (herstory?/theirstory?), and sociocultural experiences. Although this book is not autoethnographic, I think it is important for the reader to know something about my background, identity, biases, and lenses. This writing emerges from my personal and professional spheres as a gay, genderqueer music educator, researcher, and vocal pedagogue (pronouns: he/him/his and they/them/theirs).

Like other children throughout the United States, I spent many summer hours at the baseball fields of a small town. I was coerced by my parents to participate, but my fond memories are of attending my older sister's games. I could buy six gummy worms for 25 cents and play "house" under the bleachers. One summer—I was probably seven or eight years old—I came up to the bleachers where my mother was sitting with a neighbor. As I climbed the benches, this neighbor said to me, "My, what a big boy you are!" I guffawed dramatically! She immediately apologized, calling me instead "a nice young man." Walking away from her, I was stunned and confused. She was apologetic for thinking her offense was in calling me a boy instead of a man, when actually it was because she didn't call me a girl. A recurring epiphany struck again: I was not a girl like my mother or sister. I was, at least outwardly and anatomically, male. I was only beginning to grasp the cultural expectations placed upon me because of my body.

In looking back on my childhood, my sense of gender was always much more closely aligned with my mother and grandmothers. I loved playing with my mother's dolls and dressing up in her clothes, especially old bridesmaids' gowns and tulle. I adored the rainbow-like colors of lipstick my grandmother kept in her bathroom drawer and the smell of her perfumes. From a very early age, I was obsessed with musical theatre, Judy Garland, and Barbra Streisand. The movie soundtracks of *The Sound of Music* and *The Wizard of Oz* were among my very favorite. All my friends in school and extracurricular activities, like 4-H, were female. Now as a middle-aged adult, my perceptions today tell me that clothes, musical interests, and friends are less central to defining gender, but in the 1980s and 1990s in middle America, it seemed that our attire, hairstyle, and hobbies dictated not only gender but access to opportunities, social groupings, and popularity. Much in our lives was determined by societally defined gender roles; to be outside the norm was unacceptable.

In fifth grade, I joined the school band, finding a new joyful activity in learning to play the trumpet. Two years later, against my parents' advice, I forewent a study hall to join choir. The choral teacher quickly helped me find my singing voice, which naturally extended to the highest notes of Julie Andrews, and within a few months, I was performing the role of Amahl (in Menotti's *Amahl and the Night Visitors*) with a local professional opera company. My life was transformed. I went from being a farm kid with little drive (and a lot of confusion in my personal self-concept) to having an identity as a musician—an operatic ("boy") soprano! Singing was the entrance to a world of art and music (and artful and musical people) previously unknown to me, redirecting my future, my identity, and my purpose in life.

Within a few years, I gained many more stage experiences, from *Die Zauberflöte* (First Spirit) and *Tosca* (Shepherd Boy) to *The Secret Garden* (Colin) and other professional and amateur productions. My sense of self was wholly defined by my identity as a singer—and not just a singer, but a soprano. When my voice began to change at around sixteen years old, I was initially devastated, thinking my treble days were forever over. Those were dark days as my identity was slipping away from me without my control. I was very fortunate that early in this vocal transition I could easily sing in falsetto, which helped sustain my self-worth within the identity that was aligned with my vocal range. I sang my last performance as Amahl just two months short of my eighteenth birthday.

In a high school of fewer than four hundred students total, I had developed a reputation as abnormal and unusual, and I was not liked by many students. Words like "fag," "sissy," and "queer" were spat at me so frequently that teachers and administration struggled to mitigate the bullying. I do not remember when I learned these words, but the first time I remember someone calling me a "fag" was in fourth grade. There was a substitute teacher in our classroom, and we were supposed to be working silently. A boy sitting nearby looked at me and said "fag" just loudly enough that only I could hear him. When I tried to rebuff, the teacher heard me, and as punishment I had to put my nose in a chalk circle she had drawn on the board. In middle school, I mostly avoided recess to circumvent the browbeating of students. In high school, threats of physical violence were so frequent that I developed the habit of walking quickly with my head down—something an Alexander Technique teacher helped me unlearn years later. On my last day of high school, as I was walking in the graduation ceremony, someone yelled "faggot" at me, and it echoed off the gymnasium walls. I might not have had perfect attendance, but I had a perfect record for hearing "fag" hurted at me every single day in high school.

I came out as gay shortly after starting college. Though I had been out to myself much earlier, external and internal homophobia kept me from outwardly verbalizing it. College brought new and amazing people to my life—friends and teachers who accepted me as gay and in my new identity as a countertenor. The first person I came out to was my voice teacher, Audrey. It was amazingly unceremonious. She immediately accepted me in my self-knowledge, and we went right along with the singing lesson, which was exactly what I wanted. Soon afterward, I was in her home and she mentioned to her husband that I had just come out. I stopped in my tracks; no one had ever outed me before. He came over, gave me a big hug, and told me he was proud of me. I barely knew him and yet he showed me acceptance in a way I had not previously known. Audrey was supportive of me in all ways, especially with regard to my vocal pursuits, which involved much tedious work in order to make the transition from soprano to countertenor—both in terms of technique and in grappling with the identity shift. I was the first countertenor at my undergraduate institution, which meant I often had to explain my vocal range to peers and teachers. Once when I was singing in an off-campus recital, the organizer added to my printed biography (without my permission or advance knowledge) that even though I sound like a "girl," I still "retain all my male parts." To this day, that was the worst performance of my life!

In 2003, a guest speaker came to my university as part of our LGBTQ+ Awareness Week. As a trans woman, she spoke about her life and the issues she faced as a result of societal transphobia. Her brave act of storytelling incited another awakening in me. She explained the concept of gender as being separate from biological sex. Gender is the inner consciousness of a person's sense of self as related (or not) to a male-female binary construct, while sex refers only to the biological makeup of a person's body. Although it should have been obvious to me before, I realized that in addition to struggling throughout my life with my sexuality, I was also grappling with my gender identity. After hearing that guest lecture, I identified as transgender, though in the many years since then, I have come to a more nuanced understanding of my gender, which seems intangibly related to recent experiences, sociocultural surroundings, and situational context. My gender derives from but is not always tethered to male or female, and though I lean heavily toward a traditionally masculine outward expression, I do not wish to be considered "one of the guys." Although I understand the impossibility of overhauling society's notion of masculinity, I long to redefine it.

I have a lot of privilege in life as a gay, genderqueer music teacher. I do not fear for the loss of my job or healthcare because of my identity. I do not fear the loss of love, community, or belonging. I do not feel gender dysphoria in my body or in my outward expression. As a white and able-bodied individual, I benefit from access, privilege, and power that many others do not. I receive systemic privilege that other colleagues are not granted. I also realize that what I write and teach from a feminist and antiracist position might unintentionally reify a colonial or imperialist mindset because my rhetoric, musical upbringing, and educational background are steeped in Eurocentric epistemologies. While sharing about my life and identity upfront in this book might seem self-centering, I offer this identity snapshot not in an egotistical way nor to garner a sympathetic ear, but to provide insight on the bias of this book.

I worry that my lens might not enable me to serve as a clear conduit for the full range of the experiences of this specific segment of the singing population. Is this research appropriate if implemented by a scholar who is not personally involved in hormone therapy? How does my personal interest in this research assist or hinder my ability to provide transparency? Can this book provide insight into teaching trans and genderqueer singers while also attempting to avoid generalizing a diverse population of people? While referencing the prominent gender theorist Judith Butler[2] in her own work, Patricia Elliot (2010) contends that we must accept our ignorance and be willing to "question and expand one's conception of humanness."[3] For me, singing is an act of humanness, and as I aim to query vocal pedagogy, I invite you to question and problematize my ignorance, my writing, and the construction of this manuscript—not only to critique it, but to foster deeper and more critical thinking.

In *The Sound of Music*, when Maria returns to the abbey as a postulant to escape Captain von Trapp, with whom she has fallen in love, the Mother Abbess tells Maria that she must face her problems. (Yes, the musical is steeped in hetero- and cisnormativity.) From my view, it is possible that vocal music education, as a discipline, is hesitant to face a primary difficulty, which is that singers and music have outgrown our historical teaching practices. It feels essential that the teaching of singers and the discipline of vocal pedagogy move beyond conservatory dogmas that continue to emphasize the *bel canto* technique for centuries old operatic repertoire. Sure, I want there to be a place for "Climb Ev'ry Mountain" in our anthologies, but our work should always strive to cultivate a musical canon that reflects an individual's self-understood, lived personhood. Welcoming different genres, new styles, and all kinds of singers within our studio feels pertinent to fostering an expanded vocal pedagogy. The research within this text illustrates how teachers and singers are broadening the landscape of vocal teaching to greater open-mindedness, compassion, and empathy for the students in their studios.

This book is written for singers and singing teachers to use as they see fit. The chapters are organized around the identities of the singers, allowing readers to explore the chapters in a nonlinear fashion. While this book is rooted in the interviews and observations of the research participants, specific pedagogical strategies and suggestions are embedded throughout. For a reader who is a novice to the discussion of gender expansiveness, consider reading this book in the standard linear fashion to capture the most comprehensive understanding. Chapter 1 offers important terminology and language for discussing the queering of vocal pedagogy and context for understanding the experiences of gender-expansive students in US schools and music education. The second chapter discusses queer as a theoretical framework and praxis, while investigating ways in which Western vocal pedagogy is already queering. Chapters 3–5 provide the in-depth case studies of the twelve participants who contributed to this study, first exploring the experience of trans women, then trans men, and finally, trans/nonbinary singers. Pedagogical considerations for gender-affirming vocal music education are explored in the penultimate chapter, looking at (1) gendering in musical spaces with specific reference to voice classification and repertoire; (2) teaching vocal technique to promote functional and expressive singing; (3) professional responsibilities of teachers; (4) self-advocacy demonstrated by trans and genderqueer singers and teachers; and (5) socio-emotional support within the applied studio. The last chapter examines queering as a habit of mind for singing teachers and ensemble directors.

Finally, my goal with this book is not to be provocative or to call out vocal pedagogues who might be unwelcoming of trans and genderqueer singers. In pursuit of a wholly inclusive discipline of vocal pedagogy, it is valuable to acknowledge that not all teachers will be ready to accept trans and genderqueer singers in their studio—just as not every teacher is ready to teach all styles of classical Western music, musical theatre, contemporary commercial music, or any style or technique outside their area of training and comfort. Nevertheless, just as each teacher should have an awareness of different musical styles and techniques, we should be aware of the many different human identities that might enter our studios. Reading this book will not make you an expert in teaching trans and genderqueer singers (and please, do not assume I am an expert in this area either), but hopefully this book will make you a learner in teaching gender-expansive singers with an increased awareness of advocacy and affirmation of trans and genderqueer singers.

Notes

1. Freya Jarman-Ivens, *Queer Voices: Technologies, Vocalities, and the Musical Flaw* (London: Palgrave Macmillan, 2016), 17.
2. Judith Butler, *Undoing Gender* (Boca Raton, FL: Routledge, Taylor and Francis Group, 2004).
3. Patricia Elliot, *Debates in Transgender, Queer, and Feminist Theory: Contested Sites* (Farnham, UK: Ashgate, 2010), 15.

1

Understanding Gender in Teaching and Learning

> "The movement to deny people their right to use the proper bathroom is telling people it's not okay to be who they are, and there's no place for them in public spaces. If you can't use a public restroom, you can't be in public for long stretches of time. It's about keeping gender-nonconforming people out of the public space."
>
> —Peter Fullerton, in conversation with the author

From Octavian in the opera *Der Rosenkavalier* to Mary Sunshine in the musical *Chicago*, vocal music has an accepted practice of onstage gender liminality. For centuries, audiences have delighted in watching a female mezzo-soprano parade on stage as Cherubino, the endearing teenaged boy in love with a countess who disguises "himself" as a "girl" to outwit a count in *Le Nozze di Figaro*. Mozart, Gounod, Offenbach, Strauss, and Strauss II supplied some of the most beloved operas that exalt trouser roles—women singers portraying male characters. In the musical *Victor/Victoria*, we applaud Julie Andrews dressing in "male" attire to then pose as a drag queen, alternating between belting and singing with a crystalline soprano voice. Musicals such as *Chicago*, *Hairspray*, and *Peter Pan* push gender roles: a man playing a woman singing soprano as Mary Sunshine, a man playing a woman singing baritone as Edna Turnblad, and an adult woman portraying a young boy as Peter Pan. These theatrical inventions are so commonplace they feel a natural aspect of the art.

The treatment of gender in musicals and operas is inherently and wonderfully queer, yet offstage in vocal studios and practice halls, a conservatory approach does not foster the same genderfluidity we applaud on stage. Vocal and pedagogical discourse is entrenched in a binary gender praxis. In the teaching of singing, voices are described as "male" and "female," leaving little room for voices outside this duality. This book focuses on the experiences and perspectives of singers who have questioned, reimagined, and/or redefined their gender. *Queering Vocal Pedagogy* offers narratives on how these singers and their singing teachers have paved a way for the vocal studio to be as open and affirming of gender expansiveness as our onstage traditions have long been.

This chapter includes the following topics:

1. A discussion of gender, trans, and queer vocabulary;
2. Background information on trans and genderqueer students in schools throughout the United States to provide a context on how gender plays a role in education and one-on-one music instruction; and,
3. The experiences of trans and genderqueer students in music education, encompassing all levels of vocal music instruction in K–12 schools, higher education, and independent vocal studios.

While there is little information in this chapter on vocal pedagogy in terms of specific repertoire and technical singing concepts, teaching trans and genderqueer students—as should be true for any student—must extend beyond thinking of the student as an instrument that requires a merely transactional experience. In teaching singers, we must have some awareness of their daily lived experiences, how they relate to others, and how they see themselves in the world around them so that we can wholly support them and provide a transformative learning experience. To this end, the treatment of vocal pedagogy in this book is broad, addressing not only the technical demands of singing but the holistic experience in teaching singers.

An Overview of Gender, Trans, and Queer Vocabulary

Let us consider language and concepts outside the standard education of vocal music teachers. Discourse on trans and genderqueer students requires a functional knowledge of gender vocabulary. An examination of gender and trans theories provide a framework for critically and thoughtfully understanding lived experiences of trans and genderqueer persons. In a similar way that music theory enables us to more profoundly appreciate our repertoire, theoretical models of gender help us to understand the human experience more deeply. Designed for a readership interested primarily in the teaching of singers, this section will provide an introduction to these theories as a starting point from which to explore teaching practices through them.

The acronym TGQ will be used throughout this text as an alternative for *trans and genderqueer*. TGQ is based on the acronym TIGQ for transgender, intersex, and genderqueer individuals, which was coined by Reuben Zellman, artistic director of New Voices Bay Area TIQG Chorus in San Francisco. Other scholars might use **transgender, trans***, or **gender expansive** as umbrella terms. The omission of intersex from TIGQ is not meant as act of intersexphobia—the discrimination or hatred toward intersex individuals—rather, the discussion of intersex singers is exceptionally important but beyond the scope of this book. The website of New Voices Bay Area TIGQ Chorus refers to the "TIGQ community,"[1] and in this way, when TGQ is written, I am speaking about trans and genderqueer as a population. Alternatively, TGQ might be employed as a general term when a person's gender is unknown. To be clear, my goal is to avoid discussing the TGQ population in a manner that suggests a monolithic, one-size-fits-all experience. The use of this acronym is for the purposes of readability, not to consign the diverse lived

Table 1.1. Important Vocabulary

Word or Phrase	Definition
Agender	Refers to an individual who rejects the notion of a male, female, or trans as a gender
Androcentrism	A hegemonic act or practice of centering a male point of view, which can occur consciously or unconsciously; for example, only studying the repertoire of male composers is an act of androcentrism
Cisgender	Denotes an individual for whom the sex and gender they were assigned at birth is congruent with their sense of self
Gender	A socially constructed concept that influences roles, expectations, and behaviors of human bodies
Gender-affirming surgeries	Medical intervention augmenting anatomical characteristics of a person's body
Gender expression	The outward representation of one's gender through cultural cues such as clothing, hairstyle, and speech patterns
Gender identity	The inner "compass" of a person's sense of self, referring to one's sense of being male, female, trans, genderqueer, or any other gender identification
Gender nonbinary	Indicates a person whose gender self-identity does not align to the male-female binary construct
Gender nonconforming	Similar to *gender nonbinary*, denotes a gender of a person that does not conform to a male or female identity
Gender oppression	Discrimination against a person(s), mostly women or TGQ individuals, based on their assumed gender
Genderqueer	The queering of gender, implying an identity beyond or between female and male, like *gender nonconforming* or *gender nonbinary*
Hormone replacement therapy	Commonly referred to as HRT, a medical intervention providing replacement hormones to modify the hormones in a person's body; might also refer to blocking the onset of hormones, such as testosterone in prepubescent bodies assigned male at birth
Intersex	A term referring to a body that does not fit a typical biological profile of male or female
Sex	Sometimes called biological or natal sex, referring to the biological makeup of a person's body, namely anatomy, hormones, and chromosomes
Sexism	Discrimination against a person(s), mostly women, based on their perceived sex
Sexuality	Refers to a romantic or intimate attraction (or not) to another being, such as gay, lesbian, bisexual, pansexual, asexual, and straight
TGQ	An acronym representing a trans and genderqueer individual or populace

Understanding Gender in Teaching and Learning / 5

Word or Phrase	Definition
Trans or trans*	A broad term usually referencing any noncisgender individual; the asterisk in trans* heightens awareness of multiple identities within this broader term
Transgender	Similar to trans or trans*, an umbrella term regarding an expansive population of individuals who do not identity as cisgender
Transphobia	Fear, intolerance or hatred toward individuals who do not match another person's binary assumptions of male or female, potentially resulting in acts of physical, emotional, or mental violence against the individuals

experiences of trans and genderqueer individuals into a single description or account.

The language in discussing the collective TGQ population is complex and developing. Though specific words will be defined throughout this chapter, table 1.1 provides a quick reference for important vocabulary.

Gender and TGQ language is emergent and ever-changing. For more and up-to-date terms, see PFLAG's online National Glossary of Terms.[2] Near the end of this book, appendix 1 offers a more extensive list of LGBTQ+ definitions provided by the Q Center of Purdue University Fort Wayne.[3] Despite my best efforts to use the most affirming language in this book, the lexicon will likely change over time, rendering some of terms used here outdated.

In addition to understanding this vocabulary, the way trans and genderqueer experiences are discussed deserves consideration. A newspaper or journal article might print phrases like "transgender issues" or "issues of gender identity." However well-meaning, the rhetoric of "issues" may place the TGQ individual or population at fault, where the "issue" is subtly and mistakenly considered a causation of the identity or behavior, instead of an issue caused by an oppressor or system of oppression against TGQ individuals. Such rhetoric comes across as violent whenever a news report reads that a TGQ person was murdered "because they were transgender" instead of framing the homicide as the result of abhorrent transphobia on the part of the perpetrator. These kinds of phrases are so idiomatic that they may go unnoticed, but they need to be called out as logical fallacies. Thus, I do not aim to discuss "issues of the trans voice"; rather, I seek to problematize the hegemonies in vocal pedagogy that exclude TGQ singers. In discussions of TGQ students, it is important to make the distinction that pedagogical issues are not inherently a result of the students' identity but rather of transphobic language, policies, actions, and ideologies embedded in culture, communities, and teaching practices.

Understanding Gender

Gender theory has been an interdisciplinary academic study since the mid-twentieth century. Theoretical models of gender offer differing and complex perspectives. For this introductory discussion, two common ideas will be examined: (1) Sex and gender are separate concepts; and (2) gender is a socially constructed concept that influences roles, expectations, and behaviors of human bodies.[4] Sex, sometimes referred to as *biological* or *natal sex*, is primarily based on a male and female binary construct, assigned to infants at birth based on anatomical appearance. (We should note that this female-male binary categorization excludes intersex identities.) This sex assignment leads to a designation of a feminine or masculine gender that is taught throughout a child's upbringing.[5] Children are often raised with expectations about the way they "should" dress, style their hair, or otherwise carry themselves in the world. **Sex** is specifically the biological composition of a body—namely, chromosomes, hormones, and anatomy—whereas **gender** is the inner identity and behavioral attributes of a body. Liz Airton explains: "Your gender is an evolving relationship among your lived experiences, your context and your feelings about your body. Many people situate their gender within the categories of masculine and feminine and find common ground with many countless others who do the same."[6]

In simplistic terms, in some cultures, babies assigned male at birth (AMAB) are often gendered through blue clothes, toy trucks, and football, while babies assigned female at birth (AFAB) are traditionally gendered to cook, clean, rear children, and wear pink dresses. In music, we see gender in concert attire, repertoire, opera and musical theatre roles, and vocal training. Toys, clothes, and musical assignments do not determine someone's gender, but these cultural items can place expectations on a child's behavior and identity. For instance, if a child assigned female at birth is taught to care for babies and sing lullabies, they might internalize this as their position in society. There is nothing wrong with child rearing, of course, but if that is the only narrative a young person is presented, it might limit the way they live their life.

Gender is a facet of our identity that is simultaneously part of our inner experience and relational to the cultures and communities in which we exist. The term **gender identity** refers to the inner compass of a person's sense of self, while **gender expression** concerns the outward representation of gender identity through cultural cues such as clothing, hairstyle, and speech patterns. Gender is a "socially contextualized activity";[7] for example, wearing a skirt in middle America is customarily considered feminine, while a similarly cut kilt is a traditional masculine garment in Scotland. A convention that is considered masculine in one culture might be considered inappropriate or transgressive for a man in another culture.

Understanding gender, however, is more complicated than just thinking about boys' and girls' colors, hairstyles, and clothes. Judith Butler, whose scholarship is central to gender theory, argues that gender is not so much a performance of gender expression but instead is rooted in cultural expectations that lead an individual to move in the world as a gendered body.[8] While the sex of a body derives from biological and tangible matter, gender as an inner identity of a person is dependent on cultural and societal conditioning and recognition. In other words, we learn gender from influences around us, and our gender is authenticated by a community that sees and accepts us for that gender. Gender is considered a "routinization"[9] of activities that lead to the construction of our self-identity, but the routineness of these activities occurs without consciousness. The routinization of gender, as Butler asserts, "is not performed by a subject: this repetition is what enables a subject and constitutes the temporal condition for the subject" to be/act/do that gender.¹⁰ Furthermore, this unconsciousness of the expectations associated with femininity or masculinity serve as a blockade for dismantling the gender oppression prevalent in our educational communities and teaching practices.

From the Latin "on the same side as," the term **cisgender** denotes an individual for whom the sex and gender they were assigned at birth are congruent with their sense of self. An individual whose sex or gender assigned at birth does not align with their sense of self might identify (or not) as **trans**, transgender, **genderqueer**, or any other gender demarcation that feels authentic to them. Here, the term *trans* will serve as the umbrella term for the broader population of individuals, including **gender nonconforming**, **gender nonbinary**, and **agender**—to name some examples of the expansiveness of gender. Broadly speaking, a **trans woman** is a woman who was assigned male at birth. A **trans man** is a man who was assigned female at birth. To be clear, I am intentionally circumventing the phrase "identifies as a woman/man" in these definitions as an attempt to rectify the notion that a trans woman, for example, is a woman because she identifies as one; cisgender women do not need to "identify as women" for their gender to be considered female.

For many TGQ individuals, transitioning from the gender assigned at birth to their authentic gender is paramount to living fully. For some individuals, this transition might mean modifying their gender expression, such as clothes or hairstyle. For other individuals, the transition might involve physical or biological changes. Medical assistance through **hormone therapy** or **affirmation surgery** that modifies a body's biology is sought by some trans individuals, though not all. Some people may align their gender expression with visible gender cues, while others might not. For some trans individuals, their gender dwells within the female/male binary, while for others, who might identity as genderqueer (or nonbinary or gender nonconforming), their gender might be beyond, between, or inhabiting traits of both masculinity and femininity.¹¹ The Gender Unicorn, designed by Landyn Pan and Anna Moore, is a fanciful yet sophisticated image to understand the differences in gender

Understanding Gender in Teaching and Learning / 9

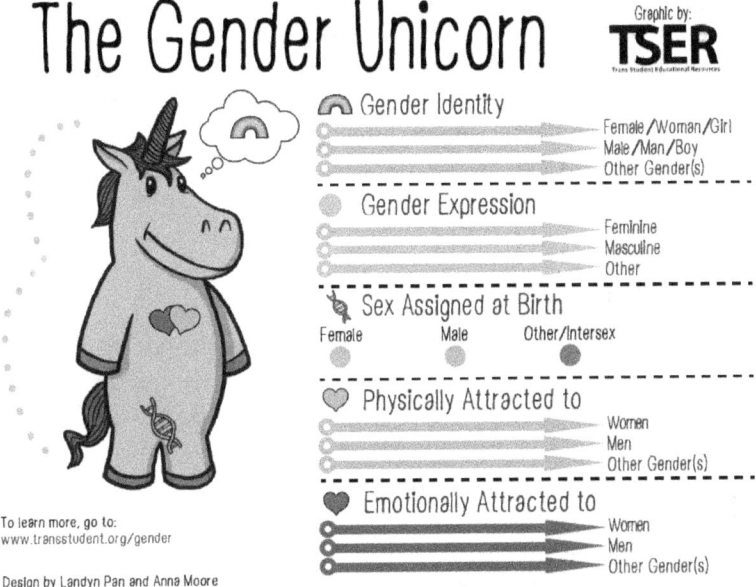

Figure 1.1. The Gender Unicorn illustrates the differences between gender identity, expression, sex assigned at birth, and physical and emotional attraction. Source: Trans Student Educational Resources (www.transstudent.org/gender)

identity, gender expression, sex assigned at birth, and sexuality (i.e., the physical and emotional attraction a person might feel for someone else). Four of the categories in the Gender Unicorn begin with an open circle moving toward an identity marker next to an arrow, signifying that gender and sexuality are no longer considered "spectrums" rooted in a female-male duality.

Remember, gender is more than a casual expectation of human bodies. Gender plays a ubiquitous and powerful role in our social status and the opportunities we are granted. Societies insist on gender conformity through legal, religious, and cultural practices.[12] Some social and cultural ideologies have accepted the archaic and hegemonic notion that men are superior to women, specifically in leadership, cognitive aptitude, and physical ability. This has led to misogyny, sexism, and a patriarchal system in which women are not given equal and equitable treatment. Our educational theories, epistemologies, and practices are built on the knowledge, policies, and histories of an androcentric—that is, a male dominated—society. This accounts for the history of Western music from the twelfth through the nineteenth centuries being dominated by white male composers. Thus, feminist theories, which are connected to gender theories, provide an important framework for reexamining long-held androcentric beliefs and systems.[13]

Understanding Trans/Transgender

Trans theories derive from feminist and queer theories and deviate from gender theories by deconstructing the normativity of the female/male binary construct. Jack Halberstam discusses the "strangeness of all gendered bodies" in thinking about the "fictitiousness" of gender that imposes hegemonic influences on expectations and behaviors in the human experience.[14] In an influential manifesto, Sandy Stone brings attention to trans as a gender identity of its own, separate from male or female.[15] Furthermore, Susan Stryker provides a definition of trans that includes, but is not limited to "identities or practices that crossover, cut across, move between, or otherwise queer socially constructed sex/gender boundaries."[16] These three pioneering scholars are influential in today's understanding of TGQ identities.

A large-scale study that surveyed 3,474 individuals, culminating in the book *The Lives of Transgender People* by Genny Beemyn and Sue Rankin, defined transgender as "a general term for all individuals whose gender histories cannot be described as simply female or male, even if they now identity and express themselves as strictly female and male."[17] Though we might find commonalities in the gender of trans and genderqueer people, no two individuals have the same his/her/theirstory, and within the TGQ population, individuals experience different levels of privilege and oppression. For example, as a person assigned male at birth and whose outward expression is male-centered, I enter spaces with an assumed cisgender status, contrary to the experience of other TGQ individuals, and thus, I receive cis privilege because I might not be "read" as non-cisgender. Beemyn and Rankin note that gender plays an enormous role in access to education, housing, healthcare, childcare, and other services commonplace in society.

Highlighting issues of marginalization and discrimination of TGQ people, Stryker shares, "I am, too, often perceived as less than fully human."[18] The medical profession, for example, has a pattern of pathologizing TGQ individuals and restricting access to hormone replacement therapy and other mental, emotional, and physical healthcare services. The psychiatric diagnosis of **gender dysphoria**—that is, the intense discomfort or distress that might occur in some TGQ individuals—is often needed for insurance purposes for individuals seeking hormone therapy or affirmation surgery. Author Declan Henry states, "Having a mental health label leads to society viewing trans people as being unwell, different or strange."[19] Unfortunately, the TGQ population is vulnerable and prone to discrimination due to being historically unheard, overlooked, and pathologized.[20]

While queer theory and feminist theory have brought important attention to realities beyond the heteronormative male existence, they have not necessarily focused on unique lived experiences within the TGQ population.[21] Julie Nagoshi and Stephan/ie Brzuzy (2010) argue, "Transgender theory encompasses and transcends feminist and queer theory by explicitly incorporating ideas of fluidly embodied, socially constructed, and self-constructed aspects of social identity, along with the dynamic interaction and integration of these aspects of identity within the narratives of lived experiences."[22]

The authors contend that trans theory enables a framework for understanding and empowering the fluid and intersectional identities of TGQ persons. As teachers of singers, we can grow our capacity for more empathy and care when we see, hear, and accept TGQ singers not only for their gender but for the intersectionality of their gender, race, age, and the multiplicity of their lives. Emphasizing individual narratives and experiences of TGQ singers as a path to crafting affirming vocal pedagogy follows in the footsteps of this theoretical framework.

Connecting Theory to Studio

As choral music educator Patricia O'Toole notes, "teachers are not immune from society's notions of gender,"[23] and the applied studio is not immune from community and cultural expectations, especially those related to gender. We need not look far to see how gender influences the teaching of singers. Our operatic and musical theatre roles can certainly reify gender (and racial) stereotypes. Repertoire anthologies for treble voices frequently contain pieces about flowers and birds or lullabies, while counterpart books for "men's voices" offer pieces about passion for young ladies and shipmates.[24] Such anthologies not only reify gender stereotypes but also reinforce heteronormativity. In other words, they tacitly bolster the notion that heterosexuality is the favored sexual orientation. Additionally, within vocal music education, voices tend to be labeled "male" or "female" without recognizing how TGQ singers might not fit within this limiting construct. Therefore, using trans theory as a lens to vocal pedagogy may lead to new insights for teaching singers, from repertoire selection to how we talk about singing and singers to informing policies and practices that impact applied studio instruction.

Singing teachers in higher education are frequently impacted by school policies or mandates—be it a compulsory curriculum, semester juries, or recital requirements. Independent studio teachers, though not necessarily beholden to school curricula, are part of a network of teachers whose musical training comes from a sometimes generational system of standards and decades-old traditions. While teachers might not be cognizant of the influences under which they operate, vocal music teaching is impacted by local communities, which in turn are impacted by a dominant cultural undercurrent. For instance, a teacher of singers might systematically select pieces from a school- or state-approved solo and ensemble repertoire list to enable students to perform in a school-sponsored competition. Understandably, a teacher wants their students to engage in important learning and scholarship opportunities. In a study of state-sponsored competition song lists, pieces suggested for competition-level performance were found to reinforce notions of gender stereotypes, sexism, racism, and colonialism.[25] Another teacher might prepare a student to be "competitive" to industry standards, unaware of the unwanted pressures of conformity being placed on the student. So-called standard repertoire is dominated by white cisgender male composers, and then we, the teachers, bolster that repertoire without considering the hidden messages about who and what is important in vocal music.

The conceptual framework of the applied studio, shown in figure 1.2, represents the teacher and student as separate yet overlapping entities. Each person brings their identity, background, and education to the shared teaching-learning space. While the teacher brings their knowledge of vocal pedagogy, the student brings their goals. Individually and simultaneously, the teacher and student are compelled by community and school dynamics, which are themselves influenced by cultural expectations. Dotted lines in the image suggest permeability. Though the applied studio is influenced by broader systems, teachers and students have the potential to reshape the contexts in which they are situated. Musicians and music teachers are not only culture bearers; they can be cultural influencers.

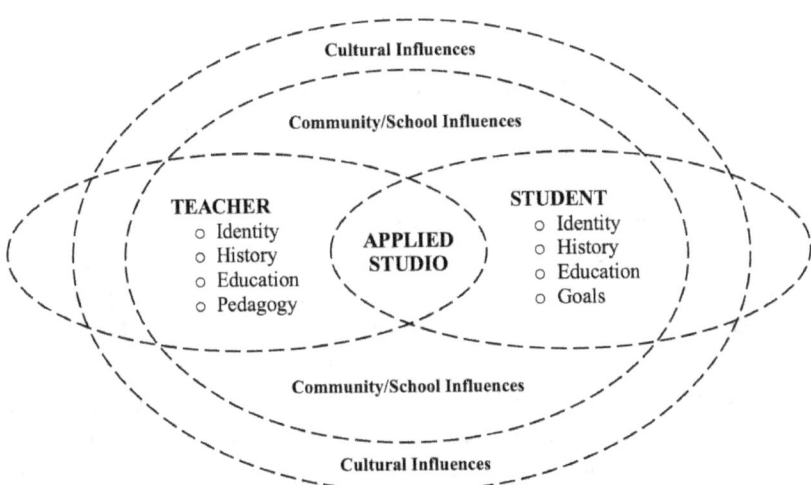

Figure 1.2. Conceptual Framework: From Theory to Studio. Source: Author

Teachers of singers know that singing emanates from the whole body, and our musical and textual interpretations are often rooted in our sense of self and our lived experiences. The whole person—including the physical, emotional, mental, spiritual, and psychological self—is not always considered in the teaching of a singer. Scholarship in vocal pedagogy has brought valuable knowledge of vocal anatomy and physiology to the field, though perhaps not necessarily conforming to or considering the cultural influences or unique identities of singers. Trans theory highlights the individual voice and stewards a broader conception of vocal pedagogy as being steeped in the lived experiences of the whole-embodied human singer.

As teachers of singers, empathetic listening is important to understanding how TGQ students use language to describe themselves. Some genderqueer individuals might identify as trans, while others might not. It is prudent that we avoid labeling others; naming (or not naming) one's gender is a personal, self-compelled process. Even cisgender students benefit when no assumptions are made about their gender or identity. Sharing and inviting pronouns, being thoughtful of a person's name, and using affirming language are vital steps in welcoming students in instructional spaces.[26]

In the case studies presented later in this book, the specific self-identity of each participant will be discussed; as such, the most appropriate language will be used to represent their identity. Pronouns used in this book will reflect the gender of the individual as they identified themselves at the time data were collected. When the pronouns of an individual are unknown to me, such as in referencing another author, the pronouns they/them/their will be used in the singular form.[27]

If it were possible to distill the gender and trans theoretical frameworks to just a few phrases, it would be this: Gender is a complex facet of human life, influenced by cultural and community expectations. Our language and the way we move through life is entrenched (or not) by our gender (or lack thereof). Sex and gender are different, yet the voice is impacted by both our sex (i.e., the chromosomes and hormones that affect physical shape and size) and gender in the way we intone our thoughts, through pitch, timbre, and inflection. In her book *Multivocality: Singing on the Borders of Identity*, Katherine Meizel contends, "The voice, as both biology and culture, reflects and contributes to the diversity of gender variance in human life."[28] Some singers see themselves within the female/male binary of sex and gender, while others do not. Finally, theory is not static. The views and definitions provided here might not feel appropriate for every TGQ person, and we should avoid boxing singers into an identity framework that is not authentic for them.

TGQ Students in US Schools

A summary of the experiences of TQG students in the US school system might seem tangential to a vocal pedagogy text, but because many singing teachers interface with school-aged children, an overview of school climate provides an important context to the formative experiences of TGQ students. Similarly, teachers in higher education might be more prepared to welcome TGQ students in universities and colleges by understanding the educational environments of these singers before matriculation.

A 2014 *Time* magazine cover article featuring actress Laverne Cox proclaimed that America had reached a "transgender tipping point," arguing that equal rights for the TGQ community is the next frontier in America's civil rights movement.[29] In the several years since that publication, TGQ academics, activists, actors, athletes, and musicians have heightened the national discussion on TGQ rights. The discourse and movement toward gender equality in the United States is complex and multifaceted, encompassing the equal rights of women and TGQ individuals. Although the Nineteenth Amendment to the US Constitution, codifying a woman's right to vote, passed more than one hundred years ago, gender bias in education and the workplace, as well as sexual harassment and assault against women as highlighted by the #MeToo movement, illustrate the continued inequitable and hegemonic treatment of women. TGQ individuals face many social, cultural, and political issues, which include the legality of changing one's name and sex on government-issued documents, bathroom usage, inclusion in sports, healthcare, and the right to serve in the military.[30] Organizations like the American Civil Liberties Union (ACLU) and the Transgender Law Center support legal reform to better safeguard TGQ individuals, while transphobic leaders espouse laws designed to legally discriminate against the TGQ population.[31]

One of the most discussed lawsuits in recent years focuses on the use of the restrooms in a Virginia school. Gavin Grimm, a teenage trans man, was forbidden to use the bathrooms assigned for male students.[32] With the legal support of the ACLU, Grimm filed a lawsuit against the school for discrimination. A decision in a lower district court and the Fourth Circuit Court upheld Grimm's claim that the school violated his rights as provided by Title IX and the Fourteenth Amendment to the US. Constitution. The Supreme Court of the United States, in declining to hear *Grimm v. Gloucester County School Board,* tacitly allowed the lower court decisions to stand.[33] Another recent lawsuit involved the Supreme Court ruling in favor of Aimee Stephens (1960–2020), a trans woman who was fired from her longtime job on the basis of being trans.[34] This historic case extends the rights of Title VII of the Civil Rights Act to prohibit businesses from firing an employee solely on the basis of their gender identity or sexual orientation.[35] The rulings in these lawsuits, and many others, may have major implications for public schools and universities in the United States, such as bathroom usage, mandatory school attire, and recreational activities that are differentiated based on gender.

A 2016 study reported that in the United States, an average of 0.6 percent of adults are trans, accounting for around 1.4 million persons.[36] The same study found that the percentage is slightly higher (at 0.66%) for adults in the eighteen-to-twenty-four age bracket, and although the study did not include adolescents, it is possible the percentage may increase as society becomes more accepting of TGQ individuals.[37] Educational policies have the power to "affirm or disavow students' identities."[38] As such, during President Barack Obama's administration, the Departments of Justice and Education issued a joint statement clarifying the language of Title IX regarding the protection of gender identity and expression in schools.[39] The federal recommendations included:

1. schools are to prevent discrimination of transgender students;
2. schools are to allow transgender students access to restrooms and locker rooms aligned with their gender identity;
3. schools are to allow students to use their chosen (not birth) name and pronouns in school records; and
4. schools are responsible for keeping a student's transgender identity, including birth name and sex assigned at birth, confidential.

Federal guidance on the protection of TGQ students in schools is currently uncertain. In 2017, these recommendations were officially rescinded, thus implicitly supporting discrimination against TGQ students in schools. However, in April 2021 President Joe Biden declared in a joint address to Congress: "To all transgender Americans watching at home, especially the young people: you're so brave. I want you to know your president has your back."[40] In June of the same year, the White House put forth a multi-initiative plan to advance equality for trans individuals. But even if governmental agencies become more robust in protecting TGQ youth, policies and recommendations are only one factor to understanding the experiences of TGQ students in educational spaces.

Transphobic practices in schools adversely affect the mental, emotional, and physical health of TGQ students. Transphobia can occur blatantly, in the form of verbal bullying or physical violence, or covertly, through unwelcoming curricula, policies, or school culture. A 2018 report from GLSEN, an organization invested in the safety of LGBTQ+ (lesbian, gay, bisexual, trans, queer) youth, examined the US school climate for LGBTQ+ students.[41] GLSEN's survey included the perspective of 23,001 students between the ages of thirteen and twenty-one. Of the students who self-disclosed in the study as LGBTQ+, 95.3 percent reported hearing homophobic remarks in schools and 87.4 percent reported hearing transphobic comments.[42] Seventy-one percent of these students heard school faculty or staff make discriminatory remarks about gender expression.[43] When narrowing specifically on the data reported by TGQ students, the story is even more worrisome. TGQ students are more likely to experience discrimination and adversity than their LGBQ peers, with TGQ students experiencing a greater number of absences and a higher level of victimization. While the survey finds some differences in school climate between students who identify as trans versus genderqueer, overall, TGQ students feel less safe than other students in schools. The GLSEN research is limited to an examination of middle and high school student populations. Less is known about the experience of younger TGQ students, despite many elementary students being aware of their TGQ gender identity even if they are unable to communicate it.[44]

Initiatives to make schools more supportive of LGBTQ+ students are often anchored in efforts related to diversity, equity, and inclusion. Updating curricula to be more TGQ affirming is key to improving school culture for TGQ students. The formation of support services and student clubs, such as gender-sexuality alliance groups, provides a "safe space" for LGBTQ+ students in schools. The concept of a safe space was born out of the 1960s and 1970s from the women's movement and now includes the LGBTQ+ community.[45] Some schools offer safe space trainings for teachers and staff, such as the one provided by Safe Zone Project.[46] While these programs promote allyship and offer valuable information in dismantling homophobia and transphobia in schools, they may fall short in providing discipline-specific information to drive curricular and pedagogical changes.

A paucity of research on TGQ students "in education is problematic because transgender people participate in the educational system at all levels."[47] The emerging research indicates that teachers are underprepared to work with TGQ students.[48] Having tools and knowledge of the ever-expanding notion of gender is necessary for teachers to support these students. Professional development for in-service teachers and preservice teacher preparation programs that provide discipline-specific training are essential to creating long-term, systemic changes in pedagogy and curricular design. Contending that schools reify **gender oppression**, Kathleen Rands outlines four models of how gender impacts pedagogy:

Understanding Gender in Teaching and Learning / 19

1. **Gender-stereotyped education** describes a model where students are treated differently based on gender, furthering inequality between male and female students.
2. In **gender-free/gender-blind education**, teachers lack a critical lens of oppression, assuming all students fit within the female/male binary, and thus unconsciously regenerate "a context that continues to favor the dominant group, that is, boys."[49]
3. **Gender-sensitive education** fosters equitable classroom policies but continues to fall along the female/male binary lines and fails to fully acknowledge TGQ students.
4. **Gender-complex education** calls on teachers to recognize and dismantle gender stereotyping, discrimination, and transphobia in curricular and pedagogical design, calling on teachers to fully embrace gender diversity within their classes.

Transphobia and other forms of oppression in US schools stem from differing histories and affect students in multiple ways. Identifying how these systemic oppressions are embedded in our traditional curricula and pedagogies serves as a first step toward dismantling them. Disassembling oppressive and marginalizing practices in schools is complex and multifaceted. A gender-complex education is important for affirming TGQ students and needs to be practiced alongside antiracist, anticlassist, antihomophobic, and other socially just pedagogies that seek to fracture systemic forms of oppression. Teaching in an applied studio context does not transcend these issues. The work of teachers wanting to undo hegemony in teaching and learning must allow these issues to be preeminent, embedded, and reiterated in every lesson, every day, and must be flexible to changes in understanding and practice.

TGQ Students in Music Education

Trans and genderqueer student experiences in music and music education have been chronicled through dissertations, research articles, opinion pieces, blog posts, and conference presentations. Although there is a growing range of scholarship and resources, research in this field is still emerging. Studies of TGQ students in higher education have focused on music teacher preparation and student teaching. Scholars have investigated the choral environment and the attitudes of music teachers working with TGQ students in pre-K through twelfth grade. Vocal pedagogues have looked at individual student experiences and outcomes, giving considerable attention to the effects of hormone therapies on the vocal mechanism.

Music Classroom Teaching

Joshua Palkki and I have explored and discussed Rand's model of a gender-complex education in music teacher preparation.[50] For music education courses in higher education, we offer practical tools for classroom and ensemble teaching, such as including children's books that highlight a gender-expansive experience, avoiding gender stereotyping in instrumental ensembles (e.g., flutes and clarinets are for girls, while trumpets and percussion are for boys), and selecting repertoire that avoids gender stereotyping. Sarah Bartolome and Melanie Stapleton provide a reflective narrative account of one trans woman as a music education major and early career music teacher.[51] Melanie, the music teacher and coauthor, shares how choir incited discomfort and estrangement for her in a musical environment that should have fostered a sense of belonging and community. Due to the imposition of traditional gender practices in a choral ensemble, such as concert attire codes and voice assignments (sopranos and altos for women; tenors and basses for men), Melanie felt unwelcomed. As a trans woman, she recounts challenges in seeking employment when her life's history (i.e., school and legal documents) disclosed her birth sex and the record of her name change. Although she successfully secured a music teaching position, she remains vigilant in presenting a "female singing voice" to avoid being misgendered.[52]

In looking at music education at the middle and high school levels, a narrative account of Rie/Ryan, a trans music student, showed that they experienced frequent bullying from peers and a lack of understanding from school faculty and staff, which ultimately forced Rie/Ryan to drop out of their music ensembles and leave school altogether.[53] Sadly, the transphobia Rie/Ryan experienced in school is not an isolated incidence. Although Rie/Ryan reported no high-level transphobia in their music classes, a survey of LGBTQ+ choral students in high school found that trans students feel less "safe" in the choral environment than their LGBQ peers.[54] A survey study with 612 participants on the attitudes of music teachers toward trans students indicated that while teachers report feeling comfortable teaching TGQ students, music educators indicate that trans individuals should be barred from the teaching profession. In that same study, 25 percent of respondents did not disagree with the statement: "Transgenderism is a sin."[55] These data suggest that although music teachers feel prepared to teach TGQ students, discriminatory and transphobic attitudes continue to prevail.

Issues of gender oppression and transphobia have been investigated in the choral setting. In discussing the experiences of women in choral classrooms, Patricia O'Toole suggests that "teachers have been found to interact differently with boys and girls, and thus their pedagogy is laden with subtle messages about who is important in the classroom."[56]

O'Toole has looked at both women's experiences in choir and the hierarchical structures of choir, where a director silences singers through hegemonic teacher-directed instruction. Through a narrative-based inquiry, O'Toole states, "Conventions of choral pedagogy are designed to create docile, complacent singers who are subject to a discourse that is more interested in the production of music than in the laborers."[57] O'Toole's line of inquiry is important in the applied studio, where we might imagine a voice teacher who unintentionally, but nonetheless systematically, stifles or dismisses a singer through their preconceived notions of what the student's goals should be.

In a narrative case study of three trans students, Palkki examines secondary high school choirs.[58] Palkki's research illustrates practices and policies in the choral classroom that cause trans students to feel unwelcome. Like Rie/Ryan, the participants in this study indicate that choir serves as an important opportunity for self-expression, but traditional choral conventions can incite dysphoria. For example, traditional choral attire such as dresses and tuxedos can make one person feel affirmed in their gender while causing another person to experience extreme discomfort. Palkki's research is bolstered by several other articles that offer strategies for welcoming and affirming TGQ students in the choral rehearsal.[59] The scholarship in choral music provides important insights on teaching TGQ students in the applied voice studio. In particular, discussions around hormone therapy, vocal identity, and inclusivity have heightened awareness in choral music education.

Palkki has explored the concept of **vocal identity**. Though not everyone may associate their gender with the acoustics of their voice, we habitually label "male" and "female" voices based on pitch and other vocal characteristics. Palkki explains, "The voice may be tied to one's gender identity and gender expression, and can be an important part of one's gender."[60] A TGQ person might seek a vocal range that aligns with their self-concept of their gender; for example, a trans man might take testosterone with a goal of lowering his vocal range to sound more like his self-concept of "masculine." Even outside the discussion of gender, in talking about voice therapy for children, Moya Andrews asserts, "Voice is a very important part of the self-concept, and our identity is projected through our voices."[61] Palkki indicates that TGQ individuals relate the sound of their voice to their gender expression in different ways. One female participant in this study said, "I'm a girl and I'm a bass and I own that."[62] For this singer, sounding like a soprano or alto is not central to her concept of being feminine. Most people have a unique relationship with the sound of their voice, and thus in teaching singers, a one-size-fits-all approach is not appropriate.[63]

Studio Teaching

Recent articles that focus on vocal technique for TGQ students have deepened the discourse on vocal pedagogy. One prominent piece of scholarship appears in *Voice and Communication Therapy*

Understanding Gender in Teaching and Learning / 23

for the Transgender/Transsexual Client, in which Anita Kozan's chapter "The Singing Voice" addresses many specific technical topics, including vocal exercises, breath support, range, and register.[64] Kozan serves as an advocate for TGQ singers, explaining:

> TG/TS [transgender/transsexual] people are literally, as well as figuratively, finding their "outer voice" with which to speak and sing, just as they are finally getting to express their "inner voice," the voice of their true identity as a human being. The most important guideline here is that there are no "rights or wrongs" in what range or ranges in which the singer chooses to sing. Our work as clinicians who specialize in care of the singing voice is to help the singer use the voice in the healthiest manner possible.[65]

While an earnest attitude to try to help a TGQ singer is valuable, Kozan suggests that having technical knowledge of TGQ voices is paramount to effectively and positively guiding singers.

A 2008 article by Alexandros Constansis addresses specific vocal concerns for trans men. As a trans man and singing teacher, Constansis discusses his own vocal transition from treble to bass clef range and provides data from his teaching of other trans students also experiencing a vocal transition from taking exogenous testosterone. The author posits that some trans men experience "entrapped" voices,[66] in which their voices experience "permanent hoarseness, lack of control and colour, and limited power"[67] due to the vocal changes brought on by the hormone therapy. Constansis advises that testosterone be taken in lower doses to enable a gradual voice modulation: "The combination of the right gradual testosterone intake together with soft exercising of the voice can help the voice not only to retain its singing quality, but also to acquire a new and aesthetically pleasing quality."[68] Constansis advises that a combination of vocal exercises, diaphragmatic breathing, and an appropriate dosage of testosterone will enable a new, lower, and more uniquely beautiful range to emerge.

Many studies on trans voices have come from speech-language pathology.[69] Practices for helping trans individuals find speech patterns congruent with their gender have developed into voice "masculinization" and "feminization" services.[70] The range of the speaking voice and elements of voice, such as timbre and resonance, are shown attention in this work. Practices and techniques employed by speech-language pathologists are shown to be useful for individuals who wish to sound more "masculine" (i.e., lower) or more "feminine" (i.e., higher). Voice masculinization and feminization run parallel to gender stereotypes, and therefore TGQ individuals may or may not find such practices useful. Henceforth, words like *feminine* and *masculine* will be shown in quotes to indicate cisnormative understandings of these words. Research and practices in voice feminization and masculinization will be discussed more in chapters 3 and 4.

Vocal technique designed for trans singers is investigated by Ioanna Georgiadou Hershberger, who promotes the efficacy of Melodic Intonation Therapy (MIT) in combination with traditional speech-language therapy.[71] MIT uses rhythm, melody, and word stress to engage a patient in communication skills.[72] Basic phrases are "intoned" within a range of three to four whole steps using a tempo slower than normal speech. Of the six trans women in the study, three of the participants received traditional voice therapy with training in "feminine" language structures and nonverbal communication, while the other three received voice therapy plus singing exercises and MIT. Hershberger found that participants who received singing exercises and MIT had slightly higher speaking fundamental frequencies than the other participants. All participants rated themselves as having more "feminine" voices at the end of their treatment, and external adjudicators also rated the voices as more "feminine" in comparing pre- and post-therapy recordings.

Hershberger's study included scalar and small intervallic patterns on voiced nasal consonants (e.g., [m], [n]) and the vowels [i], [o] and [u]. Nasal resonance is mentioned throughout singing literature as one of the key components to healthy singing.[73] Resonance is understood as the enhancement of sound as it passes through a cavity. In singing, these cavities are chiefly the throat and mouth, but the nasal passages enhance resonance as well.[74] In the case of Hershberger's study, participants were given exercises to foster a more forward tone, such as humming or singing on closed vowels to promote nasal resonance. Vowel formant frequencies are connected to resonance, and "feminine" voices tend to have higher formant frequencies,[75] thus Hershberger's exercises support singing as a useful tool in vocal feminization work.

The vocal exercises crafted by Hershberger align with the recommendations of Constansis, who reported struggling with exercises on open vowels as he first began to explore his lower range. Constansis recommends vocal "sirens" on a "ng" hum [ŋ] as well as exercises on voiced fricative consonants such as [v], [ð] and [z]. The 1833 Italian *bel canto* lessons of Niccolò Vaccaj are recommended by Constansis, though he cautions that a singer must not try to sing with too full a voice until the voice is ready for more difficult repertoire. Kozan recommends crafting vocal exercises with small intervals and using a glissando from one pitch to another. Kozan also emphasizes the importance of soft, supported singing and suggests it is "the first step in successive approximations toward the goal of firmer vocal fold adduction."[76] Her series of exercises increase in difficulty and use more open vowels throughout. Kozan recommends situating exercises within the comfortable range of each individual singer, suggesting that trans women should vocalize across their entire range, but no lower than E3 (approximately 165 Hz), as this is considered the perceptual threshold of a "male" voice.[77]

Neither Hershberger, Constansis, nor Kozan recommend any specific repertoire. Constansis mentions the Vaccaj études from 1833, and Kozan suggests the use of folk songs but provides no specific examples. Kozan also advises avoiding previously learned repertoire, as the song might be fraught with habits from before the vocal transition. It is also suggested that repertoire be taken slowly, at least at first, to ensure the singer has ample time to breathe and adjust to their new range. Furthermore, Constansis and Kozan recommend that teachers adjust the key of the song to match the singer's ability. One of Hershberger's participants suggested all participants in voice therapy should learn a song as a reference point for pitch when speaking.

In 2017, the *Journal of Singing* published five articles focusing on trans singing. Loraine Sims wrote two of these articles.[78]

In her first article she gives an overview of considerations in working with TGQ singers. She first introduces essential vocabulary and protocols to ensure TGQ students feel supported and welcomed in the voice studio. The impact of testosterone on trans male voices is discussed, along with certain technical concepts intended to promote efficient singing. Regarding trans women, Sims explains that some women may want to seek a higher range, while others are content with their lower voices. She also brings attention to the challenges that might arise if a student is receiving voice feminization therapy for speaking but continues to sing in a tenor or bass range. She notes that "teaching transgender voice students is not so different than teaching any student. . . . [C]hoose repertoire that will help them grow as musicians in the genre that is appropriate and encourage[s] them to find the means to become communicative, artistic, and stylist performers."[79] Sims's first article serves as a valuable advocacy and educational piece for teaching TGQ singers.

Her second article chronicles the voice change of one male student from soprano to tenor. She provides detailed month-to-month information on his voice modulation, giving specifics about fluctuations in range during a one-year period when the student was developing his newly emerging low range while simultaneously cultivating his falsetto voice. Sims is meticulous in her details regarding the vocal transition, documenting range and register modification. She is also candid in mentioning mistakes she made regarding her student's pronouns. The reader is reminded that all effort should be made to properly refer to the individual with the correct gender, and yet even with the best intentions, blunders may occur. Sims also reflects on working with a female student with a bass-baritone range who developed a functional falsetto. In both articles, Sims serves as an advocate of trans singers, providing concrete technical information while also encouraging teachers to embrace working with this student population.

Two articles prepared by Brian Manternach provide perspectives from both teachers and trans singers.[80] The first article provides knowledge from three voice teachers having varied levels of experience in working with trans singers. Manternach collected short depictions from the teachers (Michael Chipman, Ruth Rainero, and Caitlin Stave) to provide a useful comparison of the kinds of challenges and joys applied studio teachers face in teaching a trans student. The teachers contribute technical knowledge for singing but also offer examples of how gender stereotyping impacts a student. In discussing operatic roles, Chipman explains that his female student finds operatic roles problematic as a bass baritone, and thus she is focusing on art song literature, which they both feel is more flexible in terms of gender presentation. The teacher shares, "I think it is a crucial part of our jobs as teachers to provide a safe space for students . . . to discover, explore, and strengthen their identity as artists and human beings."[81] Rainero discusses a male student who had a long full-time career as a mezzo-soprano before beginning hormone replacement therapy at age fifty. The teacher explains that the singer's pretransition vocal range was more than three octaves with no discernable registration breaks. After the onset of testosterone, the singer's range diminished to less than an octave (E3 to C4) and "he developed register difficulties, lack of stability in tone production, and loss of breath control."[82] Through ongoing voice lessons and androgen therapy, the student's range has expanded (C3 to E-flat 4), but it is unclear whether he will sing professionally again.

Stave, the third teacher in the collaborative article, discusses a beginning male student who had been on testosterone for three years before commencing voice lessons. Stave describes working with the adult singer's voice like that of a teenage baritone, employing exercises with smaller intervals, while keeping the larynx relaxed and promoting a warm timbre. One vocal challenge observed by this teacher was an increase in vocal fatigue. All three teachers provide awareness to the varied kinds of vocal technical needs of trans students, contributing to the notion that there is no one-size-fit-all method.

In Manternach's second article, the students of the teachers from the previous article articulate their perspectives on the vocal training they received. This provides a beneficial glimpse of the student perspective, which illustrates that each student's voice is a vital aspect of their self-expression. One student shares, "I think that music has always been front and center to my transition. I mean, it was thanks to music I had the courage to come out, and it's thanks to the people who love and support me and are connected to me through music that I have the courage to continue to transition. . . . It is also thanks to music that I am able to express who I am."[83]

Another student comments, "My singing voice is very important to me as a way to express my character."[84] Manternach notes that teachers need an understanding of trans voices since the possibility of a voice teacher working with a TGQ student is "increasingly likely."[85]

In a fifth article from the *Journal of Singing*, Nancy Bos suggests that it can be helpful for a cisgender teacher to provide TGQ students with singing role models from among a list of current, well-known performing artists.[86] Bos provides a list of TGQ singers along with brief descriptions of each artist. As a teacher with experience in trans vocal pedagogy, she asserts that "the teacher has the obligation to create a safe place where students can sing ... with their authentic voices."[87] Bos's opinion seems shared among all the contributors to the emerging scholarship that appeared in 2017. Teachers need to be aware of the technical challenges TGQ vocalists encounter but also have the social skills to warmly accept these students for their authentic identities, serve as advocates for them, and create safe space within their studios for them to heighten their self-expression.

In addition to the five articles from the *Journal of Singing*, Emerald Lessley's doctoral dissertation serves as a pedagogical resource to singing teachers in working with the TGQ population.[88] The author provides an overview of extant literature as well as observations from her personal experience in working with several TGQ singers. The document is organized into trans female voices and trans male voices, giving an overview of the voice modification in both populations. Writing with the voice teacher as the intended reader, Lessley provides vocal exercises and suggested repertoire. Lessley's research supplements the aforementioned scholarship and establishes the usefulness of semi-occluded exercises, gliding between pitches, and using closed vowels such as [u] and [i] to foster consistent resonance.

One of the most preeminent texts on teaching trans singers is the book *The Singing Teacher's Guide to Transgender Voices* by Liz Jackson Hearns and Brian Kremer.[89] This valuable and clearly written book offers technical information organized into different categories, such as voice classification, pitch, registration, and resonance. Hearns and Kremer also discuss hormone therapies and psychological perspectives specific to the TGQ population. Their ability to synthesize the various paradigms among TGQ singers makes their text important in this growing area of research. Scholarship on trans vocal technique has become more abundant in recent years, laying a foundation for this book.

Outside the field of vocal technique or pedagogy, Katherine Meizel shares that "any voice may be considered a social practice of being-in-the-world (Heidegger, 1962) and of acting in the world."[90] In the book *Multivocality*, Meizel contends that the voice is both an "epistemology and ontology" that embodies a person's multiple and intersecting identities.[91] This notion of "vocality" suggests that our voice is a way of knowing and of being/becoming in the world. Thus, "transvocality" in this context is the intersection of identity and gender, which Meizel illustrates through descriptive portraits of two professional trans opera singers, Lucia Lucas and Breanna Sinclairé.[92] Lucas, a female baritone, and Sinclairé, a female soprano, are examples of trans singers navigating the realm of classical Western music. A teacher of singers may find the narratives of these singers an important tool in teaching and understanding vocal identity.

Scholarship in music and music education has laid the groundwork for using narrative-based research as a component in vocal music education. The experiences of TGQ musicians like Lucia and Breanna, Ryan/Rie, Melanie, and Alexandros, along with the scholarship of Lessley, Kozan, Manternach, Palkki, Sims, and Hearns and Kremer, provide valuable insight for teaching TGQ students. This discourse highlights pedagogical approaches to the technical aspects of teaching singers and points to the socioemotional support students might need. Vocal pedagogy should continue to be forward-looking in the development of best practices and strategies for welcoming TGQ singers. Affirming students and dismantling transphobia is more than simply the inclusion of TGQ individuals into a traditional narrative—it involves reexamining, reimagining, and rebuilding the core structures of our discipline.

Chapter Takeaways

Adrian Angelico. Shea Diamond. Laura Jane Grace. Lucia Lucas. Holden Madagame. Alex Newell. Lucas Silveira. Breanna Sinclairé. Reuben Zellman. This short list of names illustrates diversity in singing and testifies that TGQ musicians sing in a variety of styles, genres, and techniques. The purpose of this chapter was to begin a conversation and construct a preliminary framework for a vocal pedagogy that holds space for all voices. As an introduction to *Queering Vocal Pedagogy*, a broad discussion on gender-expansive language, an overview of gender and trans theory, and an inquiry on how these theoretical frameworks are applicable and necessary to teaching TGQ singers were provided. A discussion of TGQ students in schools helped draft a broad context to understand the heightened levels of bullying, discrimination, and marginalization gender-diverse students experience. Teachers of TGQ singers can benefit from knowing about the kinds of day-to-day adverse encounters a student might face. This chapter concluded with a robust review of previous literature in music education, including group settings in K–12 schools and higher education as well as studio teaching. The literature advocates affirmative practices, inclusive policies, and the crafting of safe learning spaces. To date, vocal pedagogy scholarship in teaching trans singers has shed light on the impact of exogenous testosterone on the voices of trans men, while less attention has been given to trans women, nonbinary singers, and TGQ youth. The emergent research in TGQ singing provides a valuable foundation and model for this book.

Here is a short list of essential takeaways from the chapter:

- Gender and sex are different. Gender is a cultural construct that influences the way we see ourselves in the world and how we live in society.

- A child is often reared on gendered expectations based on their anatomy.
- TGQ students experience high levels of bullying, while school cultures and curricula are often laden with gendered expectations.
- A 2016 study found that 1.4 million people in the United States are trans or genderqueer, with potentially many more young people not included in this estimation.
- Research from music education indicates that music teachers need to be prepared to teach TGQ singers.
- Vocal pedagogy and traditional voice teaching is entrenched with gendered language and repertoire, which can exclude some singers.
- A long-standing acceptance of gender liminality onstage is not fostered in the applied voice studio context.
- Understanding the lived experience of TQG singers will aid singing teachers in being more welcoming and affirming in their instructional practices.

Notes

1. "New Voices Bay Area TIGQ Chorus," San Francisco Community Music Center, accessed June 1, 2020, https://sfcmc.org/new-voices-bay-area-tigq-chorus/.

2. "PFLAG National Glossary of Terms," PFLAG, October 29, 2021, https://pflag.org/glossary.

3. "Glossary of LGBTQ+ Terms," Q Center—Purdue Fort Wayne, accessed November 27, 2021, https://www.pfw.edu/q-center/.

4. Jack Halberstam, "F2M: The Making of Female Masculinity," in *The Lesbian Postmodern*, ed. Laura L. Doan (New York: Columbia University Press, 1994): 210–28; Candace West and Don H. Zimmerman, "Doing Gender," *Gender & Society* 1, no. 2 (1987): 125–51.

5. Carrie Paechter, "Learning Masculinities and Femininities: Power/Knowledge and Legitimate Peripheral Participation," *Women's Studies International Forum* 26, no. 6 (2003): 541–52, https://doi.org/10.1016/j.wsif.2003.09.008; Carrie Paechter, "Masculinities and Femininities as Communities of Practice," *Women's Studies International Forum* 26, no. 1 (2003): 69–77, https://doi.org/10.1016/s0277-5395(02)00356-4.

6. Liz Airton, "Untangling 'Gender Diversity': Genderism and Its Discontents (i.e., Everyone)," in *Diversity and Multiculturalism: A Reader*, ed. Shirley R. Steinberg (New York: Peter Lang, 2009), 224.

7. Ibid., 232.

8. Judith Butler, *Gender Trouble: Feminism and the Subversion of Identity*, 2nd ed. (New York: Routledge, 1999).

9. Harold Garfinkel, *Studies in Ethnomethodology* (Hoboken, NJ: Prentice Hall, 1967), 161.

10. Judith Butler, *Bodies That Matter: On the Discursive Limits of "Sex"* (London: Routledge, 1993), 95.

11. Katrina Roen, "Transgender Theory and Embodiment: The Risk of Racial Marginalisation," *Journal of Gender Studies* 10, no. 3 (2001): 253–63, https://doi.org/10.1080/09589230120086467.

12. Raewyn Connell, *Gender: A Short Introduction* (Cambridge, UK: Polity Press, 2002).

13. Chris Brickell, "Performativity or Performance? Clarifications in the Sociology of Gender," *New Zealand Sociology* 18, no. 2 (2003): 158–78.

14. Halberstam, "F2M," 226.

15. Sandy Stone, "The Empire Strikes Back: A Posttranssexual Manifesto," *Camera Obscura: Feminism, Culture, and Media Studies* 10, no. 2 (January 1992): 150–76, https://doi.org/10.1215/02705346-10-2_29-150.

16. Susan Stryker, "My Words to Victor Frankenstein above the Village of Chamounix: Performing Transgender Rage," *GLQ: A Journal of Lesbian and Gay Studies* 1, no. 3 (1994): 237–54, https://doi.org/10.1215/10642684-1-3-237, 251.

17. Genny Beemyn and Susan R. Rankin, *The Lives of Transgender People* (New York: Columbia University Press, 2011), 6.

18. Stryker, "My Words to Victor Frankenstein," 234.

19. Declan Henry, *Trans Voices: Becoming Who You Are* (London: Jessica Kingsley, 2017), 21.

20. Barb J. Burdge, "Bending Gender, Ending Gender: Theoretical Foundations for Social Work Practice with the Transgender Community," *Social Work* 52, no. 3 (2007): 243–50, https://doi.org/10.1093/sw/52.3.243.

21. Julie L. Nagoshi and Stephan/ie Brzuzy, "Transgender Theory: Embodying Research and Practice," *Affilia: Journal of Women and Social Work* 25, no. 4 (2010): 431–43, https://doi.org/10.1177/0886109910384068; David M. Halperin, *Saint Foucault: Towards a Gay Hagiography* (New York: Oxford University Press, 1995); Nikki Sullivan, *Critical Introduction to Queer Theory* (New York: New York University Press, 2003).

22. Nagoshi and Brzuzy, "Transgender Theory," 432.

23. Patricia O'Toole, "A Missing Chapter from Choral Methods Books: How Choirs Neglect Girls," *Choral Journal* 39, no. 5 (1998): 13.

24. Joan F. Boytim, *Roses, Laughter and Lullabies: 18 Classical Songs for Mezzo-Soprano Ages Mid-Teens and Up* (Milwaukee, WI: Hal Leonard, 2008); Joan F. Boytim, *Young Ladies, Shipmates & Journeys: 21 Classical Songs for Young Men Ages Mid-Teens and Up* (Milwaukee, WI: Hal Leonard, 2008).

25. Nicole Hanig and William R Sauerland, "A Content Analysis of State-Sponsored Solo and Ensemble Vocal Solos Lists," *A Content Analysis of State-Sponsored Solo and Ensemble Vocal Solos Lists* (unpublished).

26. Joshua Palkki, "Inclusivity in Action: Transgender Students in the Choral Classroom," *Choral Journal* 57, no. 11 (2017): 25–33.

27. Travis M. Andrews, "The Singular, Gender-Neutral 'They' Added to the Associated Press Stylebook," *Washington Post*, March 28, 2017, http://wapo.st/2nuXMMf?tid=ss_mail&utm_term=.f9d27ba8097f%C2%A0.

28. Katherine Meizel, *Multivocality: Singing on the Borders of Identity* (New York: Oxford University Press, 2020), 157.

29. Katy Steinmetz, "The Transgender Tipping Point: America's Next Civil Rights Frontier," *Time*, June 9, 2014, 38–46.

30. Ann E. Marimow, "Transgender Student Gavin Grimm's Battle over Bathroom Access Returns to Court," *Washington Post*, May 26, 2020, https://www.washingtonpost.com/local/legal-issues/transgender-student-gavin-grimms-battle-over-bathroom-access-returns-to-court/2020/05/22/571073c8-9b8e-11ea-a2b3-5c3f2d1586df_story.html; Michael Levenson and Neil Vigdor, "Inclusion of Transgender Student Athletes Violates Title IX, Trump Administration Says," *New York Times*, June 16, 2021, https://nyti.ms/2zwOAjh; Selena Simmons-Duffin, "Transgender Health Protections Reversed by Trump Administration," NPR, June 12, 2020, https://www.npr.org/sections/health-shots/2020/06/12/868073068/transgender-health-protections-reversed-by-trump-administration; Nico Lang, "Navy Grants Waiver Allowing Transgender Sailor to Serve Openly," NBC News, May 17, 2020, https://www.nbcnews.com/feature/nbc-out/navy-grants-waiver-allowing-transgender-sailor-serve-openly-n1208651.

31. Curt Guyette, "Inside the Supreme Court's First Transgender Rights Case," ACLU of Michigan, December 20, 2019, https://www.aclumich.org/en/news/inside-supreme-courts-first-transgender-rights-case; Dawn Ennis, "Idaho Governor Signs the Nation's Most Anti-Transgender Measures into Law," *Forbes*, March 31, 2020, https://www.forbes.com/sites/dawnstaceyennis/2020/03/30/idaho-governor-signs-the-nations-most-anti-transgender-measures-into-law/#17d0688a7a12.

32. Marimow, "Transgender Student."

33. Hannah Natanson, "Virginia School Board Will Pay $1.3 Million in Settlement to Transgender Student Gavin Grimm, Who Sued over Bathroom Policy," *Washington Post*, August 31, 2021, https://www.washingtonpost.com/local/education/transgender-bathroom-settlement-gavin-grimm/2021/08/26/0f186784-0699-11ec-a266-7c7fe02fa374_story.html.

34. Aimee Ortiz, "Aimee Stephens, Plaintiff in Transgender Case, Dies at 59," *New York Times*, June 16, 2020, https://nyti.ms/2SZ3eGa.

35. Ariane de Vogue and Devan Cole, "Supreme Court Says Federal Law Protects LGBTQ Workers from Discrimination," CNN, June 15, 2020, https://www.cnn.com/2020/06/15/politics/supreme-court-lgbtq-employment-case/index.html.

36. Andrew R. Flores et al., "How Many Adults Identify as Transgender in the United States?" UCLA School of Law Williams Institute, June 2016, https://williamsinstitute.law.ucla.edu/wp-content/uploads/Trans-Adults-US-Aug-2016.pdf.

37. Beemyn and Rankin, *The Lives of Transgender People.*

38. D. Chase Catalano, "'Trans Enough?' The Pressures Trans Men Negotiate in Higher Education," *TSQ: Transgender Studies Quarterly* 2, no. 3 (2015): 411–30, https://doi.org/10.1215/23289252-2926399, 425.

39. Catherine E. Lhamon and Vanita Gupta, "Dear Colleague Letter on Transgender Students" US Department of Justice and US Department of Education, May 13, 2016, https://www2.ed.gov/about/offices/list/ocr/letters/colleague-201605-title-ix-transgender.pdf.

40. Brooke Sopelsa and Jo Yurcaba, "Biden to Transgender Americans: 'Your President Has Your Back,'" NBC News, April 29, 2021, https://www.nbcnews.com/feature/nbc-out/biden-transgender-americans-your-president-has-your-back-n1265836.

41. Joseph G. Kosciw et al., *The 2017 National School Climate Survey* (New York: GLSEN, 2018), https://www.glsen.org/sites/default/files/2019-10/GLSEN-2017-National-School-Climate-Survey-NSCS-Full-Report.pdf.

42. Ibid., vxiii.

43. Ibid., xix.

44. Stephanie Brill and Rachel Pepper, *The Transgender Child: A Handbook for Families and Professionals* (Jersey City, NJ: Cleis Press, 2008).

45. Malcolm Harris, "What's a 'Safe Space'? A Look at the Phrase's 50-Year History," *Splinter*, November 11, 2015, https://splinternews.com/what-s-a-safe-space-a-look-at-the-phrases-50-year-hi-1793852786.

46. Meg Bolger and Sam Killermann, "Free LGBTQ+ Curriculum, Activities, & Resources!" Safe Zone Project, accessed June 1, 2021, https://thesafezoneproject.com/.

47. Kathleen E. Rands, "Considering Transgender People in Education," *Journal of Teacher Education* 60, no. 4 (2009): 419–31, https://doi.org/10.1177/0022487109341475, 421.

48. Julie C. Luecke, "Working with Transgender Children and Their Classmates in Pre-Adolescence: Just Be Supportive," *Journal of LGBT Youth* 8, no. 2 (2011): 116–56, https://doi.org/10.1080/19361653.2011.544941; Jeananne Nichols, "Rie's Story, Ryan's Journey," *Journal of Research in Music Education* 61, no. 3 (2013): 262–79, https://doi.org/10.1177/0022429413498259; Elizabethe Payne and Melissa Smith, "The Big Freak Out: Educator Fear in Response to the Presence of Transgender Elementary School Students," *Journal of Homosexuality* 61, no. 3 (2014): 399–418, https://doi.org/10.1080/00918369.2013.842430.

49. Rands, "Considering Transgender People," 425.

50. Joshua Palkki and William R. Sauerland, "Considering Gender Complexity in Music Teacher Education," *Journal of Music Teacher Education* 28, no. 3 (December 2018): 72–84, https://doi.org/10.1177/1057083718814582.

51. Sarah J. Bartolome and Melanie E. Stapleton, "'Can't I Sing with the Girls?': A Transgender Music Educator's Journey," in *Marginalized Voices in Music Education*, ed. Brent C. Talbot (New York: Routledge, 2018), 114–36.

52. Ibid., 132.

53. Nichols, "Rie's Story, Ryan's Journey."

54. Joshua Palkki and Paul Caldwell, "'We Are Often Invisible': A Survey on Safe Space for LGBTQ Students in Secondary School Choral Programs," *Research Studies in Music Education* 40, no. 1 (2017): 28–49, https://doi.org/10.1177/1321103x17734973.

55. Jason M. Silveira and Sarah C. Goff, "Music Teachers' Attitudes toward Transgender Students and Supportive School Practices," *Journal of Research in Music Education* 64, no. 2 (2016): 138–58, https://doi.org/10.1177/0022429416647048, 145.

56. O'Toole, "A Missing Chapter from Choral Methods Books," 13.

57. Patricia O'Toole, "I Sing in a Choir but 'I Have No Voice!'" *Visions of Research in Music Education* 6 (2005), 2.

58. Joshua Palkki, "'My Voice Speaks for Itself': The Experiences of Three Transgender Students in American Secondary School Choral Programs," *International Journal of Music Education* 38, no. 1 (November 2019): 126–46, https://doi.org/10.1177/0255761419890946.

59. Ari Agha, "Making Your Chorus Welcoming for Transgender Singers," *Voice* 41, no. 2 (2017): 18–23; Ryan Aguirre, "Finding the Trans Voice: A Review of the Literature on Accommodating Transgender Singers," *Update: Applications of Research in Music Education* 37, no. 1 (2018): 36–41, https://doi.org/10.1177/8755123318772561; Jane Ramseyer Miller, "Creating Choirs That Welcome Transgender Singers," *Choral Journal* 57, no. 4 (2016): 61–63; Palkki, "Inclusivity in Action"; Molly Rastin, "The Silenced Voice: Exploring Transgender Issues within Western Choirs," *Canadian Music Educator* 57, no. 4 (2016): 28–32; William R. Sauerland, "Trans Singers Matter: Gender Inclusive Considerations for Choirs," *VOICEPrints: Journal of New York Singing Teacher Association* 15, no. 5 (2018): 95–105.

60. Palkki, "'My Voice Speaks for Itself,'" 128.

61. Moya L. Andrews, *Voice Therapy for Children: The Elementary School Years* (London: Longman, 1986), 3.

62. Palkki, "'My Voice Speaks for Itself,'" 131.

63. Ibid., 139.

64. Anita Kozan, "The Singing Voice," in *Voice and Communication Therapy for the Transgender/Transsexual Client: A Comprehensive Clinical Guide*, ed. Robert K. Adler, Sandy Hirsch, and Michelle Mordaunt, 2nd ed. (San Diego, CA: Plural, 2012), 411–58.

65. Ibid., 439.

66. Alexandros Constansis, "The Changing Female-to-Male (FTM) Voice," *Radical Musicology* 3 (2008), http://www.radical-musicology.org.uk/2008/Constansis.htm, para. 4.

67. Ibid., para 5.

68. Ibid., para. 32.

69. Lisa Carew, Georgia Dacakis, and Jennifer Oates, "The Effectiveness of Oral Resonance Therapy on the Perception of Femininity of Voice in Male-to-Female Transsexuals," *Journal of Voice* 21, no. 5 (2007): 591–603, https://doi.org/10.1016/j.jvoice.2006.05.005; Adrienne B. Hancock, Julianne Krissinger, and Kelly Owen, "Voice Perceptions and Quality of Life of Transgender People," *Journal of Voice* 25, no. 5 (2011): 553–58, https://doi.org/10.1016/j.jvoice.2010.07.013; Adrienne Hancock, Lindsey Colton, and Fiacre Douglas, "Intonation and Gender Perception: Applications for Transgender Speakers," *Journal of Voice* 28, no. 2 (2014): 203–209, https://doi.org/10.1016/j.jvoice.2013.08.009.

70. Shelagh Davies and Joshua M. Goldberg, "Clinical Aspects of Transgender Speech Feminization and Masculinization," *International Journal of Transgenderism* 9, no. 3–4 (2006): 167–96, https://doi.org/10.1300/j485v09n03_08.

71. Ioanna Georgiadou Hershberger. "The Effects of Singing Exercises and Melodic Intonation Therapy (MIT) on the Male-to-Female Transgender Voice" (Master's thesis, University of North Carolina at Greensboro, 2005).

72. Robert W. Sparks and Audrey L. Holland, "Method: Melodic Intonation Therapy for Aphasia," *Journal of Speech and Hearing Disorders* 41, no. 3 (1976): 287–97, https://doi.org/10.1044/jshd.4103.287.

73. James C. McKinney, *The Diagnosis & Correction of Vocal Faults: A Manual for Teachers of Singing & for Choir Directors* (Nashville, TN: Genevox Music Group, 1994); Richard C. Miller, *The Structure of Singing: System and Art in Vocal Technique* (Belmont, CA: Wadsworth Group, 1996).

74. McKinney, *The Diagnosis & Correction of Vocal Faults*, 134.

75. Carew, Dacakis, and Oates, "The Effectiveness of Oral Resonance Therapy."

76. Kozan, "The Singing Voice," 437.

77. Ibid., 434.

78. Loraine Sims, "Teaching Lucas: A Transgender Student's Vocal Journey from Soprano to Tenor," *Journal of Singing* 73, no. 4 (2017): 376–75; Loraine Sims, "Teaching Transgender Students," *Journal of Singing* 73, no. 3 (2017): 279–82.

79. Sims, "Teaching Transgender Students," 282.

80. Brian Manternach et al., "Teaching Transgender Singers: Part 1," *Journal of Singing* 74, no. 1 (2017): 83–88; Brian Manternach, "Teaching Transgender Singers: Part 2," *Journal of Singing* 74, no. 2 (2017): 209–14.

81. Manternach et al., "Teaching Transgender Singers: Part 1," 84.

82. Ibid., 85.

83. Manternach, "Teaching Transgender Singers: Part 2," 210.

84. Ibid., 213.

85. Ibid., 214.

86. Nancy Bos, "Forging a New Path: Transgender Singers in Popular Music," *Journal of Singing* 73, no. 4 (2017): 421–24.

87. Ibid., 424.

88. Emerald Lessley, *Teaching Transgender Singers* (DMA diss., University of Washington, 2017).
89. Jackson Liz Hearns and Brian Kremer, *The Singing Teacher's Guide to Transgender Voices* (San Diego, CA: Plural, 2018).
90. Meizel, *Multivocality*, 6.
91. Ibid.
92. Ibid., 138.

2

Shifting Perspective
Theoretical Framework and Methodology

> "Queer is by definition *whatever* is at odds with the normal, the legitimate, the dominant. *There is nothing in particular to which it necessarily refers*. It is an identity without an essence. 'Queer' then, demarcates not a positivity but a positionality vis-à-vis the normative . . . a horizon of possibility."
>
> —David M. Halperin in
> *Saint Foucault: Towards a Gay Hagiography*

For some people, the word *queer* means odd, strange, or unnatural. This colloquial and limited definition fuels its use in and as hate speech, rendering it synonymous with perverse or repugnant. A more erudite definition of queer suggests a shift in perspective—to view a situation from a different angle. As a theoretical framework, queer and feminist theorist Annamarie Jagose explains, "Queer is widely perceived as a calling into question conventional understandings."[1] Coined in 1990 by Teresa de Lauretis as a provocative renaming of gay and lesbian studies,[2] "queer theory challenges the normative social ordering of identities and subjectivities."[3] Though queer is an identity marker for some LGBTQ+ persons, as a praxis, queer is a catalyst for new perspectives and understandings. "As a wish and a hope for a different kind of thinking and engagement,"[4] queer as a verb fosters a questioning, inspecting, and shifting of interpretations, traditions, and conventions. Queering our teaching—as a way of querying pedagogy with an integrated perspective of TGQ voices in its approach—is a necessary process toward making vocal instruction wholly welcoming and affirming for gender-expansive singers. Drawing on the introductory quote, queering our teaching cultivates new horizons for diverse and exciting possibilities.

Applying queer theory to vocal pedagogy draws attention to queer identities in our music studios and suggests a shift in our focus as vocal music educators. As an indeterminate, nonnormative practice, queer theory opens possibilities and enables many pedagogies to coexist.[5] Queering, as a form of querying, our teaching provides space to view a reality outside a stable, normative existence, unfettering a pathway for teaching singers with diverse goals, potentials, and identities. Jagose offers that queer is a practice of "anti-normative positioning."[6] Thus, queering pedagogy is similar to critical race theory by promoting counter- and nonnormative narratives and bringing awareness to marginalized and minoritized perspectives and students.[7] In a sense, queering presents students and teachers a means of "proudly reclaiming a marginal space."[8]

Queering Pedagogy and Curriculum

Music educator and researcher Freya Jarman-Ivens argues that queer is not an identity, but rather a process or invitation for inquiry (*in-queer-y*). The author asserts, "Once we see queer as an open-ended practice—not the exclusive property of any one group that is organized around a collective and stable identity, and not connected per se to any such identity—it becomes possible to reinsert queer into a framework concerned with subjectivity."[9] Jarman-Iven's interpretation of queer is supported by the vision that "queer marks an opportunity for reinterpretation. In this sense, queer is not an identity, a thing, or an entity but an *activity*. Queer names a practice, an approach, a way of relating."[10]

In keeping with these interpretations, queering is iterative, beckoning us to reexamine our beliefs, systems, and routines. Thus, one intent of queering pedagogy is to maintain a close and critical observation of our practices and pedagogies. In conceptualizing the teaching of singers as an open-ended and iterative process of critical interrogation and reflection, queering vocal pedagogy is more than an act of inclusion or a formula of "best practices" in teaching. A queer pedagogy for teaching singing is more than merely diversifying repertoire or modifying instructional habits; it includes "an inquiry in the conditions that make learning possible or prevent learning."[11] Queering vocal pedagogy seeks inquiry and interrogation in all domains of vocal teaching—from the socioecology of the studio to the technical know-how of singing, from teacher and student rapport to repertoire selection. As a disruption of the status quo, queering vocal pedagogy might dismantle inequality, invisibility, and marginalization in the teaching of singers. Fundamentally, queering calls for a repetitive process of investigating and innovating vocal music education to make vocal pedagogy more affirming for TGQ students.

The notion and practice of queering pedagogy in music is not new, having been discussed in music education,[12] music therapy,[13] and musicology.[14] In heightening queer identity in music, Wayne Koestenbaum writes in the book *Queering the Pitch*, "Think instead of the queer students: silently queer, bruised and attentive, faithful to the full phrase, to the metronome and the composer's intention."[15] In few words, Koestenbaum highlights the marginalization of queer identities under the tutelage of the maestro. Queer theory has been employed in music therapy to understand the "intersections of the physical voice, the psychological voice, and the body,"[16] allowing the concept of voice to be integrated and interwoven with a person's body and perspectives. In music education, Elizabeth Gould summons us to think beyond inclusion of queer identities into an image of "co-creating a vital, always in process table [. . .] where music education messmates commit to practices of regard and response . . . in ways that compel us to learn from and about each other."[17] Gould argues that inclusivity may fall short in affirming TGQ students if the act of inclusion only enables TGQ singers to participate in a cis-normative space; instead, we must rebuild the processes of teaching and learning with TGQ students at the core.

Queering Vocal Pedagogy

Vocal pedagogy, in short, is the exercise of teaching singers. Coming from Latin and Greek for the teaching of children (historically, boys), in vernacular form, *pedagogy* means the method, science, or art of teaching. Vocal pedagogy literature draws attention to specific technical aspects of singing, such as range development, breath support, and register negotiation. Since the influence of Manuel Garcia II, "the father of modern voice science,"[18] there has been an emphasis on understanding the anatomy and physiology of the voice, not so much as a teaching tool per se in the specific movements of laryngeal muscles, but as foundational knowledge on the mechanics of vocal production. Situated within a Western, classical music sound, Garcia's research has inspired many pedagogical books and materials.

In a conventional sense, the vocal pedagogue is responsible for training "the voice." Therefore, a teacher's role might be to detect and correct the vocal or postural wrongdoings of a singer. Vocal pedagogue author James McKinney refers to the "vocal faults" of a singer, where a teacher's primary role is to correct vocal errors.[19] This custom of detection and correcting vocal issues derives from a focus on "the voice" as a detached instrument to be trained. It is idiomatic in our language to say, "voice teacher." Jarman-Ivens asserts, "Operatic and other highly trained professional singers are often heard to talk about 'the voice' as opposed to 'my voice,' implying that they perceive the voice as an instrument that is not exactly and entirely part of them."[20] Singers might employ this vernacular to mitigate self-blame when their vocal production does not match their perceived ideal sound. As vocal production is a function of our physical bodies, our sense of self-worth might be interconnected to the quality of our vocal artistry. Let me be clear that *we are more than our voice*, and as vocal artists, we have many different forms of self-expression available to us. Though vocal sounds are a manifestation of our body, "the voice" does not determine our worth. For the teacher, queering vocal pedagogy enables a focus away from teaching "the voice" to teaching singers as whole and emotional individuals.

In promoting a queering of vocal pedagogy, I do not mean to suggest that vocal pedagogy is in any way static or digressive. Recent and exciting measures have been taken to enhance vocal pedagogy through greater knowledge of vocal science and acoustics.[21] Another relatively new movement is a broader welcoming of non–*bel canto* styles in vocal pedagogy, including musical theatre belting and other popular styles of singing, often referred to as contemporary commercial music (CCM). The National Association of Teachers of Singing (NATS) has advanced discussions at regional and national conferences on rap, hip-hop, CCM, and other non–*bel canto* musical styles.

In a survey study by Jeannette LoVetri and Edrie Means Weekly, data revealed that 96 percent of teachers of singers who teach contemporary commercial music also teach classical music.[22] The authors discovered that only 45 percent of the respondents who teach musical theater singers had any specific training to teach this repertoire. There is also a question as to whether the kind of repertoire changes the technical requirements of sound production. LoVetri and Means Weekly argue that "there is ample scientific evidence [to show] that the biggest difference [between classical music and CCM singing] is technical."[23] Since many CCM teachers have been trained through classical music programs, we might infer that even if they are teaching different approaches to vocal technique, the nature of their instruction has not necessarily been revamped.

Research on the nature of applied studio instruction depicts a master-apprentice approach, where a novice student seeks training from a "master" teacher.[24] The scholarship of Robert Duke and Amy Simmons found nineteen common elements of master teachers in applied lessons, divided into three categories: goals and expectations, effecting change, and conveying information. Their study of a conservatory approach to applied lesson instruction narrates a teacher-centered pedagogy, where the teacher defines the structure, goals, and pacing of the lesson. Duke and Simmons observed that teachers understand and communicate "excellent fundamental technique" and the ability to convey technical issues to impact change.[25] They also found that teachers frequently give negative feedback and determine repertoire assignment.

A replication of this study with a different population of teachers by Kelly Parkes and Mathius Wexler found that applied music instructors "teach along the teacher-centric guidelines that they are familiar with and that have been held as part of the accepted master-apprentice roles in the applied setting."[26] This scholarship revealed, however, that teachers seem to tailor their strategies to fit the specific needs of their students, providing guidance regarding technique and interpretation but also offering emotional support. Parkes and Wexler report, "Teachers are meeting students at their current level of achievement and moving them forward, scaffolding skills from the familiar to the unfamiliar, at a pace that does not cause frustration, low motivation, or lower efficacy in students."[27] Addressing individual students needs demonstrates a movement toward learner-centered teaching in the applied studio, providing space for students and permitting them to assert more leadership in their educational growth and musical development. In this model, teachers lean toward acknowledging each student as a unique learner in need of specific strategies and practices.

Student-centered teaching not only emphasizes a need for student-directed learning but underlines the importance of teacher-student rapport and student motivation as components to successful applied lessons. Piano pedagogue and psychologist Lucinda Mackworth-Young highlights the effectiveness of student-centered learning within the applied studio, finding that student-centered instruction places a greater emphasis on student goals, which increases student motivation.[28] Student-centered teaching emphasizes the importance of self-problem solving, where students are equipped with the tools and ability to practice between lessons, and where lessons serve as joint problem-solving sessions.[29]

Queering vocal pedagogy allows non-master-apprentice models of pedagogy to surface, broadening our ways of teaching and learning. In addition to student-centeredness, Christine Brown considers a "humane approach" to studio teaching in underscoring the importance of teaching with concern, respect, and empathy. Brown provides an example of how humane music teaching might look:

> The mentor guides by gradually leading the student to form his own strategies and monitor his own progress while practicing. She engages the student by watching, listening, and responding to the student from the perspective of the experience. She might also employ rhapsodic communication when a student needs an imaginative illustration or inspiring thought.[30]

In this model, the teacher is still an expert in the field and facilitates learning, but there is greater attention given to the student, who has a role in self-guiding their learning. Brown further illuminates that the pedagogy is "an ongoing collaborative project of artistic and personal growth built on unconditional approval, student choice, and mutual respect."[31] By this characterization, humane music instruction serves as a source for queering vocal pedagogy in that a teacher is summoned to evaluate, modify, respond, and collaborate distinctly with each individual student. The teacher is in an iterative and constant state of learning and reflection about either the functionality of singing or the goal of the singer.

Issues of systemic hegemony in the teaching of *bel canto* singing is discussed by Emily Good-Perkins, who argues, "Bel canto technique is not merely a study of vocal production, it is also a prioritization of a specific vocal sound," one that is representative of the dominant white, Eurocentric culture.[32] The teaching of singers is not only about the production of vocal sounds, but the reception and perception of the sound by the teacher, which implies a level of value judgment. "The act of listening to singing involves both the external objective sound and internal subjective perception," Good-Perkins asserts, and this perception of sound is based on a teacher's "experience and cultural and social context."³³ *Bel canto* singing has frequently been argued to be *the* single most healthy technique for singing, though it is prudent to recognize that its roots are steeped in the bias of "refined" white civilization. As a singer and teacher whose success is based on this style of singing, I am not arguing that *bel canto* singing is injurious or wicked, but it may disseminate a style of singing derived from cultural values that might not align with the goals and interests of all students.

Though only circuitously related to the main topic here, the conventional admittance process to a music conservatory in the United States is a huge barrier for some students, promoting a specific kind of singing—one that emanates primarily from the *bel canto* tradition. Both music performance and music education majors are often upheld to the same audition repertoire requirements, which focuses on classical Western music. In Julia Koza's essay "Listening for Whiteness," the author contends that music schools underpin patterns of racial bias by predominantly admitting students who match criteria based on performance practices of the Western European canon.³⁴ Though preprofessional classical singers may need to be held to the narrowness of this repertoire in the admittance process, the criteria might be unnecessary for music education and music therapy majors, who will be teaching a variety of musical styles in their professions. Furthermore, prospective music students with musical interests outside Western music, or those who have not had the opportunity to study this repertoire, may not receive admission into these degree programs due to the audition repertoire requirements. Though preparing professional musicians is a primary target in higher education, queering our teaching might enable us to listen with open ears and provide educational opportunities to students who might not fit a specific mold. Applying queer theory to vocal pedagogy allows recalibration of audition requirements to accept diverse musicians whose vocal artistry might be distinctive or idiosyncratic.

Perhaps yet another way to meditate on queering vocal pedagogy is in investigating the socioecology of the applied studio. More than just the environment of the studio or teacher-student rapport, the socioecology represents a synergetic connection between teacher and student. The kinship formed in this space often exceeds ordinary rapport. Though teachers of singers are not by trade trained in mental health counseling, the nature of one-on-one instruction calls on teachers to be more than just voice technicians. Teachers must be concerned with not overstepping their roles, but queering vocal pedagogy might enable room for teachers of singers to have greater knowledge in trauma-informed instruction[35] or compassionate pedagogy.[36]

Compassionate music teaching is considered a form of "experience-sharing" undermining the traditional master-apprentice model.[37] Derived from Latin for "suffering with," compassion entreats teachers to journey alongside their students, to share in their enthusiasm and their struggles. Karin Hendricks explains:

> Compassionate music teachers act as guides, supports, and champions of students' self-selected dreams, using the students' own aspirations for musical expression as a catalyst for emphasizing the practice of diverse technical skills. Facilitating this kind of learning requires that we listen, that we empathize, that we truly put ourselves in students' shoes and consider what learning looks like from the student's perspective.[38]

Hendricks outlines six elements of compassionate teaching, including (1) trust, (2) empathy, (3) patience, (4) inclusion, (5) community, and (6) authentic connection. Although Hendricks's concepts of compassionate music teaching are not designed specifically for teaching of singers, the application supports the notion of queering vocal pedagogy. In the applied voice studio, Claudia Friedlander affirms the importance of compassion, asserting, "When we show our students kindness and help them to feel supported and seen, we send a message that their voice, what they have to say, who they fundamentally are, matters."[39] We see similar philosophical perspectives in vocal pedagogy framed as a holistic approach to teaching.

Finally, in discussing a "holistic" approach to teaching singers, Karen Sell contends that vocal pedagogues would benefit from knowledge of developmental psychology.[40] Making a case that teachers need more than technical know-how, Sell's scholarship supports the idea of teachers of singers learning pedagogy outside the traditional vocal music education curricula. The importance of "wholistic" teaching is also highlighted by W. Stephen Smith in his book *The Naked Voice*, where he says, "Because our entire person is our instrument, everything about us—our physical, emotional, intellectual, psychological, and spiritual state of being—affects the physical and acoustical aspects of singing."[41] Pedagogy that emphasizes compassion or (w)holistic mindfulness serves as a model for accepting all students, including TGQ singers, in a way that affirms their wholeness and authenticity. Models of teaching that steer away from judgment, competitiveness, and labeling provide a foundation for queering vocal pedagogy.

In a cultural landscape where music education seems to be undermined by outcome-driven educational trends that accentuate science, technology, engineering, and mathematics, it might feel self-sabotaging to question the nature of our work. Queering vocal pedagogy destabilizes the traditional master-apprentice model, calling on teachers of singers to be learners in an ongoing mode of critical and close observation. Queering vocal pedagogy solicits a critique on all aspects of our practices. For example, how might vocal pedagogy change if success could be measured by the number of students who live a fulfilled life of singing instead of by how many of our students major in vocal music, win competitions, or find material success in the professional industry. If we were to detach vocal pedagogy from attainments, queering vocal pedagogy might seem less daunting. In *Marginalized Voices in Music Education*, Brent Talbot affirms, "As music teachers, we have the power to create new situations, even when we may feel the pressures to confirm to the dominating practices of our spaces for teaching and learning."[42] Queer, innovative thinking and critical reflection may help vocal pedagogy stimulate new situations and relevancy, alongside evolving trends and technologies, to reshape the landscape of vocal music education in the United States.

Design and Methodology of This Book

The purpose of *Queering Vocal Pedagogy* is to explore the experiences and perspectives of TGQ singers taking one-on-one singing lessons. This book examines the specific practices and pedagogies of their singing teachers to provide insight within the applied studio. Composed of six case studies made up of a teacher-student pair each, this book represents various identities within the TGQ population. The following research questions guided this qualitative study: (1) How do musical spaces shape the identity of TGQ singers? (2) How do TGQ singers describe their vocal training in voice lessons? and (3) How do teachers of singers characterize the training of TGQ students?

The values and benefits of a case study approach in examining vocal pedagogy enables a deep look at the social situation of the participants, richly exploring the perceptions that construct the singer's experience in the applied vocal studio. This approach enables the inquiry to be "grounded in the value of information-rich cases and emergent, in-depth understanding."[43] Making meaning from this process is derived through inductive analysis. A single case study is "a thing, a single entity, a unit around which there are boundaries,"[44] and thus, the bounded context for this study is the applied studio where the teacher and student interact. Qualitative data for these case studies were collected during a defined duration of time, offering a snapshot of the vocal training experience rather than a longitudinal perspective. Gender is fluid, and therefore a depiction of a singer that was fitting at the time of the study might not accurately represent the singer's perceptions or vocal abilities throughout their entire singing lives. Strategies and approaches to training singers are complex and varied. While data on vocal technique might be transferable, this study does not yield a comprehensive assessment of vocal technique for all TGQ singers. Every applied music lesson is unique, and accordingly, generalizing can be problematic.

Six singers and six teachers comprise the study for this book. Although I established criteria for inclusion in the study, there remains a diverse pool of participants. Of the TGQ singers, two

Table 2.1. Participant Overview

Name	Role	Corresponding Participant	Gender
Isabella	Student	Martha	Transgender teenage woman
Martha	Teacher	Isabella	Cisgender woman
Chrys	Student	Nicola	Transgender woman
Nicola	Teacher	Chrys	Cisgender woman
Forest	Student	Darius	Transgender man
Darius	Teacher	Forest	Cisgender teenage man
Emmett	Student	Naomi	Transgender man
Naomi	Teacher	Emmett	Cisgender woman
Kelly	Student	Peter	Nonbinary
Peter	Teacher	Kelly	Transgender man/nonbinary
B	Student	Eli	Trans/nonbinary
Eli	Teacher	B	Transgender man

are transgender women, two are transgender men, and two are trans/nonbinary. The teacher population includes two transgender men, two cisgender straight women, one cisgender gay man, and one cisgender lesbian woman. The criteria for teacher participants included membership in a professional music organization and a record of sustaining an independent applied voice studio. Table 2.1 provides a cursory overview of the student and teacher participants. Pseudonyms have been used to protect confidentiality.

I observed two lessons of each singer-teacher pair, providing approximately twelve hours of observation data in total. Lessons were scheduled based on teacher and student availability. Field notes taken during lessons provided information on strategies and approaches to vocal training, documenting specific vocal exercises, student range, repertoire, communication, and rapport between student and teacher. I assumed a nonparticipant role—some lessons I observed in person, while other observations were made using a videoconferencing platform. A "grand tour" form of observation was adopted in the first lesson to enable the identification of "major features."[45] The second lesson enabled a "mini-tour"-style observation during which I drew comparisons between the lessons and focused on specific data observed during the first observation.

In-depth, semi-structured student interviews occurred before the observation of lessons. The interviews incorporated a varied line of inquiry, including Experience (open-ended) Questions, Mini-Tour Questions ("Walk me through . . ."), and Native-Language Questions ("Tell me about . . .") to clarify the language and perceptions of the singers.[46] Teacher interviews occurred after the observation of both lessons, which enabled me further access to understanding the strategies and approaches observed in the lessons. These interviews also provided the opportunity to ask clarifying questions and further probe the experiences and perceptions of the students, as understood by their teacher. Each interview was approximately sixty to ninety minutes in duration, yielding approximately fifteen hours of interview data. All interviews were audio-recorded, and a word-for-word interview transcription was sent to each interviewee for feedback to increase validity of the content.

Narrative inquiry and emancipatory storysharing[47] have been used in capturing authenticity in research with marginalized populations.[48] Similar to these approaches, portraiture analysis was employed in this study, which enabled me to document the participant's perspectives and visions—"their authority, knowledge, and wisdom."[49] The use of portraiture analysis has been effectively employed in contemporary music education research to illustrate the subject's lived experiences.[50] Portraiture analysis "enables the reader to experience a deeper level of understanding and empathy that would be exceedingly difficult to achieve if one were writing as a dispassionate, detached observer."[51] By highlighting an individual's strength and resilience, portraiture analysis seeks to present the successes within a case study, as opposed to investigating only setbacks and challenges. Thus, while the current study presents multiple individual portraits of TGQ singers in the applied studio, there has been an explicit attempt to seek and understand the joys alongside difficulties in the lived experience. In other words, portraiture analysis helps avoid the pitfall of discussing "transgender issues," as discussed in chapter 1.

Issues of trustworthiness with regard to validity, reliability, and transferability in this study are considered. Efforts to accurately depict the concepts, feelings, and actions of the participants through interview transcripts, as well as by directly including the participants in the creation of the portraits, were implemented to further strengthen the study's validity. Participants were offered multiple occasions to modify their interview transcripts and their narrative portraits. In some cases, participants changed their interview responses and portraits several times to accurately reflect their perspectives; other times, participants requested no changes post-interview and observations.

While I aim to realistically depict the experiences of TGQ singers and their voice teachers, as a trained singer with a background in *bel canto* technique, I acknowledge my own biases with regard to teaching vocal technique. My understanding of the participants' experiences is through the lens of my own teaching, training, and gender. While the interviews seek to deeply understand the participants' perceptions, I am aware of issues inherent in interview data collection, such as inclusion, construction, or delivery of specific interview questions might unintentionally influence the participant's response. I also recognize that participants might tend to respond in a manner that they may think is agreeable to me, though that might not accurately represent their authentic lived experience.

In pursuit of queering vocal pedagogy, this book is not organized around vocal issues such as breath management or registration, like other vocal pedagogy books, but rather around the identities of the singers. Chapters 3 through 5 each investigate the lived experiences of two transgender women, two transgender men having undergone androgen therapy, and two trans/nonbinary students. This presentation hopefully provides readers an insider's view of their lessons to understand their pacing, vocal exercises, repertoire, and process toward vocal development. Chapter 6 discusses practical steps and measures that all teachers can take to make their studios welcoming and affirming. The last chapter examines queering as a habit of mind for studio teachers and ensemble directors.

As the discipline of vocal pedagogy begins to embrace different gender identities, we also need to be prepared to teach different styles of singing, from classical to musical theatre, and contemporary styles to experimental music. Queering vocal pedagogy is a framework for reimaging vocal music education to ensure that gender and musical diversity is fully integrated. Queering as a mindset for teaching singers dismantles a master-apprentice model so that teachers of singing no longer serve as the only authority in the studio; teachers who put querying at the center of their teaching give power and voice to the students who seek vocal development and expression.

As vocal pedagogues in the twenty-first century, we must find ways to move beyond a teacher-driven, master-apprentice experience toward a model that celebrates a dynamic, pluralistic exchange of knowledge and ideas. Queer pedagogy in the music studio fosters fluidity in joint problem-solving, shared construction of knowledge, and a more democratic approach that allows for multiple possibilities and outcomes. Queering vocal pedagogy seeks an iterative state of learning, critical thinking, and reflection—steering away from a "teacher knows best" attitude into a direction that beholds a student as a whole, emotional, worthy human. The case studies within are intended to illustrate various examples and practices of queering vocal pedagogy. In 1921, James Francis Cooke recorded interviews with great Western classical singers, and in his introduction states, "Any method or scheme of teaching the art of singing that does not seek to develop the inherent intellectual and emotional vocal complexion of the singer can never approach a good method."[52] Queering vocal pedagogy is neither a method or scheme; but as Cooke suggests, it is our role to guide our students along vocal paths that enable them to express their authentic intellectual and emotional ways of knowing. Though it might be easier to focus on vocal technique, in queering vocal pedagogy, our capacities for care and artistic development are much more profound.

Chapter Takeaways

In Jerry Herman's 1983 musical *La Cage Aux Folles,* the drag queen protagonist Albin/Zaza announces: "Here at *La Cage* we live life—how should I put it?—on an angle."[53] This chapter explored the application of queer theory on vocal pedagogy to imagine the teaching of singers from a different angle. Queer theory not only brings attention to LGBTQ+ individuals in educational experiences, it also fosters a shifted perspective to a nonnormative, nontraditional lens. First, this chapter provided a short background on the history and distinctness of queer theory as an academic discourse, then it looked at how queer theory, when applied to pedagogy, allows for new ideas and capacities in learning and teaching to prosper. The notion of *queer* as a verb (as in *queering*) set in motion a dismantling of vocal pedagogy from practices that reify gender norms—thus marginalizing TGQ singers—toward a reconstruction of vocal pedagogy where all voices and identities are equitably included. Later, this chapter examined how vocal pedagogy has already shifted from a traditional master-apprentice hegemonic approach of Western classical music, toward models that foster humane, student-centered, holistic, and compassionate teaching. Finally, this chapter outlined the methodology of the research and data collection for this book, and then introduced the research participants whose case studies comprise the heart of the next three chapters.

Essential takeaways from this chapter include:

- Queering, as an act of querying conventional beliefs, carves space for new perspectives and understandings in opposition of a cis- and heteronormative system.
- Queer can serve as an identity marker for some individuals, and act as an iterative practice of critical inquiry against any normative pattern.
- While related vocal pedagogy research has discussed the need for inclusive pedagogy, queer theory enables a refashioning of vocal pedagogy with TGQ students at its core.

- Pedagogies that include student-centeredness, antiracism, and humane and compassionate teaching are already queering the master-apprenticeship model of applied lesson instruction.
- Queering our teaching, as a practice of continual learning, benefits not only TGQ students, but all students who have felt excluded from traditional cis- and heteronormative approaches.
- Queer theory serves as a nonnormative lens for the experiences and perspectives of TGQ singers offered in the next three chapters.
- Data for the case studies presented within this book were collected through interviews and lesson observations, shared here through portraiture analysis, to offer an insider's view of the teaching and learning.

Notes

1. Annamarie Jagose, *Queer Theory: An Introduction* (New York: New York University Press, 2010), 97.
2. David M. Halperin, "The Normalization of Queer Theory," in *Queer Theory and Communication: From Disciplining Queers to Queering the Discipline(s)*, ed. Gust A. Yep, Karen Lovaas, and John P. Elia (New York: Harrington Park Press, 2003), 339–43.
3. Kath Browne and Catherine J. Nash, "Queer Methods and Methodologies: An Introduction," in *Queer Methods and Methodologies: Intersecting Queer Theories and Social Science Research*, ed. Kath Browne and Catherine J. Nash (London: Taylor and Francis, 2016), 5.
4. Hannah McCann and Whitney Monaghan, *Queer Theory Now: From Foundations to Futures* (London: Red Globe Press, 2020), 3.
5. Gust A. Yep, Karen Lovaas, and John P. Elia, "Introduction: Queering Communication: Starting the Conversation," in *Queer Theory and Communication: From Disciplining Queers to Queering the Discipline(s)*, ed. Gust A. Yep, Karen Lovaas, and John P. Elia (New York: Harrington Park Press, 2003), 9.
6. Jagose, *Queer Theory*, 98.
7. Richard Delgado and Jean Stefancic, *Critical Race Theory: An Introduction* (New York: New York University Press, 2017).
8. Susanne Luhmann, "Queering/Querying Pedagogy? Or, Pedagogy Is a Pretty Queer Thing," in *Queer Theory in Education*, ed. William F. Pinar (Mahwah, NJ: Erlbaum, 1998), 124.

9. Freya Jarman-Ivens, *Queer Voices: Technologies, Vocalities, and the Musical Flaw* (London: Palgrave Macmillan, 2016), 17.

10. Tyler Bradway and Ellen L. McCallum, "After Queer Studies: Literature, Theory and Sexuality in the 21st Century," in *After Queer Studies: Literature, Theory and Sexuality in the 21st Century*, ed. Tyler Bradway and Ellen L. McCallum (Cambridge, UK: Cambridge University Press, 2019), 3.

11. Luhmann, "Queering/Querying Pedagogy?" 130

12. Joseph Michael Abramo, "Queering Informal Pedagogy: Sexuality and Popular Music in School," *Music Education Research* 13, no. 4 (2011): 465–77, https://doi.org/10.1080/14613808.2011.632084.

13. Candice Bain and Maevon Gumble, "Querying Dialogues: A Performative Editorial on Queering Music Therapy," *Voices: A World Forum for Music Therapy* 19, no. 3 (2019), https://doi.org/10.15845/voices.v19i3.2904; Maevon Gumble, "Gender Affirming Voicework: An Introduction for Music Therapy," *Voices: A World Forum for Music Therapy* 19, no. 3 (2019), https://doi.org/10.15845/voices.v19i3.2661.

14. Philip Brett, Elizabeth Wood, and Gary C. Thomas, *Queering the Pitch: The New Gay and Lesbian Musicology* (New York: Routledge, Taylor and Francis Group, 2011).

15. Wayne Koestenbaum, "Queering the Pitch: A Posy of Definitions and Impersonations," in *Queering the Pitch: The New Gay and Lesbian Musicology*, ed. Philip Brett, Elizabeth Wood, and Gary C. Thomas (New York: Routledge, 1994), 5.

16. Gumble, "Gender Affirming Voicework," para. 1.

17. Elizabeth Gould, "Companion-Able Species: A Queer Pedagogy for Music Education," *Bulletin of the Council for Research in Music Education* 197 (2013): 63–75, https://doi.org/10.5406/bulcouresmusedu.197.0063, 69.

18. James Stark, *Bel Canto: A History of Vocal Pedagogy*, 2nd ed. (Toronto: University of Toronto Press, 2003), xxii.

19. James C. McKinney, *The Diagnosis & Correction of Vocal Faults: A Manual for Teachers of Singing & for Choir Directors* (Nashville, TN: Genevox Music Group, 1994).

20. Jarman-Ivens, *Queer Voices*, 165.

21. Kenneth Bozeman, *Practical Vocal Acoustics: Pedagogic Applications for Teachers and Singers* (Hillsdale, NY: Pendragon Press, 2013).

22. Jeannette L LoVetri and Edrie Means Weekly, "Contemporary Commercial Music (CCM) Survey: Who's Teaching What in Nonclassical Music," *Journal of Voice* 17, no. 2 (2003): 207–15, https://doi.org/10.1016/s0892-1997(03)00004-3.

23. Ibid., 214.

24. Robert A. Duke and Amy L. Simmons, "The Nature of Expertise: Narrative Descriptions of 19 Common Elements Observed in the Lesson of Three Renowned Artist-Teachers," *Bulletin of the Council for Research in Music Education* 170 (2006): 7–19; Kelly A. Parkes and Mathius Wexler, "The Nature of Applied Music Teaching Expertise: Common Elements Observed in the Lessons of

Three Applied Teachers," *Bulletin of the Council for Research in Music Education*, no. 193 (2012): 45–62, https://doi.org/10.5406/bulcouresmusedu.193.0045.

25. Duke and Simmons, "The Nature of Expertise," 11.

26. Parkes and Wexler, "The Nature of Applied Music Teaching Expertise," 56.

27. Ibid., 59.

28. Lucinda Mackworth-Young, "Pupil-Centred Learning in Piano Lessons: An Evaluated Action-Research Programme Focusing on the Psychology of the Individual," *Psychology of Music* 18, no. 1 (1990): 73–86, https://doi.org/10.1177/0305735690181006.

29. Richard Kennell, "Toward a Theory of Applied Music Instruction," *Quarterly Journal of Music Teaching and Learning* 3, no. 2 (1992): 5–16.

30. Christine A. Brown, "A Humane Approach to the Studio," in *Humane Music Education for the Common Good*, ed. Iris M. Yob and Estelle R. Jorgensen (Bloomington: Indiana University Press, 2020), 100.

31. Ibid.

32. Emily Good-Perkins, "Rethinking Vocal Education as a Means to Encourage Positive Identity Development in Adolescents," in *Humane Music Education for the Common Good*, ed. Iris M. Yob and Estelle R. Jorgensen (Bloomington: Indiana University Press, 2020), 162.

33. Ibid, 164.

34. Julia Eklund Koza, "Listening for Whiteness: Hearing Racial Politics in Undergraduate School Music," *Philosophy of Music Education Review* 16, no. 2 (2008): 145–55, https://doi.org/10.2979/pme.2008.16.2.145.

35. Carin A. McEvoy and Karen Salvador, "Aligning Culturally Responsive and Trauma-Informed Pedagogies in Elementary General Music," *General Music Today* 34, no. 1 (August 2020): 21–28, https://doi.org/10.1177/1048371320909806; William R Sauerland, "Sound Teaching: Trauma-Informed Pedagogy in Choir," *Choral Journal* 62, no. 3 (2021): 32–43.

36. Karin S. Hendricks, *Compassionate Music Teaching: A Framework for Motivation and Engagement in the 21st Century* (Lanham, MD: Rowman & Littlefield, 2018).

37. Ibid., 5.

38. Ibid.

39. Claudia Friedlander, "Content versus Compassion in the Voice Studio," The Liberated Voice, last modified January 16, 2020, https://www.claudiafriedlander.com/the-liberated-voice/2020/01/content-versus-compassion.html.

40. Karen Sell, *The Disciplines of Vocal Pedagogy: Towards an Holistic Approach* (Burlington, VT: Ashgate, 2005).

41. W. Stephen Smith, *The Naked Voice: A Wholistic Approach to Singing* (Oxford, UK: Oxford University Press, 2017), 18.

42. Brent C. Talbot, *Marginalized Voices in Music Education* (New York: Routledge, 2018), x.

43. Linda Bloomberg and Marie Volpe, *Completing Your Qualitative Dissertation: A Road Map from Beginning to End* (Los Angeles: Sage, 2016), 148.

44. Sharan B. Merriam, *Qualitative Research and Case Study Applications in Education* (San Francisco: Jossey-Bass, 1998), 27.

45. James P. Spradley, *Participant Observation* (New York: Holt, Rinehart and Winston, 1980), 77.

46. James P. Spradley, *The Ethnographic Interview* (New York: Holt, Rinehart, & Winston, 1979).

47. Thomas Barone, "Persuasive Writings, Vigilant Readings, and Reconstructed Characters: The Paradox of Trust in Educational Storysharing," *International Journal of Qualitative Studies in Education* 8, no. 1 (1995): 63–74, https://doi.org/10.1080/0951839950080107.

48. Vanessa L. Bond, "Like Putting a Circle with a Square: A Male Alto's Choral Journey," in *Marginalized Voices in Music Education*, ed. Brent C. Talbot (New York: Routledge, 2018), 137–52; Jeananne Nichols, "Rie's Story, Ryan's Journey," *Journal of Research in Music Education* 61, no. 3 (2013): 262–79, https://doi.org/10.1177/0022429413498259.

49. Sara Lawrence-Lightfoot and Jessica Hoffmann Davis, *The Art and Science of Portraiture* (San Francisco: Jossey-Bass, 1997), xv.

50. Mary Jo Clemmons, *Rapport in the Applied Voice Studio* (EdD diss., Teachers College, Columbia University, 2007); Christianne Knauer Roll, *Female Musical Theater Belting in the 21st Century: A Study of the Pedagogy of the Vocal Practice and Performance* (EdD diss., Teachers College, Columbia University, 2014); Colleen Anne Quinn Sears, *Paving Their Own Way: Experiences of Female High School Band Directors* (EdD diss., Teachers College, Columbia University, 2010).

51. Donald G. Hackmann, "Using Portraiture in Educational Leadership Research," *International Journal of Leadership in Education* 5, no. 1 (2002): 51–60, https://doi.org/10.1080/13603120110057109, 53.

52. Harriette Brower and James Francis Cooke, *Great Singers on the Art of Singing* (Mineola, NY: Dover, 2018), 3.

53. Harvey Fierstein, Jerry Herman, and Jean Poiret, *La Cage Aux Folles* (New York: Samuel French, 1983), 49.

3

Trans Feminine Singers

> "It is revolutionary for any trans person to choose to be seen & visible in a world that tells us we should not exist."
>
> —Laverne Cox, on Instagram

Chapters 3 through 5 of this book provide an examination of six trans and genderqueer singers, their teachers, and their experiences and training in the applied studio. For nonsingers or nonsinging teachers encountering this book, an introductory discussion on the mechanics and function of singing is provided to help the reader understand the exercises and activities that occur in a singing lesson. Next, this chapter reviews traditional "female" voices as discussed in previous vocal pedagogy literature, followed by a discussion of voice "feminization" in speech-language pathology. The bulk of this chapter takes an in-depth look at two trans feminine singers, Chrys and Isabella, to learn more about their perspectives, vocal development, and musical lives.

A Brief Overview of the Functionality of Singing

The existence of sound requires four components: (1) a power source, (2) a vibrating object, (3) a resonating cavity, and (4) an object to receive the soundwaves.¹ In speaking or singing, the power source is the exhalation of air; the vibrating object is the vocal folds, which are in the larynx; and the resonating cavity is the vocal tract, primarily consisting of the throat and mouth. The larynx, sometimes referred to as the voice box, is made up of nine different cartilages, including the thyroid, cricoid, and arytenoid, which the vocal folds are housed within, shown in figure 3.1.

Source-filter theory of vocal sound production views the "source" as the airflow through the glottis (i.e., vocal folds) and the "filter" as the vocal tract through which vibrations are modified to make different spoken or sung sounds.² When a spoken or sung sound is produced, this is called phonation. As the vocal folds adduct—in other words, come together—subglottic air passes through the glottis, assisting the vocal folds to vibrate. The sound is consequently amplified as it moves through the throat and mouth. It is from this basic yet extraordinarily refined process that—through variations of short and sustained vibrations and articulations—the expressive art of singing is derived. A singing teacher typically offers a student techniques and practices to help make this sound-making process more efficient and expressive.

Commonplace voice types for singing include soprano, alto, tenor, and bass, though in addition to this standard quartet, various vocal classifications exist for specific voice types (sometimes called a vocal *Fach*), like coloratura soprano, contralto, countertenor, heldentenor, or basso profundo. (For a longer discussion on traditional Eurocentric voice types, see chapter 7 of James McKinney's *The Diagnosis and Correction of Vocal Faults*.) The range of a person's voice extends from the lowest to highest pitch (or, more accurately, the slowest to fastest frequency that a person's vocal folds vibrate). For bodies assigned male at birth, the natural release of testosterone during puberty commonly triggers a lowering in vocal range due to an increase in vocal fold mass and a lengthening of the vocal folds. The larynx tips forward slightly, exposing the thyroid notch (colloquially called the "Adam's apple"; note the gendered language). The vocal fold length for an adult assigned male at birth is typically

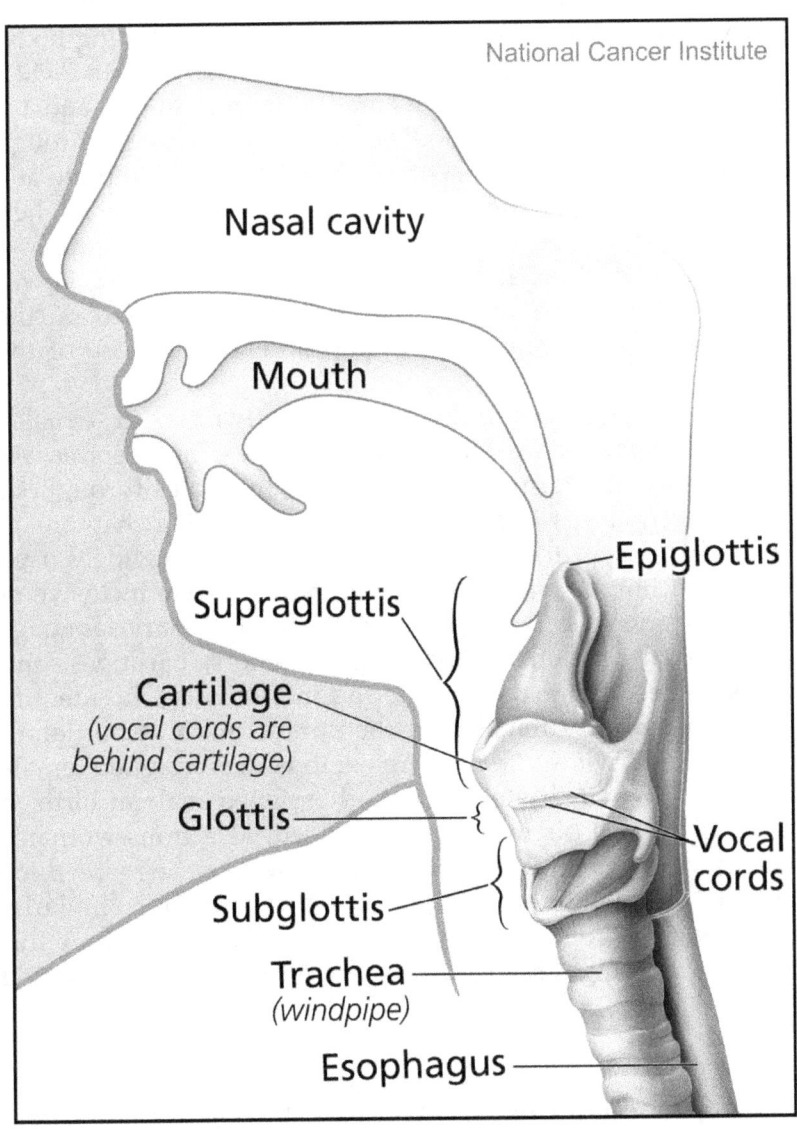

Figure 3.1. The Main Parts of the Larynx (Supraglottis, Glottis, and Subglottis) and Other Nearby Structures. Source: National Cancer Institute, 2007 (https://visuals online.cancer.gov/details.cfm?imageid=4357)

between 17.5 to 25 millimeters.[3] The voices of bodies assigned female at birth also change during puberty, with an increase in laryngeal size consistent with the overall developing body. Vocal fold length for an adult assigned female at birth is 12.5 to 17 millimeters.[4] Even such a small difference in size equates to different vocal ranges. Bodies that have advanced through puberty without high levels of testosterone tend to vibrate at a faster frequency, producing a pitch that we perceive as higher. Likewise, longer and thicker vocal folds typically vibrate at a slower frequency, producing pitches perceived as lower. Lower versus higher ranges are relative to each body based on the complete, unique biological makeup and habitual use of the voice.

Vocal pedagogy literature conventionally refers to "female" and "male" voices to denote biological sex, not gender. As noted earlier, the term "female" is used in quotes throughout the next section—as "male" will be in the following chapter—in acknowledgement that this language, which is so widely used in vocal technique and pedagogy literature, is not inclusive of all gender identities and voices. This strictly binary language is problematic, often ignoring female tenors, baritones, and basses; male sopranos and altos; and individuals who identify as neither male nor female. For the purposes of this portion of the literature review, "female" refers to bodies assigned female at birth and "male" refers to bodies assigned male at birth. It is important this distinction is addressed, as a trans woman's voice is "female" and "feminine" no matter the range in which she most easily phonates—be it as a soprano or bass. Similarly, a trans man's voice is "male" and "masculine," even if his speaking and singing range falls more comfortably in the treble range.

Traditional "Female" Voices

Traditional solo voice classifications of "female" voices are soprano, mezzo-soprano, and contralto. (The term *alto* is typically used only for choral divisions, usually sung by contraltos

Figure 3.2. *Vocal ranges for traditional "female" voices.*

or mezzo-sopranos.) In his book *The Diagnosis and Correction of Vocal Faults,* McKinney indicates that each voice type has a "practical" and "ideal" range.[5] A contralto ideally sings from G3 (below middle C) to G5, encompassing a two-octave range. A mezzo-soprano's ideal range is a whole step above the contralto, thus covering A3 to A5. The ideal range for a soprano is C4 (middle C) to C6, and higher sopranos might extend to the F above or higher. Figure 3.2 shows the "ideal" ranges of these voice types.

Voice registration refers to the shifting of the intrinsic vocal muscles that naturally occurs when a singer ascends or descends over their full range.[6] The act of shifting the gears in a vehicle might provide an adequate, albeit crude, metaphor for registration in the singing voice. The point of the shift, known as the *passaggio,* is the area of the range during which the intrinsic muscles of the larynx modify, which might result in a change of timbre. In *bel canto* vocal technique—the traditional training for Western classical music—singers aim to learn to make this muscular shift imperceptible to the listener. The discussion of vocal registers is problematic as it is hotly debated, both in terms of the number of vocal registers each singer might possess and in the language used to define them. Common language used to name vocal registers include the *chest* and *head* voices, but other descriptive terms include lower or higher, modal or falsetto, heavier or lighter, and thyroarytenoid-dominant or cricothyroid-dominant. Some teachers discuss the *voix mixte,* or mixed voice, as a blend of the head and chest registers. Writing on the speaking voice, the renowned vocal pedagogue and author Richard Miller posits, "Speech habits of females tend to fall into three types: (1) head voice is almost exclusively used; and chest voice may be nearly non-existent; (2) both chest and head voices are used for speech inflection, with a preponderance of head; and (3) chest voice is chiefly used."[7]

In *bel canto* singing, a combination and balance of the head and chest registers is employed. Contraltos may use more chest voice than their mezzo-soprano or soprano counterparts, but all standard "female" voice types typically use a combination of both registers. Miller describes "female" voices as having two *passaggi* points: lower and upper. Each voice is different, but in general, contraltos experience the lower passaggio around G4 and the upper passaggio at D5. The lower passaggio for mezzo-sopranos is E4 or F4, with the upper passaggio one octave above. Sopranos tend to experience the lower passaggio at E-flat 4 and the upper passaggio at F-sharp 5. Lastly, a part of the voice known as the flageolet register, or whistle tone, is a higher extension above the upper passaggio. This high range is produced by "a high rate of longitudinal tension of the vocal ligaments, considerable damping of the posterior portion of the vocal folds, limited vibrating mass of the vocal folds, and high subglottic pressure and airflow rate."[8] Not all conventional "female" voices produce a whistle tone, and phonation in this range is generally used sparingly by singers.

Voice Feminization for Trans Women

Research on the vocal production of trans women has received attention in speech-language pathology as early as the 1970s, but with substantially more discussion since the early 2000s[9]. Some trans women engage in estrogen hormone therapy to modify biological characteristics of their body, such as changes to skin quality and hair patterns. The introduction of estrogen in the body seems to have no major effect on the physiology of the adult voice, and thus, surgical procedures and speech-language therapies (recently being renamed "gender affirming voice care") have been developed as effective forms of **voice feminization**. The aim of these therapies is to help a trans woman develop her voice in way that aligns with her ideal sound, which might include changes in range, timbre, inflection, or language choice.

For trans women seeking voice feminization, a rise in the fundamental frequency (e.g., the average pitch of a person's speaking voice) and changes to secondary vocal characteristics, such as timbre and articulation, are often sought. This section first looks at research related to surgical procedures in voice feminization. Next, scholarship regarding voice therapies is reviewed, followed by the resultant voice perceptions of trans female clients.

It is important to note that this book does not seek to emphasize feminization therapies or surgeries over the lived experiences of trans women. The growing use of the phrase "gender affirming voice care" as an alternative to therapy or pathology removes the connotation of a trans women's voice being injured or diseased.[10] Published scholarship continues to use alternating terms, and some voice care practitioners might need to refer to their work as therapy for the purposes of the client's insurance, should their services be covered at all. The discussion that follows aims to provide singers and teachers of singers with background knowledge of voice feminization, not to objectify or pathologize trans women or to suggest that trans women need these treatments to make them more feminine.

Surgical Procedures

Research suggests that adults assigned female at birth have a mean speaking fundamental frequency of 196–224 Hz (approximately G3 to A3, below middle C), while adults assigned male sex at birth have a mean fundamental frequency of 107–46 Hz (approximately A2 to D3).[11] (As a reference, A4 is 440 Hz.) One goal of therapy is to enable the trans woman to approximate her mean fundamental frequency closer to the range of adult natal women. Surgical methods for raising of the fundamental frequency of trans women have included three fundamental principles: increasing vocal fold tension, decreasing vocal fold length, or decreasing vocal fold mass. While speech pathology has been able to feminize the voice to a degree, this form of vocal therapy alone is considered by some scholars to be insufficient. It has been argued that attempts to raise fundamental frequency can cause dysphonia or other voice issues.[12] It has also been observed that the "male" voice can emerge during laughing, coughing, or any spontaneous vocal sound, such as a startle.[13] There have been discrete surgical procedures designed to raise the fundamental frequency.

In a procedure called the Wendler glottoplasty, the vocal folds are shortened by de-epithelizing the anterior part of the vocal folds and suturing the corresponding tissue to obtain a V-shaped anterior commissure. In other words, the front of the vocal folds nearest the thyroid notch have been shortened. Ten patients who underwent this operation demonstrated a 9.2-semitone increase of the mean spontaneous speaking fundamental frequency, increasing their fundamental frequency closer to that of adults assigned female sex at birth.[14] In these same patients, a reduction in loudness over all frequencies was seen in at least the first three postoperative months. Three of the ten clients desired a louder voice, and this was restored through postoperative voice therapy. One patient experienced a splitting of their stitches due to smoking immediately after surgery, coughing, and not observing required vocal rest.

Similar studies were carried out to investigate the effects of vocal surgeries in trans women. A study headed by Marc Remacle followed Wendler's technique and also assessed preoperative and postoperative voice use by looking at fundamental frequency, frequency range, maximum phonation time, and other voice measurements.[15] Comparisons made between pre- and postoperative vocal use of the fifteen participants showed a significant rise of the median speaking fundamental frequency. Grade of dysphonia, vocal jitter, and subglottic pressure all increased post-operation, but maximum phonation time and other measurements showed no significant changes. In another study, Nicholas Mastronikolis and colleagues came to similar conclusions, but also suggest that Wendler glottoplasty surgery might be more successful in younger patients.[16] All three studies assert that postoperative voice therapy is an important element to further voice feminization.

An alternative operative procedure produces a higher fundamental frequency by the lengthening and tensing of the vocal folds. Kerstin Neumann and Cornelia Welzel performed a procedure, developed by Nobuhiko Isshiki, Tatsuzo Tairo, and Masahiro Tanabe, in which the cricoid and thyroid cartilages are backstitch-sutured together using wire and metal plates.[17] By bringing these cartilages closer together, the vocal muscle experiences increase tension. Neumann and Welzel found that if the thyroid notch is made more prominent by this procedure, an excision of cartilage can be made on the front of the thyroid cartilage to reduce the protrusion. Neumann and Welzel operated on sixty-seven patients, of which 93 percent experienced a rise in fundamental frequency by five to six semitones. Postoperative acoustical analysis showed 28 percent of participants had a fundamental frequency in the "female" range, while an additional 39 percent fell into the neutral range (neither "female" nor "male"). Patients expressed confidence in their voices, better mental health, and more acceptance as women. Some clients might prefer this procedure to Wendler glottoplasty, as there is no invasive effect on the vocal folds themselves. One disadvantage is potential scarring on the front of the neck. While results are favorable, follow-up examination of forty-five participants after approximately one year post-surgery show that in some individuals, the long-term effects were not as positive as initial reports indicated. Ten women underwent a follow-up surgery, of which half had to have the plates and wires removed entirely.

While voice feminization surgeries may show positive results regarding an increase of the fundamental frequency, most research indicates vocal therapy is still an important part of the voice feminization process. When considering voice feminization surgery, singers or anyone doing professional voice work (whether as a telemarketer, teacher, or stage performer) should proceed with extreme caution. Research on the outcomes of the singing voice after feminization surgery remain inconclusive; thus, anyone using their voice professionally should consult a professional, such as a speech-language pathologist and/or laryngologist, who specializes in working with trans patients before proceeding with any type of voice feminization surgery.

Vocal Therapy

There is a growing body of research related to voice therapy as a stand-alone intervention. Some literature supports the notion that speech pathology alone can be as effective as surgical procedures for voice feminization. A contribution to this scholarship by speech-language pathologist Georgia Dacakis examined changes in mean fundamental frequency in trans women following therapeutic interventions and evaluated long-term maintenance of fundamental frequency gains made in therapy.[18] Dacakis showed results of an increase in fundamental frequency between 20 and 50 Hz in voice feminization therapy alone. The ten participants in the study by Dacakis had received between ten and ninety therapy sessions and were evaluated an average of 4.3 years after discharge from therapy. None had undergone any kind of surgical procedure for voice feminization and no one was under the care of a doctor for any voice-related issue, but all clients reported occasional huskiness or hoarseness of the voice after prolonged use. The results of this long-term maintenance study indicate that subjects overall were maintaining a higher mean speaking fundamental frequency than before therapy sessions, but not as high as the analysis done immediately after therapy. None of the ten participants reported high satisfaction with their pitch level. Participants in other studies have shown similar experiences,[19] with one study suggesting that satisfaction shown in voice therapeutic sessions might come from the supportive nature of intervention rather than an indication of successful voice change.[20] Dacakis provides no details regarding the exercises or lessons given in voice therapy sessions, as the study is focused on long-term maintenance instead of the techniques employed in voice therapy.

In another study by Lisa Carew, Georgia Dacakis, and Jennifer Oates (2007), the authors investigated the effectiveness of oral resonance therapy on the perception of femininity in female trans participants to evaluate acoustic differences in vowel formant frequencies and the speaking fundamental frequencies (F_0) from pre- and posttreatment, and to determine client self-perceptions pre- and posttherapy, as well as their levels of satisfaction with their voice.[21] Ten trans women, none of whom had received any prior voice feminization therapy, received five forty-five-minute sessions of oral resonance therapy at weekly intervals. Oral resonance therapy includes the practice of bringing the tongue carriage forward in the mouth and using a lip spread (as opposed to lip rounding). Participants in the study were asked to practice specific vocal exercises fifteen to twenty minutes per night. Audio recordings were collected throughout the sessions. Listeners were asked to rate the femininity of the voice in the pre- and post-treatment recordings of each participant. Additionally, the participants themselves were asked to rate the quality of femininity with their voice from pre- and posttreatment recordings. The recordings were acoustically analyzed to provide data on the formant and fundamental frequencies of the recordings. Acoustical analysis of the recordings indicates the speaking fundamental frequency was much higher in posttreatment recordings than pretreatment. Regarding the perceptions of the listeners, seven participants were perceived as sounding more feminine post-therapy. All ten trans participants perceived themselves as sounding more feminine. The study suggests oral resonance therapy can be used to enhance vowel formant and fundamental frequency in voice feminization.

A further study by Marylou Pausewang Gelfer and Bethany Ramsey Van Dong explored the use of vocal function exercises (VFE), developed by Joseph Stemple, for a group of trans women seeking voice feminization.[22] The participants received one-hour individual voice therapy sessions twice a week for six weeks (for a total of twelve sessions) and were required to perform Stemple's VFE two times each, two times a day, for the entire six-week experiment period. In addition to the vocal therapy sessions, one training session for the VFE and one follow-up session were conducted for each client to ensure proper implementation at home. Acoustical analysis of the recordings indicates that the participants' voices were perceived as significantly less masculine in the post-test. The results of perceptual analysis indicate listeners perceived none of the speakers as being female in the pretest, and posttest results indicate only 7.4 percent of the voices were perceived as females. All speakers were rated by listeners as being significantly less masculine in posttest. The addition of the VFE did not appear to have a markedly positive effect on raising the speaking fundamental frequency when compared to other studies that did not use VFE. These participants felt the vocal function exercises were a positive part of therapy but did not feel it was a replacement for other voice therapies.

The vocal function exercises developed by Stemple are similar to other semi-occluded vocal tract exercises (SOVTE), such as phonating on a lip buzz, tongue trill, voice fricative consonants like [v] or [z], and humming. In teaching trans singers in the choral classroom, Matthew Garrett and Joshua Palkki discuss the usefulness of SOVTEs, in particular a technique of singing through a narrow straw developed by Ingo Titze.[23] Garrett and Palkki note, "Considering that TGE [trans and gender-expansive] singers may be working with limited ranges, choral conductor-teachers may find it useful to limit the range of vocal glides or slides with straw singing to intervals on a major third or a perfect fifth to start, and then move to wider intervals or voice range extremes as students develop additional skills with straw singing."[24] Though the authors are not discussing vocal therapy per se, the use of exercises akin to Stemple's vocal functions seem to be increasing in popularity.

Self-Perceptions of Voice

Most voice feminization research focuses on raising the fundamental frequency either through surgical modification or by retraining of habitual voice use through voice therapy. While research has considered frequency as a fundamental signifier of a person's gender, raising the fundamental frequency for voice feminization might not directly correlate with the client's post-therapy voice contentment. Emma McNeill, Janet Wilson, Susan Clark, and Jayne Deakin investigated the relationship between a participant's happiness with the fundamental frequency of their voice and their self-perception of vocal femininity versus the perception of femininity by speech-language therapists and lay observers.[25] This study found that trans women can evaluate the femininity of their voices in the form of perceived pitch, but happiness with their voices is not directly related to it. Furthermore, client voice satisfaction may not correlate with perceptions of the professional voice therapist. The study suggests that therapists can reliably evaluate how the lay public perceives the voice and emphasizes that subjective measures of patient satisfaction are a more valuable tool for therapeutic success than acoustical analysis alone.

A Transgender Self-Evaluation Questionnaire (TSEQ) was used in a study by Adrienne Hancock, Julianne Krissinger, and Kelly Owen to explore voice likability, femininity, and voice quality of life for trans women.[26] The authors of this study suggest it is valuable to distinguish voice femininity from voice likability. Twenty trans women living full-time as female completed the questionnaire and provided a speech sample. Twenty-five undergraduate listeners rated the audio samples for voice femininity and voice likability. Hancock, Krissinger, and Owen found that a trans women's self-perceptions of her voice, more so for likability than femininity, is more valuable information for a voice therapist than how her voice is perceived by others. The McNeill et al. study, alongside the findings of Hancock and colleagues, supports subjective measures, including perceptual scales and voice quality measures, in voice feminization therapy. A newer questionnaire has been created for trans women by Georgia Dacakis, Shelagh Davies, Jennifer Oates, Jacinta Douglas, and Judith Johnston to provide a more reliable measure of self-reporting of vocal functioning and the impact of the voice on the everyday lives of trans women.[27] This new questionnaire reveals a wide range of individual variability in perceptions of vocal functioning and voice-related difficulties.

While none of the above studies on voice feminization bring much attention to the singing voice of trans women, the more recent studies focus more on the clients' perceptions and support a student-centered approach for working with trans individuals. These client-centered studies align with the music studio teaching frameworks of Richard Kennell and Lucinda Mackworth-Young, where student-centered learning in the applied music studio is emphasized and student perceptions are valued.[28] The two case studies below offer insight to specific singing voices, vocal development, and the individual perspectives of two trans women engaged in one-on-one singing lessons.

Two Case Studies of Trans Feminine Singers

Case Study: Chrys (student) and Nicola (teacher)

Student Portrait

Born in Connecticut, raised in Ohio, and having lived in both Florida and California, Chrys (she/her/hers) has a broad understanding of people and cultures from across the United States. Now in her mid-fifties, Chrys is a trans woman and genderqueer. She uses feminine pronouns and transitioned from "male to female" (her words) nearly twenty years before our interview. Though her father is an amateur pianist, making music did not become important to Chrys until her early twenties. Influenced by the vocals of Jon Anderson and the progressive rock band Yes, Chrys's early musical experiences were of jamming in a band during college. Her seriousness with music developed in these jam sessions, during which time she began taking voice lessons. Having earned both bachelor's and master's degrees in mathematics, she moved from Florida, where she felt "really out of place," to California, where she has lived since.

Though Chrys does not speak much about her childhood, she implies that it was "no picnic." Her upbringing was punctuated by adverse experiences: "When I entered the world as a young adult, I did not possess a normal level of self-confidence and self-esteem." Though being trans was part of her consciousness as a youngster, she relays that there was not a working vocabulary in her milieu to enable her to process her gender. In reflecting on her upbringing, she discloses, "I definitely felt different, and not in a way that I was comfortable with, and not in a way that I wanted anyone else to know. I did not come out of my development with a sense that the world is a safe place." Music has helped her become more confident and comfortable with herself. Having been studying with her current singing teacher, Nicola (she/her/hers), for over ten years, she jests, "Everything about life I learned from my voice teacher." Vocal studies have given Chrys purpose, drive, and a desire to keep improving.

Song writing has been central to Chrys's identity as a singer. During her early days of college band jam sessions, she wrote nearly all the songs for their group. She explains that composing is an important part of her self-expression. In talking about her vocal training, she offers, "It's my interest in my own music and what I have to express that has motivated me." She continues by sharing that "it was always in my mind that supporting my voice was supporting my compositions." Heavily influenced by the high voice of Jon Anderson and with a naturally high tenor range herself, Chrys's music and singing echoes the sounds of progressive rock and folk music—not overly pushed but sung with high personal intensity and integrity.

As a singer, Chrys is comfortable with her singing range, which she explains would be classified as a "leggiero tenor" if she were in the classical realm. She freely admits that there is "no congruence" between her gender expression and her vocal range, though she shares, "If I have to have a male voice, at least it's the lightest, most agile voice." Years earlier she engaged in speech language pathology to "feminize" her voice. During these sessions, she and a voice coach worked on modifying range, inflection, and word choice. She discovered through these sessions that the mean tone of her natural speaking is in the middle between voices perceived as "male" and "female." Reflecting on her voice, she says, "It's too bad what testosterone did to my voice, but it is what it is." While at a younger age she was more concerned about appearing and sounding feminine—she even had at one time a femininity trainer for movement—as a middle-aged woman, she has jettisoned the notion of trying to appear or sound different from what is natural to her.

Taking voice lessons stems from Chrys's demanding standards for herself as a singer-songwriter. "Having very exacting standards for the quality of vocals is very important to me," she shares. "My goal is to [sing] as technically proficiently as I can." In her early years of singing, she cowrote a song with a guitarist during her college-era jam sessions. Working with this musician was beneficial because, as she says, "Someone was actually taking me seriously as a musician." Those early years of "jamming" helped her develop her ear and a desire "to metabolize higher standards" for her singing. Over the many years of vocal training since those jam sessions, she discusses the ways in which she has become a more grounded singer. "My singing has become more expressive as I've assimilated better and better technique," she explains, allowing her to vocally move around more freely, take on challenging vocal leaps, feel comfortable in a higher range, and sing florid passages with more clarity and ease. The road to vocal acuity has not always been easy. She confides, "I've such, such moments of feeling so defeated, but I didn't ever stop showing up." She has always been the driver of her vocal training, never willing to compromise her compositions because her voice is not vocally able to achieve her musical writing. Her songwriting has served a source of inspiration for constantly improving her vocal technique.

In speaking about the intersection of gender and vocal expression, Chrys articulates, "Unlike any other musician, we don't get to choose our instruments. A necessary thing for any singer is that we have to accept the voice we have." She adds to this idea, "The voice, you might say by design, is sexual dimorphism," suggesting that biological makeup of any body is a determining factor of vocal range and timbre. Offering advice to other trans or genderqueer individuals who might feel discomfort in their voice, she notes, "Get comfortable in yourself and everything else follows." In making suggestions to voice teachers working with gender-diverse singers, Chrys highlights the importance of teaching self-acceptance.

Having spent time in her life learning to modulate her voice with a speech pathologist, learning to move with greater femininity with a movement coach, and taking feminizing hormones, she relays the story of a time in her early thirties when she was shopping for lipstick. A toddler of three or four years old in the same aisle as Chrys turned to her mother and said, "How come there's a man looking at that lipstick?" Despite money and energy spent in presenting as a woman, Chrys acknowledges that even children (at least in this place, at this time) understand societally defined gender norms. It is moments like this that have led Chrys to greater self-acceptance. She cautions that that level of embracing herself "took decades to accept." She summarizes with laughter, "I have no f*cks to give with what other people think."

Teacher Portrait

Opera. Ska. Musical Theatre. Punk rock. These four different musical styles form a part of Nicola's portrait. A straight, cis woman (pronouns: she/her/hers), Nicola was raised in the Midwest in a household of eclectic musical tastes. Her mother was a professional backup singer for a celebrity rock 'n' roll country singer during the 1960s. Having grown up singing, Nicola's earliest formal vocal training began with classical music and musical theatre soprano repertoire. Performing in musicals and competitions provided Nicola validation as a younger performer. Her interests in singing, dancing, and acting seemed an ideal fit for musical theatre, until a dance professor told her as a teenager that she needed to lose weight if her interest in performing professionally was serious. "Completely crushed" by the words of this instructor, she switched her focus to earning a degree in humanities, during which time she began singing ska music, rooted in the musical styles of Jamaica, Caribbean calypso, and American jazz. Like many people after college graduation, Nicola did not know what to do with herself, so she followed a friend to the West Coast. Despite having not sung any Western classical music in several years at that point, she auditioned for an opera company, which hired her for their opera chorus, guiding Nicola to engage in singing lessons and refocus on her early love for *bel canto* singing.

Moving to a larger city on the West Coast, Nicola pursued performing in operas and musicals. She went back to college for a second bachelor's degree and a master's degree, this time in music. During this time, she worked with several different teachers and coaches who provided her a solid foundation in Western singing styles and languages. Nicola had an interest in pursuing young artists and apprenticeship programs, but in her early thirties, she had already aged out of many of these training opportunities. Her life pivoted to teaching singing, while she also focused on family life and being a mom.

As a teacher, Nicola is employed by a local community music school, where she teaches singers of all ages in singing a variety of styles. She works with a lot of singer-songwriters and students who want to sing contemporary music and Broadway. She began working with Chrys in her earliest days as a singing teacher, years before discussions on teaching trans singers were becoming more commonplace. Having grown up in an urban environment and been part of an underground punk rock scene during her undergrad years, Nicola has a lot of LGBTQ+ friends. She describes the LGBTQ+ community as her "people" and although she had little knowledge about teaching a trans singer prior to working with Chrys, she was never afraid or hesitant.

In talking about her own sense of gender, Nicola describes herself as female, but she is mindful to share that her notion of femininity is fluid. She describes, "Sometimes I can be super hyper-'feminine' and wear a frilly flowery dress, but then I might also shave my head and wear combat boots and feel totally comfortable." This flexibility in her personal gender expression influences her teaching of singers. Instead of aiming for a particular Eurocentric sound that matches a singer's gender expression, Nicola concentrates on helping them find a "free sound" that enables them to sing a style that promotes their expressivity as a vocalist—whether for an eighty-year-old singer, a young student wanting to pursue *bel canto* singing, or Chrys, her longest student. As a self-identified "super liberal cis woman," Nicola ponders why women are sometimes trained "to have a light, very unthreatening tone to be 'feminine.'" It is not that she is unaware of the biological impact on voices, nor is she against a "very light and melodious" sound. She is quick to add, "If that's what your voice sounds like, that's beautiful . . . I love that," but for singers who do not fit within this model, Nicola wants to create a studio space that appreciates and honors all colors and manners of voices.

Teaching a diverse pool of singers, Nicola modifies her teaching style to suit students' needs. Having struggled herself during lessons and having felt overwhelmed or put down by feedback, she confesses that "a lot of how I teach is sort of an opposition to how I was taught." She does not speak of those teachers badly; indeed, she reveres them, but she is cognizant that she gives feedback and enables change differently. She explains, "Some of the vocal exercises I teach are from my very first teacher.... I still use some exercises and tools, but my approach is different." As we will see in the description of Chrys and Nicola in lessons, Nicola is quick to give positive feedback and allows students to guide their learning.

As the mother of an autistic child, Nicola applies lessons she has learned with her child in the studio, which includes empowering students by giving them self-agency and autonomy. For example, while Nicola guides students through vocal exercises to foster a free sound, she often allows students to pace themselves through exercises. Though she will pause and help a student adjust their technique as needed, she is not attempting to micromanage their experience. She is careful not to provide too much constructive criticism, which may overload a student with too much information. The sequencing of the vocal exercises works like an étude, where instead of supplying feedback frequently, Nicola allows several keys to progress before pausing the student for a check-in—that is, if the student is not singing in a damaging or harmful way. This not only allows the student an opportunity to vocally adjust as they feel necessary, it also gives the student "momentum in the exercises." She explains that by not stopping recurrently, a student can "really build up breath technique if you ... [let them] breathe, engage, and sing, and have this circular motion." In working with Chrys, who is incredibly intentional and driven in her own vocal development, Nicola notes that occasionally during warm-ups, "I have to pull her back" to help her focus on a specific technical aspect of singing. For all students, Nicola tells them, "This is your lesson," and thus, while she is guiding the learning, she is purposefully eschewing a master-apprentice "authoritarian" model. She acknowledges that "you've got to take people where they are" at each lesson. Although attention is placed on finding a balanced and expressive technique, Nicola is intentionally "not looking for perfection at each moment," so that feedback does not dominate every moment of singing.

Nicola's diverse musical upbringing and experiences have provided her an important firsthand insight to different styles of singing. Working with a singer-songwriter like Chrys has driven Nicola to meet each student where they are, letting the student's artistic intentions come forward. In exploring a self-composed song with a student, Nicola is quick to explain: "I'm hesitant to make specific suggestion because it's their song. It's their music. I want them to be happy with how they're singing it, and then I usually ask them afterward, 'How did you feel about that?' or 'Was there something that was difficult for you?' I point out the things I like. We work from there."

Being present and "very sensitive" with each student is a tenet of her teaching. Nicola shares that serving as Chrys's teacher for over a decade is an honor and that she has learned much along the way. Always striving to foster independence in students, Nicola has, at times, encouraged Chrys to study with other people and to work with an "Alexander Technique teacher or someone who does bodywork." It is this model of openness that has likely kept their affiliation ongoing for so many years.

Voice Lessons

Due to COVID-19, Nicola is facilitating voice lessons on Zoom. Seated at a piano in her home studio, Nicola begins the lesson promptly by asking Chrys about her week and about how she is feeling today. Chrys is positioned in front of a microphone wearing headphones. As the lessons are taking place online, Chrys can see herself and Nicola on her computer screen. Issues of sound delay have prompted Nicola to create audio files of the vocal exercises instead of playing them from her keyboard. Chrys also is responsible for crafting the exercise audio files to her needs by modifying the tempi to fit her ideal pacing.

Prior to both lessons I observed, Chrys had already warmed up by singing through the sequence of exercises.

Figure 3.3. *Five-tone descending scale on vowels.*

Since Chrys is already warmed up, they can immediately start to focus on fine tuning technical aspects within the exercises. In the first vocal exercise, as shown in figure 3.3, a five-tone descending scale using [u] and [i] on pairs of eighth notes cascades to five half notes on [i], [ɛ], [a], [o], and [u]. This exercise promotes forward resonance and alignment of vowels. Chrys begins in D major (D3 below middle C) and finishes nearly an octave higher in D-flat major with the highest note an A-flat 4 (above middle C).

The next exercise asks Chrys to vocalize a five-tone ascending and descending scale on [jo], which fosters jaw release and forward tongue carriage. The [o] vowel has also shown to promote a lower laryngeal position, which might be necessary as the exercise ascends higher and higher. Figure 3.4 shows the exercise on [jo], which Chrys sings begins at F major (beginning on F3) and ascends to D-flat major with the top note of A-flat 4.

Some tension, or "crunchiness"—as Nicola calls it—develops at the top of Chrys's range during this exercise. This is musically a simplistic exercise but a difficult exercise for Chrys to maintain openness and a steady tone as it approaches the upper part of her range. As a way of exploring more freedom in the upper range, Nicola invites Chrys to sing a slide of a major fifth (Do to Sol) on [i] to [o], mimicking the vowels of above exercise. The [i] encourages forward tongue placement and resonance while [o] helps mitigate a high larynx. As Chrys ascends the interval, Nicola suggests a knee bend to counter the sensation of going higher. Nicola also invites Chrys to place her hands near

Figure 3.4. *Five-tone ascending and descending scale on [jo].*

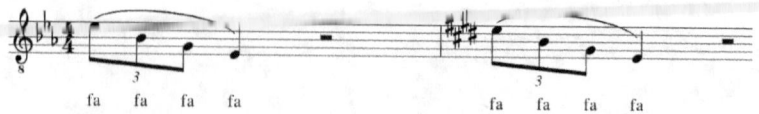

Figure 3.5. Descending arpeggio on [fa].

her mouth and forehead to gain greater kinesthetic awareness. Finding "a little more space between the tongue and roof of the mouth" on [i] enables this slide to be sung with greater ease.

The next exercise is constructed of a descending major arpeggio, (high) Do-Sol-Mi-Do, on [fa]. Chrys begins this exercise in E-flat major, with a starting pitch of E-flat 4 above middle C. She finishes this exercise one octave higher, with the highest starting pitch of E-flat 5. After singing through multiple keys in full voice, she begins mixing the starting note around B-flat 4 with the most upper notes sounding more like an upper register (in traditional terminology, the upper register would be referred to in this case as "falsetto").

Figure 3.5 shows the exercise, which is sung very slowly and with legato. The unvoiced fricative [f] promotes releasing the breath throughout the duration of the exercise, while [a] welcomes openness. Throughout these exercises, Nicola allows Chrys to provide her own feedback and constructive commentary. When appropriate, the exercise is repeated, and on certain occasions, Nicola encourages Chrys to focus on a specific key or range as they work for greater freedom, bringing attention to the tongue, jaw, breath, or any key area of vocal technique that might enable more efficient singing.

Four additional vocal exercises complete the full sequence. On the words "I know," the next exercise asks the singer to ascend a full octave preceding a descending major arpeggio. This exercise is similar to the exercise just before it, but it begins on low Do before the octave leap. The diphthong in "I" and the

Figure 3.6. Ascending octave and descending major arpeggio on "I know."

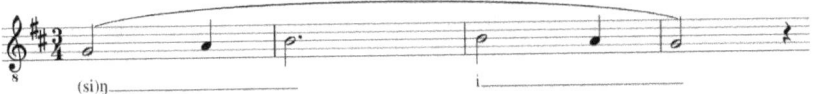

Figure 3.7.   (Si)ng – [i] on a three-tone scale.

nasal [n] of "know," which is produced by the tip of the tongue making contact with the alveolar ridge, is challenging as the upward movement of the tongue provokes the larynx to ascend correspondingly.

The next exercise asks Chrys to vocalize a three-tone pattern on the word "sing" and then the vowel [i]. The exercise is constructed so that the "ng" [ŋ] is sustained instead of the vowel. The voiced velar nasal of the "ng" enables a singer to feel forward vibrations, but it also encourages a lower soft palate as the tongue and velum make contact.

The penultimate exercise is a combination of technical feats achieved in prior exercises, consisting of a five-tone descending scale on [di], [dɛ], [da], [do], [du] that precedes a slide on [u] that ascends and descends a fifth (Do to Sol to Do). Similar to the [n] in "I know," [d] is a plosive alveolar consonant requiring the tongue to connect with the hard palate. Like an [o] vowel, [u] cultivates an elongated vocal tract and a low laryngeal position. Sung slowly, this exercise also seeks a steady release of breath over the three-measure phrase. Chrys finds some difficulty in maintaining [u], demonstrating a tendency to move toward [y], as in a German "ü" vowel. Nicola brings attention to this technical demand as the exercise moves to higher pitches.

The last exercise returns to an octave arpeggio from low Do to high Do and back down over a triplet. Though this exercise is commonplace, Nicola allows Chrys to choose the words or vocables on which to sing it. In one lesson, Chrys sings this arpeggio on the words "nothing can," remarking that the [k] sound in "can" will test her ability to not overly increase the

Figure 3.8.   Five-tone descending tone with a slide on a fifth.

speed of breath for the plosive consonant. As she is singing into a microphone, Chrys is aware that plosive consonants, like [k], [p] or [g], can "pop" in the microphone if performed with too much breath.

These exercises provide Chrys the opportunity to self-assess her singing at multiple layers, from checking in with range, register negotiation, breath, phrasing, and physical alignment. Much of Nicola's teaching is rooted in asking questions such as, "How did it feel?" or "What feedback do you have?" On other occasions when Chrys might want more guidance, Nicola offers specific direction for the tongue or jaw, or more general feedback, like, "Think up and over" for accessing higher notes. Kinesthetic actions like bending at the knees or placing a hand near the mouth or forehead give Chrys greater physical awareness. Chrys records all her lessons, and Nicola sometimes suggests looking at previous recorded lessons to assess how her technique has changed. Constructive criticism is given alongside specific and positive feedback, so that Chrys can focus on technical achievements and opportunities for change.

Nearly forty minutes into the hourlong lesson, Nicola and Chrys pivot to repertoire. As Chrys is a singer-songwriting, she works exclusively on her original compositions. Working on a piece called "Mary Jane," she sings the piece to a backing track, which is inaudible to Nicola as the sound of the accompaniment is only coming into Chrys's headphones. Chrys is wearing noise-canceling headphones throughout the duration of the lesson; thus, she is receiving her sound in an objective way, just as Nicola is hearing her sound. "Mary Jane" is an intense, demanding belt rock song that concludes with a high melismatic passage, which is where they put their attention. They isolate the final phrases to address groundedness, breath, and vowels. Singing it again, out of the context of the song, the final phrases become easier and more poignant when Chrys is able to sing these lyrics with greater expressivity:

> *How I free myself every day, everyway . . .*
> *I am open . . .*
> *And the dreams become alive . . .*

After Chrys has sung the entire song through a second time, Nicola offers some musical coaching through the song text, making a suggestion on word stress and musical phrasing. Her guidance here, once again, is derived through asking questions of Chrys—such as, "How did that feel?"—which allows Chrys to offer her own feedback. This form of teaching through inquiry does not preclude Nicola from offering specific ideas or recommendations, but it allows Chrys to drive the experience and for the two of them to collaborate and learn together. While these lessons are focused, professional, and pointed to the task of singing, they are open, supported, and punctuated with laughter, smiles, and moments of good rapport between Chrys and Nicola.

Case Study: Isabella (student) and Martha (teacher)

Student Portrait

Isabella (she/her/hers) is an intelligent, articulate, thoughtful, and talented sixteen-year-old trans Latina woman. Fluent in Spanish and English, she lives in a metropolitan area on the West Coast of the United States. She started singing in choir around the age of five after hearing her older sister rehearse in the choral ensemble. Although she was technically too young to join the choir, the director, Martha, allowed her to sing in the ensemble after Isabella correctly demonstrated all the vocal warm-ups and repertoire. In middle school, she started one-on-one singing lessons with Martha, her current voice teacher, through a community music academy. Isabella is currently attending a performing arts high school, and music is her main activity in life. In addition to music lessons in school and with Martha, Isabella has participated in shows and singing programs through after-school programs.

For as long as Isabella can recall, singing has been a part of life. She remembers singing nonstop during her childhood—essentially "out of the womb," she jokes. As a youngster, she was cast as an angel in a Christmas pageant (a combination of the Las Posadas and Las Pastorelas traditions). Dressing up in white and wearing wings, Isabella shares, "As far as gender expression goes, I was living for it." For Isabella, the performing arts is more than a hobby, social activity, or opportunity for play. She imparts, "It's the way I process my world . . . and a lot of my emotions are [processed] through song and I'll find myself singing all the time." As a child, Isabella experienced gender dysphoria, and until recently, she has blocked some of the painful memories of not being understood, of discomfort, and of not feeling comfortable in her identity.

As a young person, Isabella received gender-affirmation care and therapy through a local hospital clinic designed for trans youth. Isabella was eventually given hormone blockers through an arm implant and estrogen replacement therapy as she began puberty. The hormone replacement therapy (HRT) disrupted a testosterone-dominant puberty, which otherwise might have caused Isabella's voice to develop into a tenor, baritone, or bass range. Throughout her teenage years, she has easily maintained a mezzo-soprano range. In talking about her voice, she shares, "I was lucky to not have been put in a situation that made me become dysphoric." She clarifies:

> I want to emphasize that when I say "lucky," I mean lucky that HRT protected me from harmful misconceptions about my voice, body, and gender. Things like, "a *real* women should have a high voice" should not impact any trans person with or without HRT. This is not to say that HRT and having no development of the Adam's apple *cannot* be affirming and life-saving, but assuming that it is or necessary for a trans woman gives a limiting picture of trans feminine voices.

Though Isabella is cognizant of how fortunate she was to have begun HRT when she did, the process has not always been easy. She affirms that she has no regrets in her decision to transition, but being on medication can be difficult, and when she forgets to replace her HRT skin patch, she can experience heightened mood swings.

She admits that, as for any teenager, life can just be challenging. Once she accidentally cut her hair too short, which gave her a "boyish" look. That experience initially created some angst for her, but after some processing, Isabella recognized that hair is only one part of her gender expression and that her femininity can be expressed in many different ways. Reflecting on the haircut mishap, she affirms, "I feel like it was also a beautiful experience—it was almost reaffirming of my gender identity—to be reminded that I am a woman." In a follow-up discussion, Isabella noted that she should not have perceived of this haircut as "boyish," but that at the time, she was still "unlearning" society's pressure to appear in a specific "feminine" way. She adds, "I think my issue was in equating my gender expression with gender identity; I can approach both gender and expression with more nuance than I previously allowed myself." Isabella notes that societal pressures of gender expression based on stereotypes—whether it's a haircut, fashion choices, or musical repertoire—can be challenging.

In speaking more on gender, Isabella talks effusively about the importance of music and singing in helping her understand her identity. "I think part of my exploration of music and gender identity was really aided by my music teacher, Martha," she offers. Martha's approach to teaching singing, as Isabella explains, fosters a natural, free sound: "When I started studying, her process was very holistic, and it encourages this very natural exploration of your voice and your own capabilities, and how your body has built you to sing the way you do." She also shares that in some ways, music has enabled her to step away, or transcend, gender to "explore raw human emotions." She continues, "Singing has definitely been a part of my journey as a transgender person, because it was one of the few ways in which I could express myself freely." The importance of freedom and openness shines in her discussion. In speaking about a recent performance, Isabella says, "It was a really magical experience to get to just sing very freely and be feminine in the way that I knew myself to be." In talking about the importance of singing in her life, she also questions why music is gendered, asking "Why do we make certain music feminine, and why does that affirm my gender?" She goes on to explain, "The fact that my voice is high shouldn't affirm my womanhood any more than anyone else's voice, and yet, it does, and we should question that."

In her singing lessons, she is currently working on pieces in German (Schubert, "An die Musik"), Italian (Mozart, "Voi che sapete"), and Spanish (de Falla, *Siete canciones populares españolas*). Her love of Western opera and art song is apparent, and she talks about the way women are portrayed through the repertoire—sometimes light and helpless, other times as strong and independent. In working on "Voi che sapete," a standard aria for a mezzo-soprano portraying a younger man, Isabella takes delight in the liminality of gender that comes in singing a "pants" role. She acknowledges, "I noticed a lot of transgender youth feel the need to express themselves very stereotypically within their gender. I think that as queer people, because we're forced out of that norm, we get to experiment and realize that there's such a wide range of expressions that we can choose." Whether singing from a more traditional gender role or from a perspective that is less confined by the gender binary, Isabella enjoys embodying different characters, viewpoints, and expressions. Isabella explains that music has never not affirmed her identity. She says, "Anyone can sing anything," so long as it feels empowering to them, while also recognizing that due to limitations set by gender expectations, "not everyone is allowed to sing everything."

Isabella comments that her lessons with Martha "always make [her] feel happy and safe and ready to make mistakes and grow from those," but sometimes she experiences self-doubt and negative self-talk in choral rehearsals and other musical spaces. In recognizing how she is different from classmates, she confesses, "I feel very uncomfortable when I make mistakes in choir." While the applied studio space with Martha offers safety and security to be vulnerable, choir does not provide that same sanctuary. In the choral environment, she suggests that directors should remember that students learn in different ways at different rates, and should embrace their students' unique voices and identities. She suggests:

> Rather than trying to conform, tell your students that your voices are going to be different and we're all moving at different paces and we all learn in different ways. It's important to

know that what works for one choir member doesn't work for another. Teachers need to do the work they promise of teaching students music; if a student comes from different background, a teacher needs to adapt their teachings, question their preconceptions of music and gender, and do better at teaching different learning styles.

She adds that a teacher's role in creating a safe space for learning is in deconstructing harmful gender stereotypes in music, and that the responsibility of this resides with the teacher—not with the trans and genderqueer students.

In further discussing the role of teachers in the experiences of trans and genderqueer students, she recommends, "Know that your work is important, and with genderqueer youth, it can change their lives." She also emphasizes the importance of understanding intersecting identities. Isabella is not just trans, nor Latina, nor a teenager, nor a passionate singer—she is all of these. She conveys how important it is for teachers to see and hear each student as whole, multifaceted, and complex. She implores teachers to "reexamine how different facets of the music world have closed doors to certain people, making it harder to excel in music when music doesn't provide any support for their voice. . . . This goes beyond gender in music, but into a multitude of identities." She adds, "Find a balance between your own knowledge of music and the needs of the students, especially because you're not working with voices, you're working with people. Music does not exist in a vacuum, it is informed by many histories and societies." It has been Martha who has served as the teacher who has seen Isabella not as a voice, but as whole person—enabling her to grow as a singer and human.

Teacher Portrait

Martha (she/her/hers) has been an influence on Isabella's musical life since her early childhood: first as Isabella's choir teacher when she was a young child, and now as her singing teacher for the last five to six years. Martha is also Isabella's godmother and a friend of Isabella's mother. A mezzo-soprano singer and instrumentalist, Martha plays flute, piano, vihuela, guitar, and drums, participating in vocal and instrumental music making of Western classical and Mariachi music. Martha's earliest memories of music are singing "for hours and hours" as a little girl in the kitchen and using one of her mother's knitting needles as a baton to pretend conducting symphonies in her bedroom. Formal music training began on the flute at sixteen years old, and then singing lessons a couple of years later. She graduated as a flute major from the University of Mexico. Following undergrad, Martha joined the Mexican navy, serving as a Lieutenant for four years and a singer in the navy chorus. As a lesbian, she laughs, describing the military as a "very macho world where all the men wanted to convert me." Following her career in the navy, she moved to a major city in the West Coast of the United States to continue her music studies at a liberal arts women's college.

The vocal training Martha received during her graduate studies were counterproductive. Working with a teacher of similar voice type, Martha explains, "I learned a technique that was not very useful for me. . . . I was needing to recover vocally afterwards." Issues of overdoing, manipulating, and pushing her voice created intonation issues. She started working with a different voice teacher who focused on a "more natural honoring of the voice." This approach brought attention to breathing and vowels. It is this technique that she now tries to teach her own students. She shares, "My voice path has been so interconnected with my flute." As a musician, she identifies as both a flautist and singer, but that this was not always easy for her. For years, in some places she was "a flautist who could sing," and in other circles she was "a singer who could play flute." One day, this bifurcated musical identity felt unnecessary, and "like coming out of the closet as a musician," as she described, she identifies as a singer and multi-instrumentalist.

Natural, healthy singing is central to Martha's work with all her students. She aims to foster respect for each student's personality, abilities, and processes through positive feedback. She explains, "I decided that I was going to be positive and not deconstruct a student, because that's very traumatizing. . . . Positive feedback can be constructive." Martha continues, "I know how devastating [negative criticism] can be for someone and how you can make a really bad mark in their lives, as much as you can make a beautiful mark their lives." Because she believes the voice is personal, she is careful to not tell a student they are not sounding "good," because that might be heard or translated by the student as, "I am not good." These tenets of Martha's teaching apply to her whole studio, treating each student as a unique individual.

In working with Isabella, Martha's remarks, "I treat her as a singer, just as I treat any student of mine who is serious in music." Yet Martha is also aware that her bond with Isabella is deeper than rapport or familiarity, providing her opportunity to check in with Isabella on a more personal level. Martha is careful to not share with me personal details of their conversations, but both she and Isabella relate that they talk about Isabella's school, music, hormone therapy, and Isabella's overall health and wellness. Mostly, however, they talk about singing.

When Isabella first started studying with Martha, her musical interests were more focused on musicals and Broadway songs. She wanted to learn to belt, which is something Martha freely admits she does not teach, nor does she having any expertise in doing. As a young girl and before beginning puberty and hormone therapy, Isabella had a naturally wide vocal range, with an easy and resonant G3 below middle C and extending above the treble staff. As soon as Isabella's voice started to change due to puberty, Martha noticed Isabella having more difficulty accessing her higher range. As her vocal training and hormone therapy continued, Isabella's voice got higher and higher to where she could sing mezzo-soprano repertoire with ease. Martha also notes that while Isabella has separate chest and head registers, her passaggio is seamless. She even had another singing teacher assess Isabella's voice to ensure it was functioning properly; that teacher confirmed her voice is healthy and unified from top to bottom with no abrupt switch in registration. Currently, Isabella easily sings from B3 (below middle C) to B5, two octaves above.

Isabella is not the only trans student whom Martha has taught. She admits to having made some blunders and learned from these students, both in terms of technical needs and social respect. With every student, whether they are a singer or instrumentalist in Western classical or Mariachi music, Martha endeavors to be a learner and role model, not just as a musician but as a human being. In discussing the difference between playing the flute and singing, she avers, "The voice is who we are." As a teacher, she aims to create space in the world where singing can "transform lives truly in a beautiful way."

Voice Lessons

With lessons taking place online to due COVID-19, Martha is wearing headphones in front of her computer and seated at an electric piano with a microphone. Isabella is on the third-floor attic of her home, standing in front of her computer for video and audio reception. When lessons begin, Martha checks in with Isabella, asking how she is feeling and what pieces she would like to work on during the lesson. These first few minutes serve as an opportunity for the teacher and student to be present with each other and to co-construct goals for their time together. Through a series of guiding questions from Martha, Isabella becomes more grounded, physically aligned, and aware of her breath. Before any singing begins, Martha engages Isabella through simple breathing exercises. There is no manipulation of the breathing process—this is instead an opportunity "to be in touch with your body," as Martha tells Isabella. Bodily awareness and an ease of breathing are common threads throughout Martha's teaching.

Vocalizing begins with "sirens" from a comfortable lower pitch (around C#4, above middle C), sliding to a comfortable higher pitch (approximately A5), and then sliding down again to the starting pitch (or thereabout), sung on a series of vowels: [i], [ɛ], [a], [o], [u] and then on a lip buzz. The next vocal exercise is a one-octave major scale up and down sung on solfege, immediately followed by a one octave ascending and descending siren on [o] (as an extension from low Do). Beginning on B major (below middle C), the exercise moves up by half steps, concluding on E-flat major, with the highest note of F5. Though this exercise requires a similar technique to the sirens of the first exercise, the scale requires more control and breath support. The second exercise uses a smaller range and sounds much more like "singing" than the initial sirens. In another lesson, this one-octave exercise is lengthened to a nine-tone major scale and siren. Adding structure in the vocal exercises little by little, the next exercise, shown in figure 3.9, is constructed on an octave arpeggio, once again beginning on B major. This exercise also moves up by half-steps for over an octave until Isabella reaches C major (with the starting pitch of C5), taking Isabella up to C6 (two octaves above middle C). Isabella changes the vowels with each key, mirroring the same order of vowels ([i], [ɛ], [a], [o], [u]) from the initial sirens, but this time preceded by the bilabial [m] consonant. In the figure below, [ma] is used as an example; Isabella also sang this exercise also on [mi], [mɛ], [mo] and [mu].

Although Isabella is slightly less confident in her singing as she extends above the staff in this exercise, she accesses this part of her range without adding much muscular tension. While an exercise constructed like this might cause some singers to bring up the chest voice too high, Isabella does not do this. With a nearly seamless sound from start to finish on this exercise, she adds very little pressure as she ascends higher. Though the tone on some vowels, mainly [ɛ] and [a], is a bit breathier on occasion, Isabella is not attempting to produce a specific quality of sound. She focuses on maintaining the vowel and releasing breath, and not attempting to make a certain kind of sound.

The next vocal exercise is based on a nine-tone scale on solfege (low Do to high Re, then back to low Do), sung slowly, starting on B-flat major (below middle C). The previous exercises have been sung without any accompaniment or keyboard support beyond a starting pitch; this exercise is sung to a prerecorded audio file made by Martha. A kinesthetic movement using the arms in the "reverse direction" of the scale—both arms

Figure 3.9. *Octave arpeggio on triplets.*

Figure 3.10. Descending thirds on [vi] and [vo] with a fast five-tone scale.

starting high and moving down as the pitch ascends and vice versa—is added to alleviate tension or a feeling of upward-ness. Martha offers images to consider, such as "sing like you are in the middle of something sad" or "sing like you are bored." These images of boredom and sadness further help Isabella mitigate tension as she ascends above the staff.

The last exercise promotes breath release and agility. Using a combination of the vocables [vi] and [vo], the exercise consists of descending major and minor thirds followed by a quick five-tone major scale, as shown in figure 3.10.

As in the previous exercise, Isabella sings this exercise to a prerecorded accompaniment track, which begins on B major (below middle C) and finishes on D major, with the highest note of A5. Isabella modifies the [i] to [I] as she sings above the staff. Due to the nature of the lessons, Martha does not interrupt Isabella much during the execution of the sequence of keys. The online learning makes it difficult for Martha to make quick comments and interjections during vocal exercises. Instead, feedback is provided as the end of each sequence. Martha always allows Isabella to share her thoughts about how she sang each vocal exercise before providing her own feedback. Even if Martha offers constructive criticism, the overall feedback is positive and supportive.

After fifteen to twenty minutes of vocalizing on exercises, the lesson pivots to working on repertoire. Currently, Isabella is working on four pieces, including "El Paño Moruno" and "Canción" from *Siete Canciones populares Españolas* by de Falla, Mozart's "Voi, che sapete" from *Le Nozze di Figaro*, and "An die Musik" by Schubert. These songs reflect Isabella's love for Western classical music. In working on "El Paño Moruno," Martha scaffolds the learning process to isolate specific challenges in the piece. As it is a newer song to Isabella, Martha asks Isabella to identify the key and time signature of the piece—this

Figure 3.11. Measure 26 of "El Paño Moruno"

is not done to put Isabella on the spot but rather to ensure that Isabella is learning more than vocal technique in her singing lessons. They discuss different strategies for being able to determine if a piece is in a major or minor key. Martha is supporting Isabella's understanding of the score and basic music theory knowledge. The process of vocalizing this piece begins with Isabella speaking the words in rhythm while keeping the pulse. After confidence and accuracy is gained at this level, they add pitches to a slower tempo. With some consistency, Isabella struggles with measure 26 of "El Paño Moruno," shown in Figure 3.11, wanting to repeat a D on "-da" instead of moving down to the C#.

Martha sometimes sings the correct pitches for Isabella, and at other times, Isabella corrects the mistaken pitches herself. Never is there a comment or glance from Martha that suggests disappointment or annoyance for these mistakes. Indeed, even with this ongoing pitch error, Martha continues to praise tone, phrasing, or expression. Finally, Martha asks Isabella to put down the music, trust her ear and heart, think about the storytelling, and sing from memory. On this last attempt, Isabella not only sings all the correct pitches, but sings with more expressivity.

Isabella sings "Voi, che sapete" with aplomb. With easy access in her upper range, she shows no sign of added tension or vocal fatigue in this aria. Talking about the way women play trouser roles like "Cherubino," it seems Isabella is pleased to explore in this song the idea of being a boy lusting for the "Countess Almaviva." Finding some pitch difficulty on the lyrics "L'alma avvampar," shown in figure 3.12, Isabella and Martha focus on this section of the aria.

Though Isabella has some difficulty in hearing the correct descending intervals, and apologizes for singing it incorrectly,

Figure 3.12. Excerpt from "Voi, che sapete."

she is not chastised nor made to feel bad for it. The musical error is acknowledged, they isolate the measure, sing it more slowly, repeat it more quickly, and then they move forward to something different. Martha also empowers Isabella to work on problem spots between lessons. Rather than shaming or blaming Isabella for an error, Martha gives Isabella opportunity to correct it during the lesson, and if the error continues, Isabella is asked to reexamine the music before the next lesson. This leads to a discussion on home practice and goals for the next week. On all occasions, the goals that Martha and Isabella create are specific, measurable, attainable, relevant, and time-bound, following George T. Doran's SMART goal model.[29]

The rapport Martha and Isabella share is obvious, and the lessons are filled with laughter and good humor. Isabella takes her vocal training seriously, and though she apologizes whenever she makes a mistake, Martha never shows disappointment or displeasure. Indeed, Martha is quick to praise with specific feedback, always noticing something technical or performance-based that warrants positive reinforcement. On one occasion when Isabella seems disheartened for making a mistake, Martha takes time to explain that moments of self-doubt are a process of "unlearning" that deserves processing, as much as learning requires. Despite some technical glitches in the online format of these lessons, a connection is undoubtedly present between student and teacher.

When I first spoke with Isabella, she expressed some doubt in her fit as a participant in this study, remarking that many people do not see her as trans. Her narrative study illustrates that not all trans or genderqueer students are outwardly visible as trans. As teachers, our role is to create learning spaces that are gender affirming for all students, whether they are trans, genderqueer, cisgender, or any other gender identity. In doing so, we can create a learning environment for students like Isabella to develop into expressive, powerful, and beautiful singers.

Chapter Takeaways

This chapter examined the trans feminine voice through two case studies. First, we learned from Chrys, a singer-songwriter and middle-aged trans woman whose tenor range serves as an important part of her self-expression. Second, we looked at a portrait of Isabella, a Western classically trained mezzo-soprano singer and teenage trans woman. Through the source-filter theoretical model, this chapter first provided a brief overview of the functionality and mechanics of the singing voice before looking at previous literature on "female" voices. Recognizing that the label "female" in traditional vocal pedagogy literature serves as a demarcation only for the voices of bodies assigned female at birth proffers a catalyst for why we might reconceive how we discuss and teach the voices of all women, including trans singers. Scholarship in voice "feminization," including vocal therapy and surgeries, illustrates some of the practices for trans women in speech-language pathology. Although singing teachers and speech-language pathologists traditionally have divergent academic backgrounds, their work might be similar when supporting a trans woman to cultivate her most desired voice.

In the first of the two portraits, Chrys taught us that her gender is independent of her voice, and though she is cognizant that her voice does not match the normative range of person assigned female at birth, her voice is a hugely important aspect of her personal expression. Having attempted voice therapy and feminine movement training earlier in life, she candidly speaks about caring less and less about how she is perceived by others. In the second case study, Isabella provides insight on how hormone blockers and hormone replacement therapy for a younger trans woman have impacted her singing voice. Her rich and expressive mezzo-soprano voice matches the quality of her female peers, yet she is also aware that her body is different, and this occasionally triggers feelings of self-doubt and negative self-talk.

The teachers in this chapter—Nicola and Martha—share similar models of constructivist teaching, allowing their students to pace their lessons, decide the repertoire they would like to sing, and take the lead in sharing feedback on their singing. Structure was provided by the teachers, who supplied the vocal exercises and sequencing, held the students accountable, participated in joint problem solving for technical or musical challenges, and offered positive and constructive feedback, refraining from any manner of chastisement or disappointment. Nicola and Martha, like some speech-language pathologists who "embrace client-centered care practices," illustrated student-centered teaching, a pedagogical approach absent in some models of applied voice instruction.[30] As will be discussed more in chapter 6, these teachers offer glimpses into teaching that dismantles the master-apprentice model of teaching by instead taking an active role as a co-learner alongside their students. Here is a condensed overview of pedagogical considerations and salient knowledge in teaching trans feminine singers.

Teaching Singers

- A trans woman is feminine if she identifies as feminine, no matter her vocal range.
- Some trans feminine singers desire a voice that aligns to a soprano or alto range, but not all do.
- Students who sing in the tenor, baritone, or bass range might want new vocal nomenclature; traditional voice classification terms might incite dysphoria.
- Student-centeredness with lesson pacing, repertoire selection, and range development might help a student feel more comfortable and cultivate greater self-expression.
- Changing song keys might allow a singer to perform a piece otherwise outside their range abilities.
- When working with an adult trans feminine student in treble range, descending exercises in middle (D4 to B4, above middle C) is a good starting place.

- Singing lessons can serve a vital role in a person's vocal (and gender) transition and expression.

Hormone Replacement Therapy

- Hormone replacement therapy for trans women has little impact on the adult vocal folds, though some individuals might notice a change with the mucosal membrane of the vocal folds.
- Hormone replacement therapy (including testosterone blockers) for adolescent trans woman when administered at or before puberty can inhibit the vocal folds from developing through a testosterone-dominant puberty, allowing the voice to retain a treble range.
- Hormone replacement therapy might cause mood swings; supportive language and extra care might be necessary.
- When an individual first begins hormone replacement therapy, studies show that the need to urinate might become more frequent. Dizziness or lightheadedness can occur.[31] Allow students to sit and take nonpunitive breaks as necessary.

Speech-Language Pathology and Vocal Surgery

- Vocal therapy sessions with a speech-language pathologist might support a trans woman's desire for a higher speaking range and secondary feminine communication characteristics (e.g., timbre, inflection, word choice).
- Vocal surgeries to increase range fundamental frequency have been developed, but little is known about the effects of the surgery on the singing voice, and thus, these procedures remain inadvisable until further studies have been completed.

Notes

1. James C. McKinney, *The Diagnosis & Correction of Vocal Faults: A Manual for Teachers of Singing & for Choir Directors* (Nashville, TN: Genevox Music Group, 1994).
2. Viktoria Papp, *The Female-to-Male Transsexual Voice: Physiology vs. Performance in Production* (PhD diss., Rice University, 2012).
3. Ingo R. Titze, *Principles of Voice Production* (Englewood Cliffs, NJ: Prentice Hall, 1994).
4. Ibid.
5. McKinney, *The Diagnosis & Correction of Vocal Faults*, 111.
6. Theodore Dimon, *Your Body, Your Voice: The Key to Natural Singing and Speaking* (Berkeley, CA: North Atlantic, 2011).
7. Richard C. Miller, *The Structure of Singing: System and Art in Vocal Technique* (Belmont, CA: Wadsworth Group, 1996), 133.
8. Ibid., 148.
9. M. A. Kalra, "Voice Therapy with a Transsexual," in *Progress in Sexology: Selected Papers from the Proceedings of the 1976 International Congress of Sexology*, ed. Robert Gemme and Connie Christine Wheeler (New York: Plenum Press, 1977), 77–84; Hyung-Tae Kim, "Vocal Feminization for Transgender Women: Current Strategies and Patient Perspectives," *International Journal of General Medicine* 13 (2020): 43–52, https://doi.org/10.2147/ijgm.s205102.
10. "About: Trans Voice Initiative," Trans Voice Initiative, accessed October 10, 2021, https://www.transvoiceinitiative.com/?fbclid=IwAR3ufMOminyC917iiIM8xawhp7RIdfmdTeRodkQFAN08_CvvSUm2net17f8.
11. Anthea I. Britto and Philip C. Doyle, "A Comparison of Habitual and Derived Optimal Voice Fundamental Frequency Values in Normal Young Adult Speakers," *Journal of Speech and Hearing Disorders* 55, no. 3 (1990): 476–84, https://doi.org/10.1044/jshd.5503.476; Stuart I. Gilmore et al., "Intra-Subject Variability and the Effect of Speech Task on Vocal Fundamental Frequency of Young Adult Australian Males and Females," *Australian Journal of Human Communication Disorders* 20, no. 2 (1992): 65–73, https://doi.org/10.3109/asl2.1992.20.issue-2.05.
12. Kerstin Neumann and Cornelia Welzel, "The Importance of the Voice in Male-to-Female Transsexualism," *Journal of Voice* 18, no. 1 (2004): 153–67, https://doi.org/10.1016/s0892-1997(03)00084-5.
13. Jennifer A. Anderson, "Pitch Elevation in Transgendered Patients: Anterior Glottic Web Formation Assisted by Temporary Injection Augmentation," *Journal of Voice* 28, no. 6 (2014): 816–21, https://doi.org/10.1016/j.jvoice.2014.05.002; Manfred Gross, "Pitch-Raising Surgery in Male-to-Female Transsexuals," *Journal of Voice* 13, no. 2 (1999): 246–50, https://doi.org/10.1016/s0892-1997(99)80028-9; Marc Remacle et al., "Glottoplasty for Male-to-Female Transsexualism: Voice Results," *Journal of Voice* 25, no. 1 (2011): 120–23, https://doi.org/10.1016/j.jvoice.2009.07.004.

14. Gross, "Pitch-Raising Surgery," 246.
15. Remacle et al., "Glottoplasty for Male-to-Female."
16. Nicholas S. Mastronikolis et al., "Wendler Glottoplasty: An Effective Pitch Raising Surgery in Male-to-Female Transsexuals," *Journal of Voice* 27, no. 4 (2013): 516–22, https://doi.org/10.1016/j.jvoice.2013.04.004.
17. Neumann and Welzel, "The Importance of the Voice in Male-to-Female Transsexualism"; Nobuhiko Isshiki, Tatsuzo Tairo, and Masahiro Tanabe, "Surgical Alteration of the Vocal Pitch," *Journal of Otolaryngology* 12, no. 5 (1983): 335–40.
18. Georgia Dacakis, "Long-Term Maintenance of Fundamental Frequency Increases in Male-to-Female Transsexuals," *Journal of Voice* 14, no. 4 (2000): 549–56, https://doi.org/10.1016/s0892-1997(00)80010-7.
19. Ralph C. Bralley et al., "Evaluation of Vocal Pitch in Male Transsexuals," *Journal of Communication Disorders* 11, no. 5 (1978): 443–49, https://doi.org/10.1016/0021-9924(78)90037-0; Judith Kaye, Melissa A. Bortz, and Seppo K. Tuomi, "Evaluation of the Effectiveness of Voice Therapy with a Male-to-Female Transsexual Subject," *Scandinavian Journal of Logopedics and Phoniatrics* 18, no. 2–3 (1993): 105–109, https://doi.org/10.3109/14015439309101356; Kay H. Mount and Shirley J. Salmon, "Changing the Vocal Characteristics of a Postoperative Transsexual Patient: A Longitudinal Study," *Journal of Communication Disorders* 21, no. 3 (1988): 229–38, https://doi.org/10.1016/0021-9924(88)90031-7.
20. Dacakis, "Long-Term Maintenance," 555.
21. Lisa Carew, Georgia Dacakis, and Jennifer Oates, "The Effectiveness of Oral Resonance Therapy on the Perception of Femininity of Voice in Male-to-Female Transsexuals," *Journal of Voice* 21, no. 5 (2007): 591–603, https://doi.org/10.1016/j.jvoice.2006.05.005.
22. Marylou Pausewang Gelfer and Bethany Ramsey Van Dong, "A Preliminary Study on the Use of Vocal Function Exercises to Improve Voice in Male-to-Female Transgender Clients," *Journal of Voice* 27, no. 3 (2013): 321–34, https://doi.org/10.1016/j.jvoice.2012.07.008.
23. Matthew L. Garrett and Joshua Palkki, *Honoring Trans and Gender-Expansive Students in Music Education* (New York: Oxford University Press, 2021).
24. Ibid., 173.
25. Emma J. M. McNeill et al., "Perception of Voice in the Transgender Client," *Journal of Voice* 22, no. 6 (2008): 727–33, https://doi.org/10.1016/j.jvoice.2006.12.010.
26. Adrienne B. Hancock, Julianne Krissinger, and Kelly Owen, "Voice Perceptions and Quality of Life of Transgender People," *Journal of Voice* 25, no. 5 (2011): 553–58, https://doi.org/10.1016/j.jvoice.2010.07.013.
27. Georgia Dacakis et al., "Development and Preliminary Evaluation of the Transsexual Voice Questionnaire for Male-to-Female Transsexuals," *Journal of Voice* 27, no. 3 (2013): 312–20, https://doi.org/10.1016/j.jvoice.2012.11.005.
28. Richard Kennell, "Toward a Theory of Applied Music Instruction," *Quarterly Journal of Music Teaching and Learning* 3, no. 2 (1992): 5–16;

Lucinda Mackworth-Young, "Pupil-Centered Learning in Piano Lessons: An Evaluated Action-Research Programme Focusing on the Psychology of the Individual," *Psychology of Music* 18, no. 1 (1990): 73–86, https://doi.org/10.1177/0305735690181006.

29. George T. Doran, "There's a S.M.A.R.T. Way to Write Management's Goals and Objectives," *Management Review* 70, no. 11 (1981): 35–36.

30. Teresa L. Hardy et al., "Associations between Voice and Gestural Characteristics of Transgender Women and Self-Rated Femininity, Satisfaction, and Quality of Life," *American Journal of Speech-Language Pathology* 30, no. 2 (2021): 663–72, https://doi.org/10.1044/2020_ajslp-20-00118.

31. "About: Trans Voice Initiative."

4

Trans Masculine Singers

> "Whether in my employment, my neighborhood, the parent governor committee, the Pride committee or at a gay bar, I do want to be known as a trans person. But, I also want to be seen as a whole person. The same comes to making friends, [or] forming relationships ... I want to have the same possible future, and be included in the battles and victories of life that everyone else in the room has."
>
> —Stephen Whittle in *Trans Voices: Becoming Who You Are*

The role and impact of exogenous testosterone on adult trans male bodies has taken center stage in trans research. Academic discourse, online forums, and video platforms have chronicled the effect of testosterone replacement therapy, also known as androgen therapy. Testosterone—whether as an exogenous supplement that is externally administered or naturally produced during puberty in bodies assigned male at birth—typically triggers body hair growth, muscular definition, and a change in vocal timbre and range. Previous research in speech-language pathology[1] and vocal pedagogy,[2] as referenced in chapter 1, has provided examples of the vocal changes incurred by androgen therapy in adult trans men, which can enable the speaking and singing voice of a trans man to drop into a tenor, baritone, or bass range.

This chapter will continue this research by exploring the lived experiences of two trans men—one man in his early twenties who began take testosterone as a teenager and one man who began taking testosterone during middle age—and the modifications their voices have endured since beginning androgen therapy. As trans British scholar and activist Stephen Whittle avers in the introductory quote, the case studies presented within this chapter aim to provide a view of the whole person. Though these case studies offer information as related to the singers' changing voices, these portraits aim to capture a more holistic understanding of their experiences and perspectives. But first, this chapter begins with a cursory overview of traditional "male" voices to illustrate how "male" voices have previously been discussed in vocal pedagogy, followed by a discussion of voice masculinization in speech-language. For an elementary introduction on the mechanics and anatomy of the human voice, review the beginning of chapter 3.

Traditional "Male" Voices

Traditional solo voice classifications of "male" voices are tenor, baritone, and bass. According to James McKinney in his book *The Diagnosis & Correction of Vocal Faults*, the "ideal" ranges of each voice type are as follows: tenor is C3 to C5, baritone is A-flat 2 to A-flat 4, and bass is F2 to F4.[3] Figure 4.1 shows these ranges on the musical staff.

Providing a brief overview of registration for traditional "male" voices is challenging, as there is debate regarding the amount of head voice and chest voice employed with the different voice types. Renowned American vocal pedagogue William Vennard notes, "Most authorities agree that basses sing largely in 'chest,' with some use of 'head' for very high notes. . . . Tenors sing in 'chest' up to F4 or F-sharp 4, above which theorists dispute."[4] In his book *The Structure of Singing*, Richard Miller proposes that a combination of the head and chest registers is

Figure 4.1. Vocal ranges for traditional "male" voices.

used for all "male" voice types.[5] Like "female" voices, he contends "male" voices have two *passaggi* (primo and secondo). "Male" voices also have a falsetto register that is distinct from the head register, according to Miller.

In chest voice singing, "the vocalis muscle is tensed, which makes it thicker and brings more tissue into motion."[6] In opposition, the production of falsetto occurs when "only the inner margins [of the vocal folds] are vibrated by the flow of air; the vibrations then occur at a higher tension and frequency."[7] Miller makes a distinction of the "male" head voice and falsetto. Thus, in Miller's perspective, the "male" head voice is neither the chest voice nor falsetto, but rather "increased cricothyroid action, vocal-fold elongation, diminution of vibrating vocal-fold mass, and constantly changing contours of vocal-fold edges."[8] The prominent vocal pedagogue research goes on to explain "that vocal-fold occlusion is not the same in head and falsetto: vocal-fold approximation is less complete in the falsetto production."[9] If traditional "male" voices use a combination of head and chest registers, the falsetto can be used as a pedagogical tool for finding greater relaxation in the head voice, in Miller's viewpoint.

A modern countertenor (opposed to the Baroque countertenor, who sang with a lower register, for range example see John Blow's *Ode on the Death of Mr. Henry Purcell*) is a nontraditional "male" singer who vocalizes almost exclusively in falsetto register without causing strain or damage to the vocal folds. While Miller's scholarship does not go into detail regarding falsetto singing, he does report that "special techniques of extending the falsetto range and in blending it . . . with the traditional low male register are required."[10] Countertenor technique and training is explored by Peter Giles, and falsetto singing might provide an opening for a trans woman or a nonbinary person assigned male at birth to sing in the soprano or alto range if desired.[11]

A countertenor should not be confused with the now nonexistent castrato. During the mid-sixteenth century through the eighteenth century, mainly in Italy, boy sopranos who showed great vocal potential were sometimes castrated. Due to a reduction in testosterone from mutilation of the genitalia, the voice and body of a castrato did not develop in the same manner as bodies with standard levels of testosterone. While a castrato grew in height, sometimes abnormally tall and with broad chests, the vocal folds maintained a soprano, mezzo, or contralto range.[12] Although a castrato was frequently regarded as a star of the opera stage, castration was often against the wishes of the child and was eventually deemed illegal in the late eighteenth century. Though there is no connection in physiology between a castrato and a trans man (or a countertenor), this history speaks to a precedent of modifying voices by changing testosterone levels.

Voice Masculinization for Trans Men

As the voice is an important part of gender identity, a trans man may wish to align his voice with the quality and timbre of voices associated with postpuberty bodies assigned male at birth. This alignment might include the desire for a lower-pitched speaking and singing voice. A trans man might take testosterone to change his body, which includes a change in voice due to a thickening of vocal folds causing a drop in fundamental frequency.[13] Testosterone has shown to be so effective in creating this vocal change that voice therapy is often not seen as a necessary element in the vocal transition.[14]

In their two-part study, John Van Borsel and colleagues examined voice problems in trans men using a questionnaire administered to sixteen trans men. They also presented longitudinal study of two trans men. All trans men who participated in the questionnaire had been taking testosterone for at least one year. Fourteen of the participants responded positively to experiencing a lowering of the pitch of their voices since the start of androgen therapy. Two participants each indicated they had always had a low-pitched speaking voice and therefore did not experience a voice change. The participants were asked about their willingness to have further voice therapy, and eleven of the respondents rejected any additional need for speech therapy, citing satisfaction as the main reason. The study also revealed that fourteen of the participants indicated that voice modification was as important to their male identity as gender-affirmation surgery. Two of the respondents commented that they could not sing as high or as well as they could before taking testosterone. Issues regarding the singing voice of trans men are also mentioned in a health publication by R. Gorton, Jamie Buth, and Dean Spade, where the authors warn that voice changes due to hormone therapy might be "significantly detrimental to vocal performance."[15]

In the longitudinal part of the study, Van Borsel and colleagues examined two trans men undergoing androgen therapy. One individual was seen on eight occasions over seventeen months, while the other client was examined seven times over thirteen months. Each participant saw a substantial lowering and narrowing of their range. The researchers posit, "This reduction appears to be the result of a loss in the high tones which is not fully compensated for by a gain in the lower frequencies."[16] Despite a reduction in range, the fundamental frequency was found to drop in both clients, which positioned their speaking voices into a range similar to adults assigned male at birth.

In a frequently cited article on trans singing, Alexandros Constansis discusses his own vocal development.[17] Following his personal journey through androgen therapy as a professional singer, Constansis provides anecdotal data of his voice modification. He discusses the experience of having "entrapped vocality," in which the vocal folds had thickened, but the larynx that houses the vocal folds did not enlarge to accommodate the increased muscle mass. He suggests that the voice of a trans man may sound weak and hoarse, lacking the harmonics of a voice in a person assigned male at birth. Constansis suggests that if androgen therapy begins at a lower dosage and increases slowly over time, the gradual masculinization of the voice is "not only more predictable but also very encouraging," and that physiological changes in the vocal tract are concomitant with changes of the vocal folds.[18] Constansis's scholarship includes substantial reporting on the training of trans singers, which was discussed in chapter 1.

Three more recent examinations of the trans male voice have come from work in the areas of linguistics and communications disorders.[19] In an acoustical and perceptual study, Jennifer Sanchez investigated trans male voices and attempted to identify the unique qualities common in their voices by looking at speaking fundamental frequency, pitch range, and formant frequencies. Acoustical and perceptional data were gathered. Sanchez's research compared voice samples of three groups of men: biological males, long-term androgen therapy users, and recent androgen therapy users. Acoustical results found that long-term users had a marginally significant lower fundamental frequency than recent testosterone users. Results of the vocal formants indicate that biological males had significantly lower formant 2 (F_2) frequencies than recent users, but no significant difference to long-term users. Formant 3 (F_3) frequencies in the biological men were found to be significantly lower than long-term and recent users. No other significant acoustical differences were found between the biological males and the recent or long-term users.

Perceptual analysis collected by Sanchez showed that recent testosterone users had a significantly lower masculinity rating than both long-term users and biological males when rated by twenty undergraduate college students on a five-point scale (1 = not masculine at all; 5 = very masculine). Yet, of the voice samples used in this study, 23 percent of the seven long-term testosterone users, 16 percent of the five recent users, and 1.3 percent of the natal men were identified as being trans; thus, while the recent users received a lower masculinity rating than the other two groups, nearly a quarter of the participants were still perceived as trans. Sanchez argues that "fundamental frequency appears to be central to perceived maleness, but further studies should be conducted to identify the elusive vocal attributes that contribute to gender identity."[20] These vocal attributes, which may include vowel length and articulation, are given consideration in the dissertations of Viktoria Papp and Lal Zimman. The results of Sanchez's research might suggest that although the speaking fundamental frequency and F_2 and F_3 were lower in biological males, additional vocal attributes play a role in the perception of a masculine voice.

The research conducted by Papp is a three-part study on the speech production of trans men.[21] Decoupling gender from biological sex, Papp's first longitudinal study shows that testosterone brings about changes to both the vocal source and filter (i.e., the vocal tract). The results of this study suggest trans male speaking voices are not situated as low in their range as they were before androgen therapy, which means their physiological range expands and lowers more than their habitual range. This study does not support the findings of Van Borsel and colleagues, which indicated that testosterone induces a narrowing of range.[22] On the contrary, Papp reports, "by the end of the first year into the androgen therapy, all subjects fully regained or even surpassed their original pitch ceiling."[23] Papp's first study suggests a greater need for speech-language pathology in the voice care of trans men and shows there may be a greater amount of conscious or unconscious choice made by an individual regarding his habitual speaking range. Papp also counters the assumption that all trans men desire to be "unambiguously masculine . . . [which] perpetuates a binary gender system as the only available gender options."[24]

While Papp first looks at the function and changes of the vocal folds, the second part of the study examines the vocal tract, or *filter*, the term preferred by this author. Specifically, Papp investigates changes in the vocal tract upon the introduction of androgen therapy. Results indicate that although testosterone in a transitioning adult male does not enable growth in overall height, the vocal tract lengthens, which supports Constansis's theory that physiological changes occur in both the vocal source and filter. In addition to skeletal changes in the ramus and lower mandible, Papp posits, "Some transmen [*sic*] experience the growth of the bony protrusion of an Adam's apple, which may be accompanied with other laryngeal cartilage shifts and growths."[25] This study advances the notion that smaller bones and cartilage might be more responsive to androgen therapy than previously assumed.

The final part of Papp's dissertation investigates the acoustic correlations of trans men and sexuality in sentence-level read speech. This section of the study looks specifically at vowel formants and articulation, mainly with consonant sounds. Papp's research provides additional data on the changes in vocal sounds during androgen therapy and further illuminates the need to consider the individual vocal experience of each trans man.

The last study to be considered in this section is the dissertation of Lal Zimman, which is a long-term ethnographic and sociophonetic study of fifteen trans men.[26] Zimman examines the voice change during the initial twenty-four months of voice modulation. In addition to observing a lowering of the fundamental frequency, Zimman provides "evidence that these speakers are engaged in various types of articulatory shifts as part of their gender role transition, which affect both formants and [s]."[27] More than investigating this phenomenon from a physiological perspective, Zimman examines the phonetic domains through a sociocultural context, which suggests voice modification helps the trans man construct his identity of maleness.

Research in voice masculinization promotes a theoretical framework to suggest that voice, in part, is a performed social construct. Although the quality of one's voice is product of biology, it is also formed by habitual use, where to some degree a person can purposefully pitch their voice higher or lower. This research further illuminates the scholarship of trans theory in which being TGQ is understood to be more fluid. Early literature on voice masculinization primarily focuses on the lowering of the fundamental frequency for trans men to "pass" as natal male bodies, while recent literature provides a wider perspective in which voice masculinization is more individual and complex, suggesting that it is an area where further sociological research would be beneficial.

Two Case Studies of Trans Masculine Singers

Case Study: Forest (student) and Darius (teacher)

Student Portrait

A twenty-two-year-old trans man from the West Coast of the United States, Forest lives in a metropolitan city with a population just under five hundred thousand. He describes himself as a "dude," offering, "I fit pretty well in the binary.... If I had been a cis dude, I would have just been a dude." His bulky frame, short hair, five o'clock shadow, and deep voice match the "dude" profile. He's a gentle guy, well-spoken, generous with his time, and introspective about his identity and life experiences. He is currently attending a community college in the city where he grew up, working toward a degree in field ecology. When discussing his choice of major, he attributes this decision to a single professor who, without hesitation, affirmed his male identity. In the margins of a quiz one day in an environmental biology class, Forest wrote a note to his professor that he was changing his name to Forest and he would start going by he/him/his pronouns. Forest reports, "He printed out a new roster and never slipped up. He was calling me [Forest] before I was used to it. It would take a couple of tries because I'm like, 'Wait, that's me!' That's honestly why I picked that major."

Though field ecology is an important aspect of his time in college, Forest is also very involved in the music and theater programs, both onstage and behind the scenes.

The performing arts have been impactful in Forest's life for several years. He was raised in a devout Mormon household and sang in the church choir. He was fourteen years old when first he began to explore his masculinity through music. He says, "There was a church choir. That was actually the first time I ever sang masculinely [*sic*]. There was an old lady in the tenor section, and I was like, 'I want to be an old lady in the tenor section.' So, I hung out with her and realized I could do this, and so I started singing tenor. I had no inkling that I was transgender. It was just, 'I like being masculine.'"

The choir was an affirming experience because it was a safe place to be "masculine for a bit," where Forest could explore his male identity without feedback or adversity from family, peers, or teachers. Though he describes the ensemble as "not a forward-thinking choir," there was no pushback from the director because there was a need for singers in the tenor section.

The need for more "boys" in various performing arts activities paved an opportunity for Forest to explore his masculinity. In addition to choir, Forest was active in his high school's theater program. He describes theater as his second foray into being masculine. Forest recalls:

> I showed up freshman year to an audition and they cast me as a male character because I had short hair. I realized I really liked it, so I kept doing theater. I remember it was about my second show where the director was giving out notes, and she was like, "You have such a masculine energy on stage," and I'm like, "Oh, that feels good." So, ever since then, I would keep playing male characters. There was never enough of them—boys in school to play them.

The performing arts provided a space for Forest to explore his identity. He shares, "Singing was always this way I could explore it safely without people trying to label me." As a youngster, he took piano and voice lessons from a "sweet old lady from church." This voice teacher allowed him to sing repertoire from a male perspective but stopped short of letting him sing romantic men's songs.

Individuals in other areas of his life showed less support. When he was a young child, he wanted to join a Daisy Girl Scout troop. He was "bullied out for apparently being too butch." During his formative years, he explains, "One of my parents' biggest fears was that I would end up queer . . . well, very specifically, their biggest fear was that I would be a lesbian. Transgender was completely off their radar. It shouldn't have been. If I tried to do particularly masculine things, sometimes people would get really worried about it. People would try to save me from that."

He notes that had he grown up in Utah or Arizona, where there is a larger Mormon population, it might have been more difficult for him. All his cousins went to a major Mormon university, and Forest says they were part of large performance groups that were very gender-based. He shares, "We don't have these big [performing arts] programs that everyone's fighting to get in to . . . in a way, that's really good because then we, as students, get to take those programs and make them what we need."

He believes that growing up in an area where the arts are "drastically underfunded" and considered of low importance essentially helped provide an environment for him to explore his masculine identity long before he recognized his trans identity.

While Forest has a good relationship with his parents, he still experiences marginalization within his family's church community. For example, on the occasion he attends a church service, he says, "I won't wear a dress for them. I won't answer to my birth name for them. I won't go to the women's meetings for them. I will sit there in a suit, and if they don't want me to go to the men's meeting with them, I will find another place to be."

Forest is resolute in his behaviors around his family and the members of their Mormon church. While he imparts this information stoically, interacting with this community while maintaining his authentic identity is emotionally challenging.

Forest has been out as a trans guy for three years. He was nineteen years old and taking a playwriting class at the same college where he is now studying field ecology when he started to realize his authentic self. He remembers:

> I was sitting there in a playwriting class and I was writing a play about this lesbian who is going to a dance and decided that she wanted to wear a tux. I'm writing this play and I'm fleshing out this character, and all of a sudden, I realized this character isn't a girl. I was doing a bunch of research, and so I dove into this character, and then the more I did the research, I was like, "Oh, I am not a girl."

Though he had played male roles on stage and sang tenor in choir for years, he had never identified as male offstage.

Although Forest had developed a tenor range in choir, he took a group voice class to further develop his singing: "I took

Beginning Voice... to explore my lower range, but in a healthier way, because singing that low and not on HRT [testosterone] was a little rough on my voice." Although he admits to being misgendered by the teacher on the first day of class, he found a community of singers and a supportive, knowledgeable instructor in voice. Forest speaks enthusiastically about his experience in this course, finding both the group instruction and the one-on-one coaching sessions with the teacher valuable. His final performance in that class serves as an example of how music and his gender intersect:

> I did "Out There" from *Hunchback of Notre Dame* and it's the last time I could have ever done it because it's got all these high A[4]s. It's a good thing I did it because at the time I didn't know I was going to be on T [testosterone] soon. I remember that recital really well. I got that feeling of being on stage... remembering why I liked being on stage in the first place and getting to sing this song, which in my mind personified how I felt as a young, just-come-out-of-the-closet trans man. It was just a really beautiful moment as an artist.

In the summer after taking the Beginning Voice class, Forest began taking testosterone. Despite characterizing his pretransition tenor voice as rich and masculine, he explains, "I couldn't hit a tenor low C[3], but I could still achieve this masculine richness and I absolutely loved it, but my voice was sort of the last bastion of femininity that I had. Even though it was so masculine, it would give me away all the time. My voice was the main reason why I decided to take HRT [hormone replacement therapy]."

Forest received little support from the medical clinic that prescribed him the testosterone. A diabetic friend of a friend showed him how to give himself the shot, as the clinic provided no training on how to administer the prescription. He also received no voice therapy. Forest believes that even if he had been offered voice therapy, he probably wouldn't have accepted it. "Even though my voice was this huge source of dysphoria," he acknowledges, "it wasn't necessarily the way I talked; it was purely just the pitch. I speak exactly the same as I did before T.

The only thing different is the pitch is lower." Thus, the only vocal coaching Forest received during this transition was from the voice teacher of the group voice class. During the following two semesters, he took Intermediate Voice and then Advanced Voice classes.

The vocal transition was not easy. About a month into Intermediate Voice, his voice began to modulate. He recalls, "It was squeaking. It was like I had to relearn how to sing because all of a sudden what I used to do to sing high wouldn't work, and I what I use to do to sing low, well, just everything was flipped around."

Forest recalls the change in his vocal range came about one month after he began HRT. As soon as the change started, his speaking and singing voice dropped quickly. He describes the experience as being strange, with no graduation in range change nor any warning of the vocal modulation. "By the end of Advanced Voice, everything had settled. I stopped shifting down, stopped squeaking," he shares. It took about than six months, more or less, for the voice to settle.

Forest is currently taking private voice instruction from Darius, the same teacher who taught him in the three voice classes. In total, they have been working together for three years. Forest's voice has lowered into a baritone range, from approximately G2 to E4, which enables him to sing a lot of repertoire originally written for cisgender "male" voices. Currently he has no falsetto/light register above E4. He jokingly comments, "I'm really angry about it. There are times I miss singing a little higher. . . . My best friend has the most beautiful falsetto and he's an outright bass." While Forest makes light of not having a higher range, he admits it would be nice to have for singing nonclassical repertoire. Nevertheless, that is not the goal for his lessons: "What I am really focusing on is learning how to maintain my vocal health because I know that I'm not going to be taking voice lessons forever. This isn't a career path for me. It's just something that I have always really, really loved."

Forest's lessons are not for college credit, and they occur intermittently throughout the semester. He performs in studio recitals and participates in a mentorship program for younger voice students. Before his transition, Forest explored his masculinity through voice lessons and church choir, but now he acknowledges it is different: "It's not my only outlet for masculinity. My whole existence is now masculine, but it's still a way that I can explore it and it's a way that I can express it as an art form."

Apart from his collegiate studies, Forest works several different jobs: as a costume stitcher in the theater department, as a pixie for children's birthday parties, and as a camp counselor. Despite earlier negative experience with Girl Scouts, Forest teaches archery and theater for their summer camp. Passionately, he shares, "It's absolutely glorious to watch these kids.... A lot of theater camps are ... very competitive, but this is theater as a communal art ... at the end of the day, it's not about the show.... It's about giving these kids an experience."

When talking about teaching, he relates: "We just sort of let them do what they're going to do.... They're students ... let them have those experiences and don't try to fix all their problems for them right away. You know, just let them be."

He emphasizes that affirming a student's identity is imperative. "Once you question them on their own identity, they question everything about you ... they question the relationship you two share," he adds.

As a person who describes himself as a "dude," the intersection of Forest's gender identity and voice exists within the masculine binary. Although he was singing tenor before transitioning, his voice was the main impetus for taking testosterone to further lower his vocal range. Vocal and theater performances serve as a space for his self-expression, and he uses his knowledge and experience to enable other young people to explore their authentic identity.

Teacher Portrait

Darius, Forest's teacher, is a full-time faculty member at a community college with a student population of slightly over twenty-five thousand. Teaching classes in voice and choir, Darius holds a bachelor of music in vocal performance, and a master of music in choral conducting. When asked how he identities, he initially laughs and responds, "Human." He also describes himself as a cisgender gay man who uses he/him/his pronouns. Darius is a well-respected choral director, voice teacher, composer, and singer. His community chorus has had the distinction of performing at a national conference of the American Choral Directors Association. As a commissioned composer, he has more than twenty titles in his catalogue, and he appears frequently as a tenor soloist in oratorios with choruses and orchestras.

The music program where Darius teaches currently offers voice instruction through group classes at three levels: Beginner, Intermediate, and Advanced. Darius teaches free, noncredit private voice lessons to students who have successfully taken the three-tiered voice classes and show an interest in further vocal training. Incorporating student-to-student mentorship in the vocal program, the students whom Darius teaches privately serve as mentors to beginning voice students, helping them learn their repertoire and guiding them through music classes. Some private students are pursuing an associate's degree in arts with music as the concentration, while other students, like Forest, are part of the music program for personal enrichment. This form of mentorship enables both mentor and mentee to learn from one another. In serving a mentor role, a student is given the opportunity to reflect on early stages of vocal development and recall their experiences in the group voice classes.

Darius speaks earnestly about cultivating rapport between students and creating rapport with his students: "I always call them singers and I try to tell them that they're beautiful people with beautiful voices to honor and respect them, especially with beginning voice students because they're coming with a load of anxiety."

Creating an environment where exploration and creativity can flourish in a mentoring environment is essential to Darius. He emphasizes the importance of a supportive space for students "from all different walks of life" to feel empowered to be lifelong learners. He also discusses the difference between "noticing and discerning." In other words, he encourages students to listen deeply and to keep their eyes and ears open to notice how they sing, but to also suspend judgment of themselves and each other.

The concept of a singer as an artist-creator is central to his teaching philosophy. He speaks enthusiastically about singers expanding their imagination and exercising skills in "audiation," so the singer can re-create the sounds they imagine in their mind. An aspect of his teaching includes "helping them manage their creative head because . . . we are all, as singers, creators." He continues, "We've got to imagine ideas in our heads and then create them and 'audiate' sounds." While these tenets of his teaching are important for all students, he believes this ability is "significant to trans students." For an individual who feels dysphoric in their body and voice, he posits that being able to imagine a potential new future is empowering: "As a vocal instructor, I think that 50 percent, if not 70 percent, of what I do is get them to access something for their future. They've created a technique based on their past and you have to break down those walls to get them to move in the direction of the future, whatever that future is for them, whatever they want to create." The notion of students being empowered to set their own goals and vocal objectives is fundamental to his teaching.

With twenty years of teaching experience, Darius underlines the need to be a constant "sponge" as a teacher, to continuously learn about teaching and about his current students. He explains, "What I do is try to listen and learn and hear through their language and their voice and their body language what's going on with them and where are they . . . and how can I help them get where they want to go. I'm listening really deeply to hear how things are occurring to them and . . . give them a new occurrence or a new experience."

Darius is specific in noting that the objectives of his students are their own, not his: "They are the students' goals, and if there are some things I've learned along the way to help them achieve their goals, then great! And, if I don't know, I know people that know . . . they help me figure it out." As an example, when Darius first started working with Forest, he called a colleague experienced in teaching trans singers to gain insight on the appropriate "social interactions."

Forest and Darius met on the first day of the Beginning Voice class. Darius was bombarded with various questions from students at the end of the first day of class. He was doing his best to answer as many inquiries as possible while also trying to engage students in the process of answering questions, knowing that many of the students' needs could be answered by their peers. An older student was asking about accessing information on the college's website, and Darius turned to Forest and said, "Maybe this nice, young lady will be able to help you out." When Forest replied, "I'm not a lady," Darius was mortified at misgendering Forest and sincerely apologized to him. Forest was gracious, accepting that he hadn't started taking testosterone yet and so his appearance was less "masculine." He also acknowledged that Darius intended no malice nor harm. Darius explained, "I didn't expect it, you know, at the time. I was just overwhelmed with answering questions. I needed to be more sensitive to that." Both Darius and Forest laugh when discussing this awkward initial introduction to one another. The rapport they now share as teacher and student is irrefutably positive.

The philosophy and pedagogy Darius discusses is evident in his private teaching: "I'm trying to get out of their way to let them figure it out, take control, and let them feel and create.... You explore it and then back away and get out of their way again ... to build upon their success."

The sensitivity and thoughtfulness of his teaching is exemplified in the vocal exercises he creates for Forest in his voice lessons. Darius offers, "I'm listening deeply to treat the warm-ups for an individual in a lesson at their stage of development." None of his students are working on "very difficult aria[s]" or preparing an opera role, and thus, voice lessons serve to enrich their lives and improve their avocational singing. In the crafting of vocal exercises, Darius talks about the importance of allowing the students to pace their singing. As observed in Forest's lessons, Darius avoids playing the rhythm of the exercises and instead plays a rolled chord to allow Forest to set the speed of his breathing and singing. He describes his vocal pedagogy as based on "getting the voice in functional order all the time, as functionally possible all the time, based on what I believe to be very healthy vocal exercises and ideas that constantly get tension off the instrument." For Forest, this currently includes phonating while sliding between two pitches on voiced fricatives, such as [v] or [ð]. These semi-occluded exercises enable the student to notice consistent breath release and changes in subglottic pressure throughout his range.

Darius recalls the difficulty Forest had with singing when he first started androgen therapy. He remembers providing emotional support and offering positive feedback to Forest during this vocal change. He said he constantly reminded him, "Don't worry. It's okay. This is today. Just keep singing, as long as it doesn't hurt." Together they worked for freedom in his singing, and to keep Forest singing during the transition, even when the voice was not responding to the technique. Darius reported that Forest's voice reminded him of the adolescent vocal *cambiata*, in that they did not know how his voice would develop during this time. He remembers that during Forest's transition, he treated Forest's instrument "like a young boy . . . going through some vocal change . . . making sure [to] build the voice in functional order . . . and just getting [him] to continue singing through the process." Darius believes the vocal transition was dependent on a combination of the testosterone, personal maturity, and vocal technique. He also recalls working on posture with Forest, who would slouch to minimize his chest size. This presented an additional challenge when working with Forest in a group voice class environment.

Darius feels Forest has many strengths as a musician and performer. His stage presence, his ability to connect with the audience through song, and the confidence he brings to the stage are his strengths as a singer. Darius is also impressed with Forest's ability to choose repertoire appropriate for his voice. They continue to work on posture to support better breathing and the management of pressure in the upper range. While Forest can sing as high as an E4, Darius notices some tension in the voice due to overpressurization as he approaches the upper part of his range. Darius also comments on Forest's continued work in cultivating richness of tone and allowing for more openness and release in the upper range.

Darius emphasizes that teaching Forest is like teaching any of his students. Approaching each student as an individual with specific needs as applied to their technique and objectives is paramount. Listening deeply to each student's goals and singing while also encouraging them to take control of their learning is an example of the learner-centered pedagogy primary to Darius's style of teaching. He talks about the importance of using future-based language with his students to get them to think about their future and empowering them to be their own teacher. "Both in their lives and their voices," he asserts, "they're more in control of what they can do for themselves" than what he can do for them.

Voice Lessons

Darius's studio is located down a long hallway that connects the music teaching spaces with the theater classrooms. His office is a hive of activity, used for teaching private voice lessons, meeting individually with students for various reasons, and hosting small groups of students to discuss class material and other academic pursuits. A glossy black upright piano is to the immediate right of the door and sits opposite Darius's desk. Above the desk and piano, extending to the ceiling, are bookshelves filled with repertoire anthologies, music textbooks, and an assortment of academic journals, binders, and notebooks. Although the space is small, an inquisitive mind could spend hours looking over the materials that fill the room.

The lessons begin with Forest and Darius discussing various topics, such as how Forest's week is going or whether he has met with the student he is mentoring. They also check in regarding Forest's voice and how his practicing is going. These few minutes are jovial, increasing rapport, developing shared language, and allowing Forest and Darius to ease into the hour they will spend together. This time is also spent on goal setting for the current lesson, with Darius probing to understand Forest's goals for the lesson (e.g., "What do you want to work on?" and "What are your goals for today?"). These questions allow Forest the opportunity to talk about his immediate goals and the challenges he discovered in the prepared repertoire. They also spend a couple of minutes speaking about practicing, repertoire, and upcoming performances. This student-teacher talk comprises five to ten minutes at the beginning of lessons.

After this initial discussion, singing begins with vocal exercises developed by Darius. The preliminary exercises bring attention to a balanced onset, using voiced fricative consonants, including [v], [z], and [ð]. Darius asks Forest to slide between Do and Sol, as shown in figure 4.2, and then from Sol to high Do to low Do, shown in figure 4.3. Darius plays scale degrees 1 (Do), 2 (Re), and 5 (Sol) underneath the exercises. "Playing 1, 2, and 5 gets a little bit more color in the voice," he explains. "I try to roll it [the chord], too. I try to give them not a rhythm, but some sort of pattern to anticipate where they're going next, which allows them time to breath and decide when to start the exercise." In addition to fostering consistent breath release, the voiced

Figure 4.2. Vocal slide 1 on a fifth for balanced onset and breath release.

Figure 4.3. Vocal slide 2 on a fourth and octave for balanced onset and breath release.

fricatives promote forward resonance and a smooth and connected sound over the intervallic leap. Normally Darius moves up or down by half steps with each exercise, but he explains that at times he may move by whole steps or to various keys, depending on the intention of the exercise.

Following these exercises, Darius introduces two vocal exercises that bring attention to vowels and resonance. One of Forest's goals for his vocal development is to develop a richer timbre. These exercises foster legato singing, incorporating vowel differentiation within a more defined rhythm. On the vocable "zinga" [ziŋa], the singer begins on the first scale degree, Do, with the first syllable, and then skips an ascending fifth to Sol on the second syllable, then descends on a five-tone major scale back to the original pitch (shown in figure 4.4). The use of [z] connects the exercise to the preceding two slides and propels breath release at the onset. The "ng" hum [ŋ], though lowering the soft palate, keeps the sound forward, while the [a] fosters jaw release and openness in the vocal tract. The second exercise employed is on the vocable [nɛomi] (pronounced like "Naomi") on each pitch of a five-tone descending major scale from Sol to Do, as seen in figure 4.5. The [n] and [m] in this exercise correlates to the [ŋ] in the previous exercise, promoting forward tone. The rapid text encourages a released jaw and tongue. The descending sequence helps avoid singing with too much weight in the upper range. This exercise also requires Darius to start on a higher pitch, which becomes increasingly more difficult as Forest approaches the upper area of his range.

While Darius allows Forest to pace the timing of the exercises, both of the above examples are sung slowly, giving time

Figure 4.4.   Exercise [ziŋa] for breath release and flexibility.

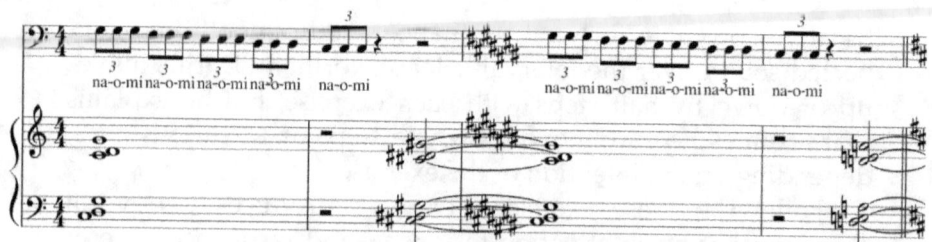

Figure 4.5. Exercise [nɛomi] for resonance and released jaw and tongue.

to focus on legato and the kinesthetic awareness of every vowel. Throughout the vocal exercises, Darius gives immediate constructive feedback to increase vocal efficiency or improve the beauty of the voice. He reminds Forest to "keep the openness" or "don't let the soft palate drop." He makes space for Forest to feel the change in his singing and to offer a reaction or response. Prompting Forest to imagine the resonating cavities and the shape of the vowels, Darius asks, "What does the space look like?" He follows this question with, "What does it feel like?" Darius uses imagery and descriptive words such as "noble," "richer," and "darkness" to effect positive change. These exercises aim to do more than merely warm up Forest's voice; they set in motion how Forest will approach his singing in the repertoire. The design of the exercises promotes greater resonance and heightened vocal efficiency.

In the second lesson observed, Darius creates a vocal exercise based on a difficult passage in one of Forest's pieces to bridge the vocal exercises to the repertoire. Forest is working on two pieces: "Tally-Ho!" by Franco Leoni (1864–1949) and "When I Was One-and-Twenty" by Arthur Somervell (1863–1937). The former captures the scene of a fox race where the narrator, a farmer, provides no assistance to the nobility in tracking the fox. The second piece is based on the poem about love written by well-known English poet A. E. Housman (1859–1936). Both pieces are new to Forest, and he and Darius spend time working on difficult rhythms or pitches. Accompanying both pieces on the piano, Darius asks what Forest feels he needs to work on. Forest offers some broad difficulties, issues related to his voice or the music, and Darius identifies a specific area in the music to address one of the identified problems on the repeated word "galloping." The plosive [p] is causing the third syllable of the word to be unintentionally stressed. Darius and Forest work to deemphasize the syllable by singing lighter and bringing attention to the amount of air needed for the [p] consonant.

Through the learning process, Darius provides ongoing feedback regarding tone and technique. A zone of proximal development is established by Darius guiding Forest through areas of growth he would have been unable to attain on his own. Darius also scaffolds the learning, where at one point he has Forest speak the text to feel the vowels without the melody. Later, he has Forest sing the melody on [va], [na], or [ga] to focus on correct pitches and consistent resonance without the complication of the lyrics. When they put the lyrics and melody together again, a slower tempo is chosen to give Forest time to process the changes in technique. Eventually they work to bring the tempo back to performance speed.

The lessons are positive in nature. While Darius frequently provides constructive criticism, he also offers supportive feedback, often praising Forest. During a challenging moment, Forest says, "It's different understanding something conceptually and actually doing it," and it is obvious Forest is frustrated with himself for not being able to achieve what Darius is asking of him. The teacher affirms his feelings and reminds him that this lesson is not the end goal, but part of the learning process. The theme of forward-thinking to affect positive change in Forest's singing outside his lessons is evident. Often Darius is working toward helping Forest hear and feel the changes he has made in his lessons so he is able to re-create this on his own. Each lesson ends with establishing goals and setting parameters for what to work on in preparation for the next lesson. Darius asks, "Do you feel successful? Do you hear a difference?" "More important," Forest replies, "I feel a difference, too."

The rapport between this student and teacher is strong. They seem to be working together toward a common goal with shared language and experiences. Forest is given opportunity throughout the lesson to give Darius feedback. Though the pacing of the lesson and the learning sequence is determined by Darius, Forest has chosen the repertoire and identified to Darius where he has had trouble during his own practice, which sets the learning in motion. Darius maintains that teaching Forest is no different from teaching any of his cisgender students; however, Darius's approach to teaching is a departure from the master-apprentice model of teaching. Forest and Darius portray collaboration in the lessons, where Darius's expert knowledge in vocal pedagogy enables him to guide Forest through the arc of learning he has established for himself.

Case Study: Emmett (student) and Naomi (teacher)

Student Portrait

When Emmett decided to undergo androgen therapy, it meant not only a transformation in voice and body but a change in career, and as a result, in lifestyle. For twenty-five years, Emmett was a full-time professional mezzo-soprano. Living in a major city in California, his career included opera, oratorio, and ensemble singing. Although Emmett has spent most of his adult life as a resident of the United States, he was born and raised in England. His childhood experiences gave him a love for singing and music.

Emmett is a trans man in his mid-fifties. When asked how he describes his identity, he says, "I'm not sure I have ever really thought about it that distinctly before." He continues, "I've always identified as male. I suppose I would say I'm a trans man . . . I guess that's how I would describe myself in terms of gender." Though his gender forms part of his overall identity, more significant to his life is his identity as a singer. Emmett discusses singing both in the here and now and also as a part of his past. He shares, "It [being a singer] is the biggest part of my identity." Moments later, when discussing his vocal range, he offers, "I did have a ridiculous range. I had a three-and-a-half-octave range with no breaks anywhere." While he still identifies as a singer, there are pieces of that identity that are behind him.

Early memories of music for Emmett are from his family home. His mother would listen to the conductor Annunzio

Mantovani and his orchestra as she was cleaning house. "My grandmother always said I was singing before I could walk, before I could talk," he remembers. He showed musical aptitude very early on. During a hymn practice at school, he recalls:

> When I was very small, about seven I think, the music teacher started playing the hymn. When we were all supposed to start singing, I was the only one singing because I knew it and nobody else did. She [the music teacher] made me stand up on stage and sing it for everyone. It just happened to be a hymn that my granny sang at church, so I learned it there. The music teacher asked me if I wanted to be in the choir, which was very confusing to me because you weren't actually allowed to be in the choir until you were nine. So that's when I started getting really interested.

Emmett confesses to not being strong at other academics. Music was the subject for which he had the most intrinsic motivation and natural ability. He started taking voice lessons at the age of fourteen and sang and played percussion in many different ensembles growing up. He remembers a music teacher suggested he take voice lessons to supplement his training at school: "It was almost in desperation that my music teacher suggested [private lessons] to my mother. Basically, he said, 'You know, he doesn't seem to be capable of doing anything else. The only thing he—she then—is interested in is singing. Have you thought of getting him voice lessons?'"

Despite a passion for music, he completed a university degree in plant biology. Afterward, he started a specialized course in vocal performance at a major conservatory in northern England. He was also the recipient of a scholarship from the Rotary International Foundation, which enabled him to study singing at a prestigious music school in the United States. After these formal studies, he moved to the West Coast, where he started his professional career.

Early on he recalls auditioning for the role of Cherubino in Mozart's *Le Nozze di Figaro*. Despite being vocally and physically ideal for the role, he was not hired, as the company cited they should hire a mezzo-soprano in the role. Despite having always trained as a soprano, his wide vocal range allowed him to do varied repertoire. Emmett decided to change the voice type listed on his résumé from soprano to mezzo-soprano, which ultimately created more work for him. "I went home," he says, "and I put *mezzo* in front of *soprano* on my résumé and didn't change anything else and worked for twenty-five years solid." Although he always felt comfortable singing both mezzo-soprano and soprano repertoire, he suggests that was confusing for many people: "People want you to tell them what you are. They don't want to just take you on face value for what you can actually do standing there. You've got to be in a [vocal] box. If you do bits of this and bits of that and some of this, they don't know what to do with you."

As an opera singer, Emmett sang a lot of "boys and old bags" roles, as he describes them. He flourished in trouser roles, like Cherubino, and older female roles, such as Meg Page in *Falstaff* or various parts in Offenbach operettas. When working as a principal artist, it was possible to choose the roles for which he would audition. As a singer in the opera chorus, he says, "I had to do whatever they said. They would never put me in any of the men sections. They would never have even put me dressed as a boy onstage." As a choral singer, he performed with the highest regional professional organizations, singing anything from second soprano to tenor, depending on the needs of the concert repertoire. Most often he sang in the alto section. Choral singing created fewer gender issues than his experience in opera.

In terms of attire, singing as a concert soloist was comparable to playing an opera role. While he identified as a man offstage to artistic staff and colleagues, his feminine birth name appeared in concert programs, and so often he would dress in "drag," as he explains, to appease audience expectations. He would wear black trousers designed for women and a beaded or sequined jacket. He adds, "I did all the makeup and all that crap. I cleaned up pretty well. It always shocked people. That was the funniest thing for me . . . it was worth it in some ways for the hilarity factor." Later he mentions, "On a few occasions when I kowtowed to worrying about what other people were thinking, I wore a frock. I always regretted it because it was so much more uncomfortable for me."

He shares that often he was more worried about what he was wearing than about his singing. "There is a difference," he states, "between wearing something that's a bit scratchy and wearing something that just makes you feel dysphoric." While he discusses his solo concert attire in jest, dressing in "drag" was an unwelcomed and uncomfortable form of expression. Eventually he changed his attire to white tie and tails or a suit, depending on the formality of the concert. One conductor who was supportive of Emmett worried that the audience might think more about his attire than his singing, but that did not bother him. Indeed, he jokingly commented, "Which depending how I was singing that night is not necessarily a bad thing!"

As he approached fifty years old, Emmett noticed the quality of his voice starting to wane. He discloses:

> I knew that my voice was going to start aging, and I could tell it had already started a little bit. I don't think anybody else really could tell, but I could tell. I knew that basically I was aging out of the roles that I was comfortable doing—that I really liked to do. There were some old bags left, but that was it, and more competition for them. So, I guess, in a way, that played a large part, but it was also like, "Well, I'm fifty years old, so it's kind of now or never." And I wasn't really going to be going anywhere else with my singing.

This decision led him to start taking testosterone. Emmett's dosage was low at first, starting with a skin gel application and moving to injections. He initially chose a low dosage, hoping it would make the vocal transition easier. He describes his transition as a "nightmare," but he continued to sing through it, despite not feeling motivated. Before the onset of androgen therapy, he was fully aware there was no way of knowing how his voice would change, but he confesses, "I ended up with a lot less range than I thought I would have to work with. Obviously, there was no way of knowing what it would be. I knew that going into it, but I went from three and a half octaves to one. That's not enough really to do anything. That's been hard."

His range lowered in frequency, which was the expected course, but he lost stamina, size of range, and flexibility. The one octave range he mentions is from approximately D3 to D4. He says he was a better tenor before his transition than he was after. In describing his changed voice, he says, "It's like trying to put a cello under the chin or something, when you used to play the violin." Emmett has been on testosterone for four years, and though his voice has developed, he still "horrendously" misses high-quality singing.

In addition to being left with a reduced range, Emmett also experiences a lack of vocal flexibility. Before transition, he could easily imitate other singers and animal sounds, which was an aspect of his personality and humor. This is impossible for him now. He has limited falsetto, which stymies imitating other voices or sounds. He had a laryngoscopy performed on his vocal folds a few times to ensure there was no damage. As revealed in previous procedures before his transition, the scope showed a partial paralysis on one of his vocal folds. Otherwise, no other discernible issues were present. Emmett believes the vocal transition was more challenging for him at middle age than it would have been if he had transitioned earlier in life. He speculates that had he been younger at the onset of androgen therapy, the transition might have been easier and more fruitful, owing to less ossification of the larynx.

Soon after transition, Emmett participated in a single-case research study conducted by a speech-language pathologist and his current singing teacher, Naomi, who, in addition to singing, works with individuals on the overall health of their speaking voices. The findings of this study have been presented at conferences but are not currently in print. The researchers examined Emmett's vocal change using empirical evaluations, such as vocal range and pitch duration, and perceptual measurements related to speech and singing behavior. This research will be further discussed in Naomi's portrait.

Emmett continues to take lessons with Naomi. He had known her before his transition, having had a couple of lessons years ago, but they have been working together more regularly since his transition. The purpose of their lessons is to find "ease and consistency" in his baritonal range. They are also working on range expansion and breath support, a concept Emmett freely admits to having never properly understood as a mezzo-soprano. Since Emmett found singing so naturally easy before transition, he never had to work diligently to build or maintain efficient vocal technique. He says, "I had no idea singing was difficult. Not a clue. To think that some people face that all the time, from the beginning. I take my hat off to them." When data were collected for the current study, he and Naomi had not seen each other for five months. Emmett admits to not being prudent in practicing or doing much vocal exploration while she was out of the country. Now that he no longer works as a professional singer, it is difficult to prioritize singing.

The vocal transition for Emmett has caused serious disruption in his life. When asked if he could undo the process, he pauses for an inordinately long time and finally responds, "Maybe not . . . maybe not." He follows up, however, by indicating that not all aspects of the transition have been unfortunate. He shares, "There are other aspects of my life that are much better, like I am not misgendered in my daily life, which use to drive me insane." He further notes, "Because I was so identified, not just self-identified, but so identified by people in general, as a singer, now that I'm not a singer anymore, I sort of feel a bit lost at sea." Where he would see friends and colleagues as a matter of course through professional engagements, he has discovered it is difficult to find time to maintain friendships and associations since he no longer works the schedule of a professional musician. Emmett is in an entirely different line of work now that, although it is not as exciting as being an opera singer, he very much enjoys.

Teacher Portrait

A California native, Naomi is a straight, cisgender female. She is an internationally respected voice teacher and a specialist on trans singing. Naomi's earliest training as a serious musician was on the flute. She earned a bachelor's degree in flute performance at an institution that fostered student creativity through collaboration with other departments. After completing her undergraduate studies, she matriculated at a major European conservatory to study traverso (Baroque flute). Naomi discovered that the more traditional conservatory training, along with the limited repertoire of the traverso, made her feel musically stifled. During her first winter in grad school, Naomi was accepted into a chamber choir of eighteen voices. She describes, "I had a very clear, nonvibrato choral voice . . . because I was in such a good choir, I started taking lessons and something started to open up." Eventually, she switched from traverso to voice and completed a master's in vocal performance and pedagogy, which has afforded her a career in teaching and performing.

As a singer, Naomi has worked with some of the highest regarded conductors in early music, both on the concert stage and in recordings. She also has enjoyed performing contemporary music and art songs and collaborating with dancers and orchestras in eclectic and unusual programs. While she studied opera in graduate school as a *Zwischenfach* ("mezzanine soprano," as she denotes her *Fach*), she feels she never had the voice or passion for opera. She had lived in Europe for fourteen years when her husband received the opportunity to complete his doctoral studies in California, and so the couple returned to her home state. While she maintained a performing profile in the United States for several years, most of her attention has been spent on teaching singers.

While still residing in Europe, Naomi was requested to work with various individuals on their speaking voice health. Although she was a singing teacher, she found that her approach to vocal technique benefited the individuals who needed speaking voice rehabilitation. She says, "People asked me to help with their speaking voices, and I found that the approach I was taking with my students—just a healthy approach to air and resonance—was working with spoken voice as well."

After returning stateside, Naomi did specialized training in vocology to support her knowledge of vocal use. She partners with laryngologists and speech-language pathologists to assist singers and nonmusical professional voice users. "It's always such a help," she shares, "when they do sing, because then they're more attuned to using their voice, and often their singing voice is actually healthier than their speaking voice." The work she does with sung and spoken voice rebuilding has led her toward collaborative research on trans singing.

As mentioned above, Naomi has been collaborating with a speech-language pathologist on a research project that tracks Emmett's vocal transition. In every session, Emmett would complete an extensive questionnaire about his perceptions. She explains, "As [Emmett's] voice started to descend, his congruence between his voice and his identity increased." She continues, "It was so striking. [Emmett] didn't even realize this because it happened so gradually." Emmett and Naomi met weekly for a one-hour session while data were being collected. Approximately forty minutes was spent on a range of diagnostic assessments, including (1) the questionnaire; (2) singing on [i] and [a] on G4, which was a comfortable pitch at the beginning of the study, as well as on whichever pitch was most comfortable at that moment; (3) testing maximum duration on G4 and that day's comfortable pitch; and (4) checking physiological range and performable range. Emmett also recorded Handel's aria "Ombra mai fu" every meeting to further examine voice modification. The remaining time was spent on vocal development through vocal exercises and repertoire. Interviews and observations for the current study were conducted many months after the data collection for Naomi's study had been completed.

Naomi recalls near the beginning of Emmett's transition, "Every single time, [Emmett] presented with a new voice; I never knew what to expect." She conveys that it was like he came to each lesson with a new instrument. It was further complicated because Emmett was such a natural singer before transition. He never really had to learn vocal technique, as it came effortlessly to him. Naomi notes, "[Emmett] was such a natural talent that this is a big stumbling block, because he never used to have to work. He had such an easy voice." Near the beginning of the transition, his voice was thin, breathy, small, and unstable. It cracked a lot and there was no continuity. Regarding his early vocal development, Naomi explains, "I just tried to find the area where he was phonating best and extend from there, [but] what would happen is that I would work his lower range at the start of the session, he'd be relaxed and be able to phonate down, but as he went along, he'd get more tense . . . then that would start to weaken." Eventually, as he started to gain a few notes, the breathiness also started to dissipate, and the breath pressure and balance began to align. While she describes Emmett's voice as becoming "solid" and "lovely," he was still limited by small vocal range.

Shortly before the data collection for this study began, Naomi returned from teaching in Europe for five months. She describes how she was surprised to find Emmett had made vocal progress in her absence: "There's been an enormous change in the meantime, both in terms of range and consistency of resonance. He told me he hadn't practiced at all and barely sung, so I can only assume that the change is due to the THT [testosterone hormone therapy]."

Later in the interview, she reiterates her surprise in his vocal development: "What I heard last week and this week was dramatically different from before I went away, and it has to be the androgen, because he hasn't been singing for five months." Currently his vocal range extends from B2 to F4, which means he can sing much more repertoire than he could five months prior. While the entire range is not necessarily free and easy, the mere presence of this expanding range indicates continued growth.

As a vocal pedagogue, Naomi honors the Socratic method of teaching. "A fundamental part of how I teach is eliciting, asking questions, and guiding," she offers, "rather than dictating from the top down." Naomi is cognizant that students benefit from understanding the process of singing: "We're all different and none of us can actually crawl into somebody else's body to figure it out . . . six days out of seven, they are on their own. They have to be making decisions, so they need to be paying attention [to what works for them]." She continues, "If I am prescribing the *what* [italicized for emphasis] instead of the *how*, they're going to be going through the motions, and it's useless." Naomi strives for her students to find "easeful-ness" in their singing, and mindfulness in their practice to explore the process of optimal singing.

Seeking ease and freedom in singing is discussed in a couple of ways, in (1) exercises and (2) repertoire. Naomi discusses the use of two exercises. One exercise is built on stacking minor thirds. The second is constructed on the pentatonic scale. She avoids the standard arpeggio, made up of scale degrees 1-3-5-8-5-3-1, as she has come to find the ascending fourth interval between Sol and Do can cause singers to lift or "winch," either in their body or larynx, producing tightness. In using the pentatonic scale, comprised of scale degrees 1, 2, 3, 5 and 6, the largest interval is a minor third, and she can "slither around," adding extra pentatonic scale degrees at the top or bottom at will. The same appeal exists in the exercise on minor thirds. She usually avoids transposing the exercise up or down by a half step but instead extends the exercises higher or lower by adding a pitch to the top or bottom. The purpose and design of these exercises will be examined more thoroughly in the next section.

With regard to repertoire, Naomi suggests having singers transpose songs or parts of songs to learn them without tension. She warns, "If you embed a sensory feeling of strain, it's hard to get that out." Instead, she suggests, "learn it where it is comfortable. Once you know the shape of that phrase and you're comfortable with the text, try it in the [original] key." Transposing a phrase to a higher or lower key as necessary enables a singer to learn it kinesthetically, without strain. "You may have to adjust the vowel, you may feel a little difference in terms of breath pressure, but you're looking for the same ease-fullness," Naomi says. She teaches Emmett in the same way she teaches all her singers: guiding them to find freedom and ease in their voices. Naomi also advocates changing song keys entirely as needed. There is a tradition, she notes, in performing repertoire in the composer's intended key, but Naomi asserts it is more important to sing well than to honor convention.

Being present and acknowledging each student as an individual is foundational in her teaching. Naomi asserts, "I think you shouldn't treat your trans singers any different from your cisgender singers. They're all different. Every time they show up, they're different, and you work with what you've got. These are individual people. Honestly, every single one of my students, every time they show up, is different. I think it's important to teach what walks in the door." She continues to advise that in working with students who are taking androgen therapy, a teacher needs to be more vigilant to acknowledge their changing instrument. She emphasizes the need for a student-centered approach in applied lessons teaching. She asks of her students, "Don't tell me what you've been doing. Show me. Just imagine you're at home right now. You're about to practice. What are you going to do? Start making noise, and I'll guide you."

This approach to allowing the student to lead their lesson gives her the ability to see how they problem-solve. It also provides insight to their understanding of process and vocal technique. She recognizes not all students flourish in student-centered pedagogy, and she adjusts her approach differently for each student based on their emotional and psychological needs. Naomi believes student-centeredness is empowering, especially for TGQ singers aspiring to align their voice with their gender.

Naomi cautions to avoid making any assumptions about TGQ singers. She mentions "how little research there is on this. . . . We're all kind of feeling our way in the dark. . . . The current research is just the tip of the iceberg." Despite having worked with Emmett for four years, there are aspects of his transition that remain a mystery. She theorizes, "I think psychologically it was very hard for [Emmett] to transition so gradually—like removing a Band-Aid painfully slowly. It might have been better to dive in more quickly. We'll never know." She further acknowledges, "Whether he will ever have sufficient range to really perform professionally, I don't know, but I'll tell you, I'm much more optimistic now than I was five months ago." For teachers of TGQ singers, she urges for further exploration. Despite nearly thirty years of experience in teaching, she wants to keep learning and researching the voice.

Voice Lessons

Naomi's studio is on the third floor of her home. The cozy, warm space is painted a light, vibrant rose color. The bookshelves are filled with repertoire books. The grand piano sits in the middle of the room, next to her desk. A large mirror hangs on one wall, adjacent the piano, providing a reflection for the students to see themselves.

Figure 4.6. Stacked minor 3rds, version 1, for rounded lips and forward resonance.

Figure 4.7. Stacked minor 3rds, version 2, for rounded lips and forward resonance.

Naomi greets Emmett with friendly rapport. Her demeanor is open and approachable. The lessons begin with a few minutes of talking about nonmusical aspects of Emmett's life regarding his job, daily commute, and energy level. The singing begins with an exercise that is constructed of minor thirds, as shown in figure 4.6. The limited range of this initial exercise enables Emmett to focus on making a resonant sound without straining over large intervals. Naomi has Emmett begin on [u] and then switch between [u] and [y] on every other pitch. The closed vowels promote rounded lips and forward resonance. Figure 4.7 shows a similar melodic sequence, except that the exercise extends the voice a little lower by adding an additional minor third to the bottom.

After these preliminary exercises, Naomi continues extending the range and difficulty of the exercise by adding more minor thirds intervals to the sequence. In figure 4.8, the exercise shows Emmett starting with [bla], slurring two pitches together. The consonant pair fosters forward resonance, a lifted soft palate, and a released tongue and jaw. From [bla], Naomi has Emmett sing the same pitch arrangement on [spɛ], which

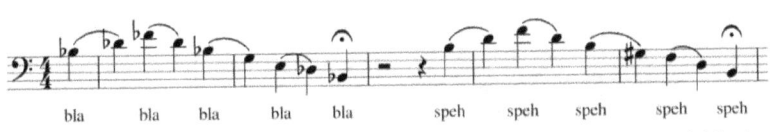

Figure 4.8. Stacked minor 3rds, version 3, for forward resonance and lifted soft palate.

136 / Chapter 4

supports similar technical functions and promotes breath release and abdominal engagement at the start of each pair of notes.

Figures 4.6–4.8 display the full vocal range Naomi guided Emmett through in this succession of exercises. While she moved by ascending half steps, she circumvented moving up or down frequently or quickly, to potentially allay unwanted tension. Instead, she concentrated in his middle range before moving up or down. It should also be noted that at Naomi's request, Emmett repeated some of these keys twice, others three times, to hone resonance or breath support before moving higher or lower. These exercises were constructed and taught with specificity to establish the technical prowess needed for efficient singing.

The next two exercises are built on the pentatonic scale. These exercises are like the previously shown exercises but use a wider range and a different arrangement of intervals. In figure 4.9, Naomi has Emmett sing the exercise on several vowels and vowel combinations. First, Emmett sings the first three measures on all vowels shown below. Then, he sings the second half of the figure on the indicated vowel combinations. This exercise fosters range development, smooth tongue movement between two vowels, and resonance enhancement on [i]. Figure 4.10 is similar in using the pentatonic scale, but the exercise is longer with a wider range, which increases the level of difficulty. Naomi starts these exercises in Emmett's middle range, which fosters a balanced resonance and suppleness of tone.

Throughout the execution of these exercises, Naomi brings awareness to Emmett's breathing. Drawing attention

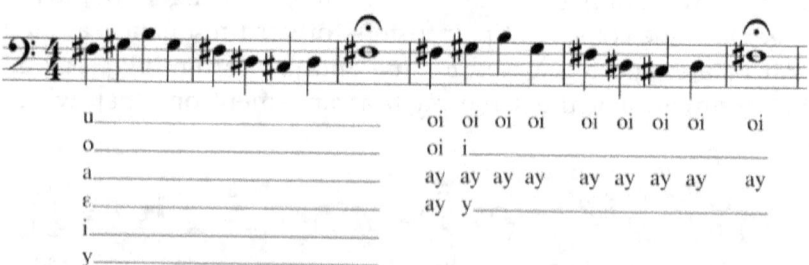

Figure 4.9. Pentatonic scale, version 1, for range development and smooth tongue movement.

Figure 4.10.   Pentatonic scale, version 2, for range development and breath control.

to inhalation, she suggests, "Don't go away from your vowel when you breathe." She uses an analogy of not putting down your instrument between musical phrases to illustrate the need for maintaining the vowel during inhalation. She frequently asks him to be mindful of his tongue, hoping it will stay released throughout the exercise. Inviting Emmett to "keep asking the tongue to release," later she suggests to him, "Close your eyes. Crawl into your mouth and ask if your tongue is happy." Naomi avoids telling him exactly how to shape his tongue but instead focuses on his kinesthetic awareness of it. During a segment of a lesson, she has him lightly touch the tip of his tongue with a finger to see if he can avoid retracting it in his mouth. She explains that he should not hold it forward, but simply notice how his tongue responds to different pitches and areas of his range.

In the first lesson observed, Naomi asks Emmett to place one hand on his abdominals and the other on the side of his ribs. He makes a comment in jest about being too heavy to feel the muscles move, to which Naomi responds that that is not true. In exclamation, he responds, "It's true." As he laughs on the word "true," his voice effortlessly jumps from A3 to A4, into a resonant falsetto. It lasts only for a second but is interesting because (1) during his interview, he reported he has no falsetto nor any ability to phonate in a lighter/higher voice, and (2) in follow-up correspondence with Naomi, she reports that in a lesson after the data collection was complete, he sang in falsetto during the vocal exercises. This suggests that even after four years on testosterone, his voice is continuing to modify.

While Naomi leads much of the lesson, with regard to exercises and pacing, she leaves room for Emmett to make important decisions, as he sees best, for his singing. During some of the exercises, Naomi solicits Emmett to choose the vowel for the exercise or to modify the vowel during an exercise. She encourages him to seek an "easy" technique, which fosters a "rich" tone. Frequently Emmett is asked what he notices kinesthetically during his singing. Naomi also regularly leaves room for Emmett to conceptualize the singing process and provides space for him to offer feedback. Recurring affirmative comments are combined with constructive feedback, while questions and guiding statements elicit positive changes.

Prior to the start of this study's data collection, Emmett had been working on Fauré's "La chanson du pêcheur" in F minor. Due to an increase in range, they read through some additional pieces, including Schubert's "An den Mond" and Schumann's "Die Lotosblume" and "Aud den östlichen Rosen." Time is spent in learning the newly selected Schubert. Naomi prints off the song text, and has Emmet sing the poetry on the pentatonic exercise in figure 4.9, without having him look at the musical score. The purpose of this activity is to gain familiarity with the text without worrying about specific pitches and rhythms. This immediately promotes legato singing. Emmett is an excellent musician, and thus to avoid him scrutinizing the score and worrying about how high or low the pitches appear, Naomi teaches the melody mostly by rote. After he is conversant with the melody, Emmett sings the poem on the melody without looking at the sheet music. Though he makes some errors regarding textual underlay, Naomi is drawing attention to how he produces sound rather than his precise rendering of the musical score. During this process, Naomi encourages Emmett to modify vowels in order to phonate with as much freedom as possible. She also suggests finding additional pieces outside the published keys if they are easier to sing.

An additional facet of vocal technique is the work spent on singing softer, not louder. Naomi does not discuss dynamics much during the exercises, but she brings attention to singing more softly during the song work. The consideration of dynamics is a characteristic of musical coaching and an aspect of vocal technique, as the softer dynamic diminishes the need to push in the lower or higher ranges. Naomi reminds Emmett that the softer singing requires more energy, "like a hamster running on a wheel."

Naomi's style of teaching with Emmett is compassionate. Emmett describes himself as self-deprecating, and the shortened vocal range Emmett has experienced post-transition has caused him to lose confidence in his singing. Naomi provides structure and a safe place for Emmett to explore his voice without judgment, using technical concepts and exercises that honor process over product. As she does with all her students, Naomi encourages Emmett to avoid going through motions while singing, but instead fully invest in the learning process so the exercises and concepts can be implemented outside the applied studio.

Chapter Takeaways

This chapter investigated the experiences and perspectives of two trans men and their singing teachers. Emmett, a middle-aged man, gave up his career as a full-time professional mezzo-soprano to live his authentic self. Emmett's decision to take a low dosage of testosterone was influenced by previous vocal research that indicates a lower dosage might allow the voice to change more slowly, thusly avoiding a massive shift for the vocal muscles and fostering an easier time with singing. Unfortunately, Emmett's challenging vocal transition stands in contrast to those recommendations, not only due to his frustration in being forced to wait so long to see or feel any physical changes, but also in not being pleased with his resulting voice or range.

The effects of androgen therapy are different for every person based on age, weight, physical makeup, and dosage amount. As demonstrated in Forest's narrative, his vocal change has been more positive, but as he is a nonprofessional singer, it is also plausible that Forest's expectations for his own voice might not be as high as Emmett. In both cases, these men eventually experienced a drop in vocal range, allowing them to sing in the baritone range. Additionally, Emmett and Forest, although working with different teachers, found positive affirmation in their lessons, giving them more awareness and confidence in their vocal abilities. Here is a condensed overview of pedagogical considerations and salient knowledge in teaching trans masculine singers.

Teaching Singers

- Singing through a vocal transition brought on by exogenous testosterone is important as it helps maintain vocal flexibility and pliability; it can also help a person relearn vocal habits as their vocal range modulates.
- Transitioning voices can become more easily fatigued.
- As is typical during puberty for individuals assigned male at birth, a voice might crack and sound raspy or breathy during the vocal transition.
- Encourage coordinated adduction through semi-occluded exercises constructed on voice fricative consonants, lip buzz, or straw singing.
- Former treble range singers might be used to singing with a higher laryngeal position. Exercises on [u] or [o] might foster a lowered larynx.
- Vocal exercises in the middle range (E3 to A3, below middle C) are a good starting place.
- The falsetto register might take many months to return, if it returns at all. Singing in the treble range, considered important by some vocal pedagogues for overall vocal health, might incite dysphoria for some trans men.
- Changing the key of a song allows a singer to embody a song that might otherwise might be out of their range or tessitura.
- Student-centeredness with lesson pacing, repertoire selection, and range development might help a student feel more comfortable.
- Singing lessons can serve a vital role in a person's vocal and gender transition.
- Some trans men might bind their torso to minimize chest size. Half-torso binders might encourage better abdominal breathing for singing. (Compression bandages are dangerous, as they become tighter and tighter when worn around the torso.)

- If a transgender man slouches, this might be to minimize his chest. Be cautious when modifying a singer's posture.

Hormone Replacement Therapy and Speech-Language Pathology

- Hormone replacement therapy is frequently called HRT; the administration of testosterone is sometimes referred to as androgen therapy.
- HRT is administered under the care of a medical professional, but the amount of support a person receives varies from clinic to clinic.
- Adult trans male singers who begin testosterone replacement therapy will experience a thickening of the vocal folds; the larynx will not enlarge due to its cartilaginous composition.
- Age, physical makeup, and testosterone dosage amount effects the vocal transition:
  - Previous research recommends a lower testosterone dosage to enable the vocal muscle to develop more gradually;
  - However, a lower testosterone dosage can heighten gender dysphoria as vocal and physical changes might take a long time to develop; a lower dosage does not ensure an easier vocal transition.
- Testosterone-induced vocal transitions (sometimes called the "second puberty") can take many months, sometimes 6–12 months, but other times much longer.
- Less is known about the singing voice of adolescent trans men, but if exogenous testosterone is administered at puberty, their voices might develop as other males their age.
- HRT is unavailable to persons under the age of eighteen without parental/guardian support.
- Speech-language pathology might help a person become more comfortable with their voice, approaching the production of sound from a space of healthy functionality.

- While trans men may want their voices to sound lower, not all men choose to receive HRT.

Notes

1. Jennifer Sanchez, "Acoustic and Perceptual Study of Female-to-Male Transgendered Voice" (Master's thesis, William Paterson University of New Jersey, 2013); John Van Borsel et al., "Voice Problems in Female-to-Male Transsexuals," *International Journal of Language & Communication Disorders* 35, no. 3 (2000): 427–42, https://doi.org/10.1080/136828200410672.

2. Alexandros Constansis, "The Changing Female-to-Male (FTM) Voice," *Radical Musicology* 3 (2008), http://www.radical-musicology.org.uk/2008/Constansis.htm; Loraine Sims, "Teaching Transgender Students," *Journal of Singing* 73, no. 3 (2017): 279–82; Loraine Sims, "Teaching Lucas: A Transgender Student's Vocal Journey from Soprano to Tenor," *Journal of Singing* 73, no. 4 (2017): 376–75.

3. James C. McKinney, *The Diagnosis & Correction of Vocal Faults: A Manual for Teachers of Singing & for Choir Directors* (Nashville, TN: Genevox Music Group, 1994), 111.

4. Richard C. Miller, *The Structure of Singing: System and Art in Vocal Technique* (Belmont, CA: Wadsworth Group, 1996), 117.

5. Ibid.

6. Theodore Dimon, *Your Body, Your Voice: The Key to Natural Singing and Speaking* (Berkeley, CA: North Atlantic, 2011), 61.

7. Ibid., 60.

8. Miller, *The Structure of Singing*, 118.

9. Ibid., 122.

10. Ibid., 124.

11. Peter Giles, *A Basic Countertenor Method for Teacher and Student* (London: Kahn & Averill, 2005).

12. Patrick Barbier, *The World of the Castrati: The History of an Extraordinary Operatic Phenomenon* (London: Souvenir Press, 2010).

13. Van Borsel et al., "Voice Problems."

14. Shelagh Davies and Joshua M. Goldberg, "Clinical Aspects of Transgender Speech Feminization and Masculinization," *International Journal of Transgenderism* 9, no. 3–4 (2006): 167–96, https://doi.org/10.1300/j485v09n03_08; Van Borsel et al., "Voice Problems."

15. R. Nick Gorton, Jamie Buth, and Dean Spade, *Medical Therapy and Health Maintenance for Transgender Men: A Guide for Health Care Providers* (San Francisco, CA: Lyon-Martin Women's Health Services, 2005), 59.

16. Van Borsel et al., "Voice Problems."

17. Constansis, "The Changing Female-to-Male (FTM) Voice."

18. Ibid., para. 15.
19. Viktoria Papp, *The Female-to-Male Transsexual Voice: Physiology vs. Performance in Production* (PhD diss., Rice University, 2012); Sanchez, "Acoustic and Perceptual Study"; Lal Zimman, *Voices in Transition: Testosterone, Transmasculinity, and the Gendered Voice Among Female-to-Male Transgender People* (PhD diss., University of Colorado Boulder, 2012).
20. Sanchez, "Acoustic and Perceptual Study," 19.
21. Papp, *The Female-to-Male Transsexual Voice*.
22. Van Borsel et al., "Voice Problems," 434.
23. Papp, *The Female-to-Male Transsexual Voice*, 67.
24. Ibid., 68.
25. Ibid., 98.
26. Zimman, *Voices in Transition*.
27. Ibid., iii.

5

Trans-Nonbinary Singers

> "There were days I felt like a girl and days I felt like a boy, and those days wouldn't always correspond with the body I was in. I still believed everyone when they said I had to be one or the other. Nobody was telling me a different story, and I was too young to think for myself. I had yet to learn that when it came to gender, I was both and neither."
>
> —Vic, the protagonist in David Levithan's *Every Day*

The trans population includes individuals who do not identify within the female/male gender binary. This subset of individuals uses multiple different gender labels, including, but not limited to: nonbinary, enby (pronounced "n-b" for nonbinary), nonconforming, genderqueer, genderfuck, and agender. These gender markers might be spelled with or without a hyphen. In a preeminent study on the lives of trans people by Genny Beemyn and Susan Rankin, which included 3,474 respondents, of the 275 participants who did not self-identify as female, male, or transgender, there were 119 different unique gender descriptors used.[1] The liminality within a nonbinary identity allows a person's gender to be fluid; one person might identify as neither female nor male, while another individual might identify as both simultaneously or freely move between and outside this dichotomy. The expansiveness of gender enables some trans folx to identity as nonbinary (or any other identity marker) or not, while some nonbinary individuals may or may not identify as trans. The expanding notion of gender queers the sociocultural constructs of identity.

Where academic scholarship and media reporting has brought attention to trans women and men, less advocacy has been paid to nonbinary individuals. Beemyn and Rankin explain, "Until recently, there have been few visible images of transgender people who do not present and identify as woman or men.... As a result, people with a nonbinary understanding of their gender have often lacked information, support, and role models, all of which makes it more difficult to adopt a genderqueer identity."[2] The researchers further suggest that as more individuals come out as nonbinary there will be an increased awareness of different forms of genderqueer expression. In his book *Trans Voices*, Irish author Declan Henry supports this notion, observing that nonbinary identities are becoming more prominent and suggesting, "Society is now seeing far fewer people feeling trapped in binary gender categories."[3] A study from the Williams Institute found that 1.2 million adults (ages eighteen to sixty) in the United States identify as nonbinary and that a majority of these adults are under age twenty-nine.[4]

The growing awareness of diverse gender identities that abandon gender conformity has helped foster a recent change in linguistics. In 2017, the *AP Stylebook* updated its policy to include they/them/their as a singular pronoun.[5] Important organizations such as the *Washington Post*, American Psychological Association, and Merriam-Webster also include the use of they/them/their as a singular gender-neutral pronoun.[6] A Pew Research study found that around 18 percent of adults in the United States know someone who uses gender-neutral pronouns.[7]

The growing use of gender-neutral pronouns includes *neopronouns* that broaden lexical norms. Generally, pronouns are used to replace a proper name. Neopronouns, also called "nounself pronouns," as reported by the *New York Times*, are created when a "pre-existing word is drafted into use as a pronoun."[8]

Neopronouns inflate gender-neutral pronoun options beyond popular alternatives like they/themself, ze/hirself, or fae/faerself. A neopronoun, as based on a preexisting noun, might be anything, such as princ/princself, wolf/wolfself, or bun/bunself. Neopronouns have gained traction through online platforms such a TikTok, Switch, and Twitter, and though many online discussions are dominated by debate over the authenticity of these pronouns, this queering of the language seems to be embraced by a younger population who wish to break down communication conventions. In the case of neopronouns, in place of saying the person's first name, the speaker or writer would say the neopronouns chosen by the individual (for example, "Jane went to the store to pick up the items by princself.").

Though neopronouns are a deviation from standard vocabulary, using multiple different names/labels/references for a single person is commonplace. A person might be referenced formally in one circumstance ("Mrs. Smith" or "Pastor Phil"), by their first name in another space, and by different terms of endearment (Mom/Dad/Friend/Lover) in a different environment. Students might use a formal approach when referring to a teacher in the classroom but call them "Coach" on the sports field. Cultural norms suggest we are routinized to code-switching—that is, referring to people differently in discrete spaces or modifying our language as appropriate in different instances. While neopronouns are not nicknames, they can easily replace he, she, or they. The growing use of gender-neutral pronouns suggests the need for nimbleness of language to affirm diverse identities. As small as they are, pronouns impart ethos, agency, power, gender, and self-identity.

While chapters 3 and 4 presented research from speech-language pathology on trans voices, there is an absence in the research on affirmative voice care that addresses the perceptions and needs of nonbinary folx. While some nonbinary people might not seek voice modulation at all, others might seek a gender-neutral voice or a higher or lower range to match their identity. Research indicates that the target range for gender-neutral speaking voices is approximately 155–65 Hz (around D#3-E3, below middle C);[9] however, vocal pitch alternation alone might be unsatisfactory in attaining the desired qualities of a person's voice. Furthermore, there is no conclusion that a gender-neutral voice is the targeted goal for nonbinary individuals. Singing voice research, like speech-language pathology, has focused on voices in transition brought on by hormone replacement therapy, rather than addressing the vocal needs of nonbinary singers.

The two case studies presented within this chapter offer insight to lived experiences of two nonbinary singers. Neither singer has engaged in hormone replacement therapy. As will be explored, coming from different backgrounds, both singers have experienced affirmation and dysphoria within the performing arts. In addition to the singer narratives, both teachers in this chapter are trans men, and so this chapter continues the conversation on trans masculine voices and offers valuable insight on teaching gender expansive singers from the perspective of two trans teachers. A review of terminology can be found in chapter 1; information on the mechanics and anatomy of the singing voice is available in chapter 3. When discussing the trans-nonbinary-genderqueer population as an entity, the acronym TGQ will be used.

Two Case Studies of Trans-Nonbinary Singers

Case Study: Kelly (student) and Peter (teacher)

Student Portrait

Kelly identifies as nonbinary trans—more specifically as genderfluid. For ease in the reading of this portrait, Kelly has requested to use they/them/their pronouns, though informally they accept he, she, and they pronouns. Assigned female at birth, Kelly asks that language describing them be as gender-neutral as possible. For example, as an individual involved in multiple performing arts activities, they like to be referred to as an actor instead of an actress. Likewise, they do not use titles "Miss" or "Mr." Kelly grew up in many different places throughout the United States because their parents moved during their childhood. They also studied abroad, having lived in Liverpool and London, and thus their cultural influences are broad. Currently, they live in a progressive, major city in the Pacific Northwest, pursuing a degree in graphic design from an online program. Singing is a major part of their life, and in addition to taking private voice instruction, they are active in a choir and in auditioning for musical theater productions.

As a child, Kelly participated in the church choir. This served as an early exposure to music and musical training. Kelly has always loved music. They recall their parents listening to older musical theater and jazz music while growing up. Attending a performing arts high school, Kelly participated in choir and musical theater workshop. They also took private voice lessons outside of school. Kelly's focus in their voice training has centered on musical theater repertoire. Although declaring that musical theater plots and songs are often rooted in gender stereotypes and heteronormativity, Kelly professes, "But, it's also my passion, so it's kind of been interesting to try and navigate that." As a student of musical theater in high school, Kelly faced marginalization early in their training.

During a high school musical theater workshop, Kelly was assigned soprano repertoire. Though they can sing in a high tessitura, they felt stifled in being given such a narrow range of repertoire. Kelly explains, "I struggled a lot in . . . the musical theater courses I took. . . . I don't know how I was pegged as a soprano, probably because I sang soprano in choir as a kid and I can sing pretty high; the teachers thought that was all I could sing. I couldn't even do alto, let alone tenor."

Admittedly having not realized their genderfluidity in high school, they blamed many of their struggles on their perceived lack of talent or on not connecting with their teacher. Kelly explains, "At the time, I didn't know [it], but looking back, a lot of [the negative experiences] had to do with a combination of gender issues, and that I wasn't allowed to explore the full range of my voice." Kelly felt stifled by not being permitted to sing outside the standard soprano range.

While Kelly was wanting to perform more contemporary musical theater, they were assigned scenes from older shows, which featured heavily gendered roles. They recall, "I was always made to feel like I wasn't good enough, especially when it came to the types of music they wanted me to sing because it was always very hyper-feminine and just stuff I cannot really relate to." Their negative experience was compounded by being assigned repertoire outside their musical interests and musical theater roles that reify gender stereotypes.

Kelly's experience in this class during their junior year was so unwelcoming, they decided to take a different class the following year, but when they found the secondary class uninteresting, they returned to musical theater workshop. Kelly remembers, "In senior year, I joined late. I specifically didn't want to do it after the experience my junior year. Before the switch, the teacher had given a big lecture on how you should never audition with a song that doesn't 'match your gender.'" Kelly notes that this teacher likely had little knowledge of how musical theater reifies gender oppression. A female friend of Kelly's who had performed several "boy" roles in outside productions was forced to remove those songs from her repertoire to adhere to class policies.

After high school, Kelly started to realize their authentic gender identity. Genderqueer, genderfluid, and nonbinary identities were introduced to Kelly through queer fashion blogs. Kelly discovered these blogs around the time they came out as gay, and Kelly shares, "I used that as an excuse to dress masculine for the first time in my life." When coming out as genderfluid to their mother, Kelly and their mom had just seen a production of the musical *Anastasia* on Broadway. They recall, "This was the first time I saw a tenor part where I was like, 'I could play this role.' I even ended up coming out [as genderfluid] to my mom at the stage door. I was just so excited and emotional, and she was wondering what the hell was wrong with me."

Kelly found themselves having an emotional response in strongly identifying with the male protagonist, Dmitry, in the show. While Dmitry is not a genderfluid character, seeing a role with whom Kelly could closely identify affirmed Kelly's identity and gave them the confidence to come out to their parents. While their parents continue to struggle with Katie's genderfluidity, they have come to accept their child for how they identify.

Despite the negative experience in the musical theater high school class, Kelly continues to explore singing and musical theater repertoire in voice lessons. They offer, "I had had a lot of negative experience in taking lessons, so it wasn't until I found Peter and wanted to go into acting and singing that I've been able to find my voice and figure stuff out."

After the initial labeling of soprano in high school, having now figured out their gender identity, Kelly hoped voice lessons would help them expand their range. Kelly enthusiastically describes their first voice lesson with Peter: "I went into the lesson and I kind of talked about [range development] with [Peter]. He starts doing just basic warm-ups with me, and . . . I am singing notes I didn't even know I could sing in terms of my lower, or even middle registers. At one point, he casually said, 'Yeah, you're a tenor.' I wanted to cry. It was like the greatest thing anyone could have said to me."

Kelly's genderfluidity was affirmed not by Peter's words alone, but in receiving vocal exercises and concepts to access areas of their range they had been discouraged to explore before. In these lessons, Kelly explores both vocal exercises and repertoire that fosters growth in their whole range, including pieces that are intended for sopranos, mezzos/belters, and tenors. Kelly says, "I just love how I've been free to explore the range, how gender hasn't been a barrier." The voice lessons with Peter have been therapeutic for Kelly, who says, "Taking voice lessons with Peter has kind of been my transition because it's helped me grow my voice. It's helped me become more comfortable with my identity, and helped me accept my own preconceived notions on gender that have been beaten into me and actually hurt me because they go against who I really am."

Kelly affirms that they have been taking better care of themselves since starting voice lessons with Peter. "It's more than just going in and singing for an hour," Kelly says. The voice lessons serve as a positive and empowering influence in Kelly's life.

Since Kelly is not undergoing androgen therapy, nor do they plan to in the future, Kelly has not experienced a change in vocal range from testosterone as some trans men do. Kelly's voice has not been modified through androgen therapy. Thus, changes in voice, including singing tenor repertoire, have been accomplished through changes in habitual use of the vocal mechanism. Kelly has also never seen a speech-language pathologist for seeking a lower or neutral-sounding voice, but they have observed some changes in their voice at speech level. Though their speaking voice has not drastically changed since starting voice lessons, they note, "At the very least, it's made me more confident with my natural voice. I'm at the point where I'm starting to hear my natural [speaking] voice. . . . I don't know how to explain that, but it was something I never really noticed before."

Their "natural voice" has not been achieved in solely finding a lower range, but by exploring their full range. They clarify, "I'm getting to the point where if I go into [a] higher register, it feels a bit more like me. I don't know if it's stronger or I'm just more confident. In high school, I would sing these songs and it sounded like someone else's voice to me." Being able to explore and strengthen their chest voice has fostered greater comfortability in the head voice. By never being given the opportunity to experiment vocally with other repertoire, Kelly never gained confidence in the higher register.

Currently Kelly is studying three songs, including one for soprano, one for alto, and one for tenor. The tenor piece is "My Petersburg," one of Dmitry's solos from *Anastasia*. The alto-range piece is "Never Never Land" by Jule Styne from the musical *Peter Pan*. These two pieces are being prepared for an upcoming studio recital. The soprano piece is "Wishing You Were Somehow Here Again" from Andrew Lloyd Webber's musical *The Phantom of the Opera*. Kelly is learning soprano repertoire not necessarily for a performance or audition, but more as a vocal étude to explore their head voice. Repertoire selection centers on Kelly being able to relate to the character or narrative of the song: "Because I don't identify strongly with any gender, all songs I can sing as myself. . . . It's been great to explore that, to see what roles I could play as a tenor . . . even what roles I could play as an alto or soprano." Later in this portrait, Kelly's repertoire will be discussed in further detail.

Kelly's experiences in singing are carried beyond the applied lessons studio. Kelly sings in a choir specifically intended for

TGQ singers. While there were a few bumps in the road for the choir in the beginning regarding the rigidity of voice parts, the ensemble has retracted the traditional model of calling the different sections soprano, alto, tenor, and bass. As an alternative, they use voice one, voice two, voice three, and voice four. Kelly sings mainly in voices one and two but also joins voice three at times. Importantly, this labeling of the choral parts is not laden with gendered expectations, and there is flexibility in singing within different sections. Regarding the ensemble repertoire, Kelly adds, "We're also trying to do songs that aren't problematic in any way. A lot of times we will change the gender of songs to make it gender neutral. There have been a couple songs we've cut because the message doesn't really align with what we stand for, which I love that we actually have that input."

While this musical experience has been affirming overall, Kelly explains they have difficulty knowing what to do during the vocal warm-ups. Since Kelly sings a wide vocal range, they often feel the warm-ups do not necessarily benefit their full capabilities. As the ensemble vocalizes for warm-ups together in octaves, Kelly must choose whether to sing with the upper or lower voices and does not feel fully warmed up for rehearsal.

Kelly speaks at length about their experiences in auditioning for musical theater. Every year, there is a citywide audition, which brings together the casting directors and artistic teams of many local theater companies. The audition form requests a variety of information, including an individual's gender using the binary male/female system. Kelly worked with the organizing company to reformat the form to be more inclusive. For auditions outside this platform, Kelly sometimes faces issues of being forced to use their legal birth name and wear gendered attire for the audition. "One day I had an audition and for whatever reason they wanted me to use my legal name," Kelly states, "[and] on top of that, I didn't have any clothes that fit my gender identity that were also professional for an audition, so I went in an outfit that didn't match my identity." Kelly is not opposed to dressing professionally, but being forced to wear traditional women's attire is problematic, especially when being cast in a show in which every actor will be costumed specific to a scripted character.

In addition to experiencing issues related to audition forms and apparel, Kelly says, "I'm still trying to figure out the language to describe my voice." Currently Kelly lists their voice as "soprano-tenor" on their performing résumé and affirms, "I am actively trying to defy the traditions . . . [by] going for tenor parts." In a recent audition, Kelly sang one piece in a head voice range and a second piece in a chest voice/tenor range. They disclose, "Even if they don't cast me, maybe they'll consider it the next time another nonbinary or transgender actor shows up." Kelly wants gender to not be a barrier or consideration in casting. Kelly wants to be seen for their voice and acting ability apart from expectations determined by inaccurate assumptions.

After one emotionally frustrating audition experience, Kelly turned to Peter, their voice teacher, for support. As a trans man, Peter provided insight on his experiences of marginalization to help Kelly feel less isolated. Kelly comments, "That was really nice to be able to talk to someone and to know I'm not alone, even though our experiences are different, and our identities aren't the same. We have a lot of common experiences."

While not all singing teachers would be able to share such similar experiences with each student, having a trans teacher has helped Kelly feel affirmed and supported in their musical training.

Teacher Portrait

Teaching approximately twelve to fourteen hours each week with twenty students in his studio, Peter is a singing teacher whose studio is composed of approximately one-third students who identify as trans or nonbinary. As a trans man himself, Peter specializes in teaching this population, though he teaches a wide range of students with regard to age, experience, and identity. In addition to having trained as a singing teacher, he holds a master's degree in gender studies, and thus the intersection of gender and the voice is his area of expert knowledge. Peter uses he/him/his pronouns, though he self-professes to not being "super masculine." He describes his gender as being fluid or flexible, and sometimes he identifies as genderqueer: "Being trans and having gone through gender transition is a big part of who I am and helps me relate to people who have gone through that." While he is still misgendered at times, he says it is usually due to the length of his hair or the timbre of his voice. His young son's friends will ask direct questions, such as, "Why do you talk like a girl?" or "Why is your voice squeaky?" Peter began androgen therapy more than eight years ago. The range of his speaking voice might be perceived as higher than the average range of a person assigned male at birth, but his vocal tessitura sits comfortably in the tenor range. Possessing a wide singing range is an advantage to him in offering vocal demonstrations for his students.

Raised in northern Virginia, Peter was assigned female at birth. His musical training began early in life. He began voice lessons at eleven, and after high school, he matriculated as a music major at a prestigious conservatory in the midwestern United States. In college, he was training as a high operatic soprano when he began to realize his authentic masculine identity. Having a difficult time connecting with his voice teacher and feeling frustrated with the kind of repertoire he was being pushed toward at the conservatory, Peter dropped the music degree and completed an undergraduate degree outside of music. He describes his undergraduate teacher as "intimidating" and not someone he could have confided in regarding his gender dysphoria. He describes his transition as being fraught with opposition from friends and family:

> I think there's a lot of cultural forces going against transition. There were a lot of voices telling me not to. A lot of people who are close to me just told me I was wrong—that I was confused about who I was. I'm not a hypermasculine guy, and I'm pretty feminine in my demeanor [in] the way I talk to people. I also looked really feminine, so the combination of my appearance and the way I behaved, I think people just didn't get it. My parents were totally confused and a lot of my friends just thought I was losing touch with reality, I think.

Struggling with his gender identity, Peter's parents took him to the gender clinic of a world-renowned hospital in Maryland.

On Fridays, the psychiatry department saw TGQ individuals. He recalls, "These people were so unbelievably insensitive." It became obvious to Peter that the hospital's intent was to collect data for research because he was always asked a "laundry list of questions they clearly just asked everybody." He elaborates, "It was very traumatic. My mom . . . expected them to tell me I was wrong, I think, that I wasn't transgender. My gender transition was in the face of all this opposition."

Beginning androgen therapy was one of the most difficult decisions of Peter's life, not just for the extreme marginalization he faced, but also in the knowledge that his singing voice, a meaningful aspect of his identity, would be forever changed.

Soon after he started taking testosterone, Peter moved to England to pursue an interdisciplinary master's degree in gender and media studies. In addition to cultural adjustments, he also found himself in a new environment where he needed to "come out" as a trans guy. "I was going to gender studies classes where nobody even knew I was trans," he shares, "and one professor said this very transphobic thing in front of me, not knowing I was trans." He also experienced a shift in how people perceived him. He recalls, "All of a sudden, I was being read as a cisgender male, and I didn't know what to do. . . . It was all so confusing." In the United States, he was sometimes seen as male, and other times as female, but in the United Kingdom, everyone saw him as masculine.

Early on in graduate school, he auditioned for a student-run production of *West Side Story*. He remembers being the oldest in the cast and the only American in this popular American musical. The audition caused him some anxiety as he was suddenly singing with his newly lowered voice. Regarding the vocal transition, he shares, "It was like someone takes your instrument and gives you a whole new instrument, and none of my technique is applying to this new voice." He mentioned to the student director that he had recently started taking testosterone. He was cast in the show, but he was not aware that the director had told the entire company of his trans identity. When this information was eventually disclosed to him, he was relieved that the cast had been so accepting of him. He quickly mentions,

"I know there's probably plenty of people who would've been horrified that that information was being circulated without my knowledge," but for Peter, it was a relief.

His participation in *West Side Story* was not Peter's first experience with musical theater. During middle and high school, he studied musical theater repertoire in his voice lessons. As a teenager, he had some discomfort with the sound of his voice and the roles he was given, but he could assuage this dysphoria by immersing himself in the character. In college, concealing this discomfort was more difficult.

While still in undergrad, Peter participated for three consecutive summers in musical theater shows produced by his undergraduate college. In the first summer, he was cast in a role he characterizes as an "angry lesbian." He explains that the role was not intended to be played that way, but it worked for the role, and so it provided him a queer facade in performance. In the second summer, he was cast in a traditionally male role. Though he sang the role an octave higher with feminine pronouns, being cast in a conventional male role gave him an outlet for masculinity. In the third summer, having now worked with the same director twice before, Peter was under the impression the company understood his shifting gender identity. He explains,

> I said on my audition form I wanted to be considered for the Wizard, which I thought could be a nongendered role. I was called back for it, but then I was cast in this "lady" role instead, and I was so intensely uncomfortable, but I felt like I couldn't say anything at that point because we were already past the audition phase. The first day we had a costume fitting was just so upsetting. Not only did I have to wear a dress, but I had to do it on stage in front of all those people. It felt humiliating. It was awful, but I just felt so much pressure to just go along with it.

Peter's experience in these musical theater productions demonstrates not only issues related to gender but also power dynamics between artistic staff and members of the cast. Attempting to be agreeable and fulfill the demands of the production led Peter to feel marginalized and subjugated. The lessons he learned from this experience shape how he creates safe space in his teaching studio.

After completing a master's degree in England, Peter had a series of jobs in arts administration. Feeling unfulfilled by his employment and now living in the Pacific Northwest, he started taking voice lessons again. His new teacher was also a voice teacher trainer, who encouraged him to work with her on learning to be a voice teacher. In the beginning, he apprenticed under her as a student teacher until he eventually opened his own studio.

In addition to studying his teacher's methods, he read multiple pedagogy books and online materials. He admits to not having a lot of knowledge in teaching at first, but through the apprenticeship program his skills advanced. Early in his teaching he resolved to not imitate the style of teaching he experienced in college. He contends, "If the system is so formulaic and systematized that the student doesn't thrive, they are blamed, as if it were the student's fault . . . , when really the system is not meeting them in a way that's helpful to them."

Peter describes his own voice studio as holistic, where a student is honored as wholly individual, not solely as an instrument needing refinement. He offers, "I am teaching a whole person, and I don't think you can really separate the person from the instrument." Lessons generally follow a structure of (1) physical stretching on a yoga mat or standing, (2) drawing attention to breathing, (3) vocal exercises, and (4) repertoire. He shares, "If you were to observe a different lesson with a different student, it may look really different." Thus, while he has an outline he follows with all students, the progression, pacing, and activities in each lesson are tailored in a way specific to each student.

Creating a safe space for all students is paramount to Peter: "I have a rule in my studio that everyone treats everyone else with respect; that while you're here, you treat people with respect. I always go over my studio policies with a new student. I get to set the rules for my space, and these are my rules: Everyone is equal. No one gets to be a diva. Everyone is on the same level, whoever they are." Peter stresses that these rules are to protect the emotional safety of himself and the students alike.

In working with his TGQ students, he shares that he does nothing different with them unless "they want to work on their speaking voice." While he does not take on many clients for speaking voice work only, he considers singing technique a viable approach for establishing a healthy speaking voice. As a singing teacher, he makes it very clear that he is not qualified in speech-language pathology, but he is also willing to help a student if they can find no better alternative for vocal coaching.

The benefits of working with TGQ students are plentiful for Peter. While he has discussed the many challenges encountered in being trans, and specific issues faced by Kelly or his other students, he finds strength in empowering TGQ voices. He emphasizes,

> It's so meaningful to provide a space where people can be themselves and not be made to feel different. I think that's one of the best things about the work that I do. People come in, maybe early in their transition, and 99 percent of the people they encounter don't see them as who they really are, and to just make a human connection where they feel seen and heard is so important. It's very personal to me because of everything I've been through and people in my life misgendering and misunderstanding me. I think even at the very basic level of just to have a space where the student can be seen, and really seen is, just tremendous. On top of that, then to use their voice in a way that reflects who they are and how they want to be seen.

He also cautions that in creating rapport with a TGQ student, a teacher must avoid "othering" the student; it is not the student's responsibility to train the teacher. "There are all these ways that we are treated by others in a gendered way that are so pervasive and so subtle," he notes. Even if a teacher has only one TGQ student, it is the educator's responsibility to learn how to best train the student without asking invasive questions or causing them to feel different. He admits that learning how to affirm each student "takes time and it takes energy," but the benefit is in creating a space that honors the student as an individual.

A common practice in some voice studios is to list voice types in concert programs. Peter warns, "If we're identifying voice type, we can't forget that there's a gender implication." Peter always asks Kelly how they would like their name and voice type to appear in print. In a recital from last year, Kelly was listed as a soprano for one piece, and as a tenor for a secondary piece. In an upcoming recital, Kelly will be listed as a tenor, even though one piece fits the conventional alto range. While this decision might defy tradition, Peter does not care so long as a student is comfortable. He says,

> I think there's so many cultural forces that push toward gender conformity. I feel like there's these erasures that happen of people, and there is huge subset[s] in the range of human diversity that is silenced. It's so hurtful and destructive. We need alternative spaces for letting people be human. I feel it's a human right be yourself. We have to offer people that; we just have to. That's part of being a decent person.

Peter actively works to create a learning environment that pushes against conformity, allowing otherwise silenced voices to emerge and be emboldened. Though he also wishes more material was written for genderfluid and unconventional gender performers, Peter supports Kelly's interests in auditioning for musical theater companies, despite the challenge of marginalization present in audition forms and requirements. He believes there is much room for "different kinds of diversity" in performance spaces, if artistic directors would keep an open mind.

Voice Lessons

Located in the lower level of his home on a residential street, Peter's studio is a calm and inviting space with carpeted floors and light, mossy green walls. The entryway provides an area for students to hang their coats and leave their shoes. The large teaching space provides ample room for physical warm-ups and singing. A piano and electric keyboard sit in a corner.

The lessons begin with Peter and Kelly checking in about the week since they last met. Kelly is working night shifts, and they discuss the impact of this on Kelly's overall energy level. Peter begins lessons with physical stretching or centering exercises to align the mind and body. Kelly chooses to start the lesson on the floor, on a yoga mat. In a semisupine position, Peter prompts Kelly to bring mindfulness to their breathing, asking the air passages to relax, and to allow the breath to freely flow in and out. After a few minutes of measured breathing, Peter asks Kelly to "sigh" on a pitch from high to low. Peter comments that breathing and singing while prostrate can disrupt the body's habitual process. Peter proceeds to teach Kelly a shoulder-opening exercise, which involves (1) extending the arms above the head, (2) forward bending, and (3) placing the palms and forearms on a flat surface like a table or countertop in front of the body. In this exercise, the back is parallel to the floor, and the body is making a 90-degree angle at the hip joint.

The vocalizing continues with a sigh from top to bottom. They also perform a "siren" (like that of an emergency vehicle) with the voice sliding from low to high to low again. These sighs and sirens figure prominently in the vocal exercises, as Peter asks Kelly to sing one or the other between every metered vocal exercise. The sigh and siren have not been transcribed because they are intentionally inconsistent, based on arbitrary pitches chosen by Kelly.

Peter begins the vocal exercises by exploring Kelly's higher range. In the first vocal exercise, Peter asks Kelly to sing a five-tone quarter-note descending scale, from Sol to Do on [a] and then on "blub" [blʌb], which helps release tongue and jaw tension. This exercise moves up and down by half-steps, warming up Kelly's middle range, from approximately C4 to E5. The descending sequence promotes a lighter sound and a mix of head and chest register singing.

In the next exercise, Peter extends the range in two-note slurs through an arpeggio, as seen in figure 5.1. This exercise initiates singing in both head and chest voices, starting in the lower register and moving into the upper register. Peter provides exercises that work each register separately, but also exercises that align the

Figure 5.1.   Two-note pairs over a tenth for stretching upper range.

voice and bridge the passaggio. Never is register discussed explicitly at this point; instead, Peter's language encourages Kelly to sing with ease and freedom, which prompts Kelly to switch registration. The purpose of this exercise is to extend breath release while stretching the upper range. The two-note slurs help mitigate tension that might build over a long exercise and wide range.

The next two exercises, shown in figures 5.2 and 5.3, are exercises intended to further open and strengthen the upper register. Figure 5.2 shows singing a fifth interval on [a], starting in A major, which ensures Kelly is singing in head voice primarily. The following exercise (figure 5.3) is described as "squeaks" to access the highest part of Kelly's range, beginning in E major and ascending by half steps, taking Kelly to F6. Peter encourages Kelly to sing these arpeggios lightly to assuage bringing weight of the bottom pitch into the upper pitches. The initial [h] and detached notes promotes a balanced onset.

One final exercise for the upper range is a nine-tone scale, from low Do to high Re, on sixteenth notes. Beginning in C major, Peter moves the scale exercise up by half steps to G major, taking Kelly to an A5. The speed of these scales keeps the voice lighter, and while the starting pitch is low enough to sing in full chest voice, Kelly lightens the sound to rapidly ascend to the top of the scale. Peter's primary concern is aligning the lowest and highest notes without inundating the middle range with tension. Less attention is given to clarity of pitches or precision in the scale, as the purpose of this exercise is to find fluidity between middle to upper range.

Figure 5.2.   Perfect fifth skips on half notes for stretching upper range.

Figure 5.3. Triad arpeggio for upper extension and balanced onset.

Although one of Kelly's aspirations is to strengthen their lower range and audition for tenor roles, Peter explains,

> I found earlier in my process of us working together, [the voice] was getting out of balance. There was a lot of belt singing and something was happening with the head voice that I thought was not a good sign, which was that it was getting tighter. I said to [Kelly], "You don't have to ever perform in head voice, if you want, but I think your voice is going to be healthier if you get some exercises in the higher end of your range."

Peter assures Kelly that they need not ever perform in the soprano range, but explains that exercising that range will help bring balance to their full voice and strengthen the lower range. Before exercising the lower range, they sing through "Wishing You Were Somehow Here Again" from *The Phantom of the Opera*, which has a range from A3 to G5. Used as a vocal étude, the piece provides challenges related to tessitura, tongue and jaw tension brought on by lyrics, and pitch issues posed by difficult melodic intervals. After singing through the entire piece, Peter coaches Kelly through the more difficult passages, highlighting places to breathe and offering suggestions for vowel modification. As this song is for exercise purposes only, they do not spend significant time on the piece.

Kelly is preparing the song "Never Never Land" from *Peter Pan* in an upcoming studio recital. This piece sits in Kelly's middle range, and while Peter gives some feedback on their performance, the piece is well prepared and performance ready. Peter invites Kelly to decrescendo on the last note of the piece. The technique required to diminuendo on a sustained pitch provides an opening for discussing abdominal muscular support. As the lesson began with mindful breathing, this is an opportunity to circle back to the start of their lesson, revisiting breath and body alignment.

As precursor to working on Kelly's tenor song, "My Petersburg" from the musical *Anastasia*, Peter inquires if Kelly would like to do some "belt" exercises first. Often Peter asks, "Do you want to . . . ?" before offering an exercise or moving onto another activity. While Kelly always positively replies to the query, it gives Kelly an opportunity to pace or redirect the lesson if necessary. In the case of working on the lower range, Peter provides similar exercises as above, but initiates them at lower pitches to induce chest voice singing. For example, the exercise in figure 5.2 is repeated beginning at B3 (below middle C) to promote chest register singing. Kelly aims to phonate the higher note in chest voice, but as they approach A4, Peter is explicit that Kelly should mix the voice more. The proceeding exercise is a similar pattern as the first exercise lesson, based on a five-tone descending scale on quarter notes sung on [jo]. Starting at G major below middle C, Kelly sings down to E3, with the [j] glide to help onset the pitch and release the jaw.

The final exercise, shown in figure 5.4, illustrates a descending slide in chest voice. This exercise has similar properties as the sigh used throughout the exercises, to reset the voice and allay any tension developed while singing. Sliding on distinctive pitches connects the undefined sigh to a specific sung sound, promoting freedom and openness in Kelly's singing.

In preparation for the upcoming studio recital, Peter and Kelly spend considerable time in working on Kelly's pieces chosen for the performance. Attention is given to identifying specific challenges, as related to pitch, rhythm, or musical interpretation. They isolate the beginning of "My Petersburg" as it requires Kelly starting on E3, at the bottom of their range. Resolving this issue comes from being mindful of feeling the resonance higher

Figure 5.4. *Descending fifth slides to release subglottal pressure.*

Figure 5.5. Excerpt of "My Petersburg" from the musical Anastasia. Source: Stephen Flaherty (music & lyrics) and Lynn Ahrens (lyrics).

for the lower passage and hearing the pitch before voicing it. They also examine the two pitches in the piece where Kelly needs to "mix" the voice, which will mitigate intonation issues and foster greater vocal freedom. During the initial vocal exercises where Peter allows Kelly to flip registration unheedingly, Peter is more focused in his instruction now. Figure 5.5 shows an example of where mixing the voice is encouraged to keep power in the upper range, without bringing the chest voice beyond where it can easily phonate.

As an individual who is actively pursuing a more masculine identity in auditions, Kelly has selected songs that represent this identity. The role of Peter Pan, though traditionally sung by women, is a male character whose repertoire fits Kelly's middle range. "My Petersburg" is a tenor solo but has been transposed up a third for a better vocal fit. The lyrics speak overtly about being a boy, and about making important changes in one's life.

Throughout the lesson, Peter is positive and affirming, offering frequent encouraging remarks. Furthermore, in serving as Kelly's pianist in the forthcoming recital, at times Peter and Kelly take a collaborative approach to rehearsing the concert literature, both offering feedback and solidifying a musical partnership. While Peter primarily steers the purpose and pace of the lesson, Kelly is given ample space throughout the hour to reshift the focus or activity. The student and teacher share common ground and strong rapport. The lessons are filled with an exchange of ideas and joyful conversation.

Case Study: B (student) and Eli (teacher)

Student Portrait

"Music has always been so key and central to me," B shares, "but it was a longer unfolding of understanding what that meant." Like music, B's sense of identity has been a process of understanding and unfurling the social constructs of gender and race. Averse to labeling themselves, B goes by a single letter. As an artist-scholar, B is an associate professor in ethnomusicology at a notable research university on the West Coast of the United States. In writing, B uses they/them/their pronouns, yet discloses that some people refer to them as "she," others as "he." Though B considers the pronoun options insufficient, using the plural third person seems most innocuous to them, and will accordingly be employed in this portrait.

While B avoids categorizing their gender, they acknowledge, "When it gets down to talking about gender, I feel very masculine." They mark their identity as "genderqueer and nonbinary or trans and queer," but the purpose of these labels is for the benefit of others, not for self-affirmation. B believes "there is a lot of power in the nonbinary space. I am not a man. I am not a woman, and that's really how I've explained it for so long." Instead of speaking of gender identity, B allows people to make their own conclusions, asserting that others will make assumptions about them, with or without self-prescribed labels.

As a person of color who sometimes identifies as mixed race and other times as black, B experiences indefiniteness in their racial identity. B believes race identity is demarcated by sociopolitical boundaries, not by biology. They explain,

> I was raised in a community where it was all mixed kids, black and white, and white single-parent mothers. Those were the people I was around most growing up. It was very distinct. It wasn't a white upbringing. It wasn't a black upbringing. It's just our own thing and feels very ungrounded culturally. More and more, I don't actually think there is a real racial "mix." The idea of someone being mixed doesn't make sense to me, if you think race is not biological, which is what I believe.

There is a sense of purposeful *in-betweenness* or of oscillation in B's sense of identity. The resolve to exist outside a box, defined either by race or gender, is a product of B's upbringing and cultural influences, and from a political certitude to create an alternative space of existence.

As a youngster, B was considered a "tomboy." Being drawn to items socially constructed for boys, B recalls assuming they were a boy until they were a little older. B shares,

> Until maybe seven or eight, I think I thought I was a boy. I was moving through the world assuming that's what people were seeing from the outside. I remember one time when I was playing with a friend of mine, we were running around with our shirts off. I think it was his mom who said, "You know, you aren't going to be able to do that much longer. You're not going to be able to have your shirt off." I was like, "What are you talking about it?" But it also made me feel bad, like she was shaming me.

This early experience "closeted" B's true sense of self, and likely stymied B at a young age from moving around the world in a way that felt most appropriate to them. When puberty began, B was unprepared for the biological changes to their body. Being attracted to girls, B coded their masculine leanings as related to sexuality. The identity of nonbinary or genderqueer was not yet realized because they had little concept of living outside the gender binary. Though during this time B had awareness of their racial identity and sexual orientation, their authentic gender identity would not emerge until college.

Music has played a central role in B's life since childhood. Their mother was a pianist and choral director, and B can remember participating in a children's choir as early as two years old. Around the age of five, B started lessons on the violin, and later piano lessons. Among their many musical activities, choral singing remained the most constant. B sang in church and community choirs growing up and describes themselves becoming a "hardcore choral singer" in high school and through college. They sang second soprano and alto in high school. Later, when singing Renaissance and late medieval music in college, they would sing the middle part, which was traditionally sung by high-voiced men. With an easy facilitation in the lower range, sometimes B would sing tenor parts, or if the ensemble was purposefully all singers assigned female at birth, B would sing the bass line. While acknowledging that the choral space was gendered, B never felt marginalized or inappropriately boxed in when singing soprano or alto. Indeed, B suggests singing higher provided them a "boychoir" experience, which framed it within a masculine paradigm.

The high school choral experience presented issues around race. B concedes that their memory or perceptions of their experience in the intersection of choral music and race might be "completely wrong," but B remembers more singers of color in the alto section, feeling "soprano was a whiter space." B sensed they did not fit either racial image—neither that of the white soprano nor having a timbre that matched the other altos of color. Also in the choral setting, B reflects on how singers assigned female at birth always outnumbered singers assigned male at birth, so there was more room and acceptability for "girls" to move into "male" spaces within the performing arts.

Recently, B and their partner have been performing *bomba*, an Afro–Puerto Rican folkloric music and dance. Within the *bomba* performance tradition, male and female dance moves are different and delineated. B explains it is becoming possible for women to perform the "male" dance moves, though it continues to be inappropriate for a man to perform the "female" choreography. B shares, "There was a huge uproar when a cis guy decided he was going to dance in a skirt. To me, there is homophobia embedded in that and assumptions made about that person's sexuality." Making a connection from *bomba* to choral singing, B feels when a woman enters a traditional "male" performing space it is widely accepted, but for a man to enter a "female" space is viewed as gender transgressive.

In college, B started taking voice lessons. They disclose, "I never felt like I was a very good singer. I always felt very strong as a choral singer . . . but the idea of singing solo . . . never really felt comfortable." Their first experience with private voice instruction was destructive. B recalls attempting not to cry during multiple lessons. They blamed themselves at the time, thinking they did not have sufficient talent or were culpable for inadequate student-teacher rapport. Looking back, B realizes they were being asked to sing repertoire that did not suit them, in terms of both gender and musical interest. Though B has a deep appreciation for Western classical music and a fondness for early music, as a solo artist their interest lies in pop and folk genres. There was no room for them to make song selections that suited their aesthetic. In addition, much of the assigned repertoire felt overly feminine.

During graduate school, B served as music director for a queer version of *West Side Story*. This production was a collaboration between a drag king troupe, a Latina theater company, and students in the grad program. Having difficulty in finding someone appropriate to play the role of Tony, B took on the role. In preparation, B took a voice lesson from a recommended teacher. While singing the song "Maria," the teacher referred to B's higher notes as falsetto but then quickly corrected her language. B elaborates,

> Falsetto was only something I had ever heard talked about with men's voices, but . . . it's not just where your voice is singing range-wise, it's how you're using it and how it's put into a piece. It's contextual. If I sang those [high] notes in a choral piece as a girl, you wouldn't call it [falsetto], but singing those same exact notes at the end of "Maria," there is a gendered construct around what is falsetto. It felt kind of good in the moment, even though she corrected herself, or what she thought was correcting herself.

Not only did the role of Tony feel appropriate, the teacher's language affirmed B's singing and framed it within a masculine construct. The portrayal of this role and the creative work in producing this alternative version was an affirming experience for B.

For the past year and a half, B has been working with their current teacher, Eli. B describes Eli as a "godsend" who has created new possibilities for their singing. B remembers their first lesson and thinking, "Oh my god, I didn't think I could sing that note, or I didn't think I could sing in this way or this loud." The impetus for taking singing lessons stems from an artistic endeavor. B sings in a queer retro band, whose mission is to create a space for "masculine-of-center" singers and to present personal narratives through music. (Here, "masculine-of-center" refers to queer/nonbinary individuals whose gender identities lean closer to masculinity.) As a founder and leader of this ensemble, B felt they needed to work on their vocal technique. They knew of Eli, as a trans man who teaches voice, and started lessons for two reasons: (1) to build better vocal habits and stamina and (2) to explore new vocal possibilities.

One technical issue addressed in B's singing deals with an ongoing pain on the right side of their throat. Off and on since college, B has experienced discomfort while singing. B explains,

> I remember doing a musical in college and singing lower, being put on the tenor part a lot, and feeling this pain in the side of my throat. Then I was singing in an all "women's" a cappella group during grad school and I was singing the bass part in that group, and I started feeling this [pain] again. But it would always go away. A couple of years ago, this pain came up and it wouldn't go away. It is not there every day, but there have been periods where it is there every day for months. I think it stemmed from me not using my voice in a good way.

An additional contributing factor to this pain might derive from emotional stress, B suggests. In addition to potentially pushing the voice too low and causing unwanted tension in the neck, it is an area of their body where they hold tension in general. While the pain mainly originates from singing, it can be exacerbated by speaking. Awareness of the tension figures prominently in lessons with Eli.

Though the purpose of B's singing lessons has been to develop vocal technique, there have been additional benefits to the lessons. B has experienced an improvement in their speaking voice. B explains, "It is not something I was seeking out, but doing the vocal work around singing . . . it's not that the range is changing, but sitting in a more comfortable place, especially in the lower realm, and more relaxed." In learning to release through singing, a "broadening" of the speaking voice has occurred. As a college professor, B speaks frequently to larger groups of people, so the voice lessons have brought an unexpected positive outcome. B also reports singing more with their students and not feeling nervous in front of them.

B's singing also serves as a vehicle for their research. Their ensemble establishes space for B and the other singers to thrive as artists, and as well as to promote narratives of gender and racial diversity through alternative artistic programs. B wonders how their narrative might have been different if a teacher like Eli had been present during their childhood. B considers, "How different it might have been if I had been working with Eli as a ten-year-old and singing in more unmarked spaces. Would I have found my voice earlier?" Continuing in this reflective state, B suggests they are still finding their authentic voice.

As TGQ individuals become more visible in popular media, B worries teachers will see gender as a "fixed space," one in which a person becomes a "man" or a "woman." B affirms that gender is an ongoing process, and thus students and teachers need to be aware of the fluidity in identity. For music educators, B offers, "I think so much is in not making assumptions, and asking a person where they are coming from or what they are wanting. I don't think anyone is going to be perfect, but I have been in so many settings where the metaphors being used or the space of character we are being asked to embody is entrenched with gender." As a teacher, B is conscientious to create space and openness in their classes to challenge assumptions and ideologies. B insists a teacher's language needs to be open and progressive to honor all perspectives.

Finally, B reflects on how their experiences in musical settings has shaped their confidence as a singer. While B can forge a pathway for themselves now, as a student, it would have been beneficial to see teachers or professional musicians who looked and sounded like them. B admits that being a musician is a challenging profession, but having a role model to emulate provides musicians with a path to follow, something TGQ musicians rarely have.

Teacher Portrait

Eli is a full-time independent voice teacher in a politically left-leaning college town in the western United States. By many, Eli is considered one of the leading experts in teaching trans singers. He identifies first as a man but also as trans, queer, and gay. He was involved in music from a young age, having participated for nearly a decade in children's choir in central Virginia. Having studied piano and saxophone early in life, his primary musical focus in high school became singing. He took private singing lessons in Western classical music but also studied jazz singing.

He attended a widely known liberal arts college in the midwestern United States, and though not a music major, he studied singing in college and participated in a high-level early music vocal ensemble. He was first accepted into the ensemble as a first soprano. Eli started androgen therapy during his junior year of college. His voice sounded hoarse at first, but he shares, "I tried my best to just keep doing whatever sounds happened." He recalls that it was difficult to find appropriate keys for art songs and arias, as he needed to change keys frequently because of his shifting voice. While some singers lose their higher range soon after starting testosterone, Eli did not. While his range gradually lowered within the first six months, he also retained his high range. Eventually his upper range diminished, and after two years, his voice settled as a first tenor. He had a supportive vocal ensemble director who had little knowledge about TGQ singers but revoiced him every semester to ensure he was in the best-fitting voice part. Eli remembers, "Specifically the moment when he said I sounded interchangeable with the other tenors of my age . . . was super affirming." Eli also explains that the repertoire he was singing did not require him to sing with a heavy sound, which helped during the transition, as he describes his voice as lighter in general.

After college, Eli moved to the West Coast and sang in professional choral ensembles while teaching singing lessons and community group music classes. Influenced by the music his parents listened to when he was growing up, the music he performs now as a solo artist is based in folk tradition. He began studying the vocal technique of contemporary commercial music and gained three certifications in Somatic Voicework™ The LoVetri Method. Eli continues to study voice with one of the leading teachers in this approach, which further enriches his practice and pedagogy. He is a singer-songwriter and guitarist, and his style of vocal pedagogy is grounded in the principles of CCM techniques.

Having received all his collegiate vocal training in Western classical singing, he understands both *bel canto* and CCM techniques. He summarizes that *bel canto* singing emphasizes (1) breath support, (2) resonance, and (3) an open/released throat. While he admits this is an oversimplification of the technique, he compares this summation with Somatic Voicework™ The LoVetri Method, which underscores the importance of vocal registration through exercises that address (1) vowel brightness/darkness, (2) pitch, and (3) volume. While a vocal pedagogue might debate semantics or the correctness in his distilled descriptions of these techniques, they provide a basis for how Eli thinks about singing and the technical elements he highlights in his teaching.

Eli notes that there is also an explicit prominence on voice functionality in teaching contemporary commercial music. Though Western classical voice training includes elements of voice functionality, Eli's collegiate teacher did not offer this knowledge, instead centering on the aesthetics of sound, with an emphasis on breath support and placement. In CCM teaching, he shares, "You listen to the singer not for what you like or dislike about their sound, but to hear what's happening functionally in their body and in their throat." One of the main elements Eli listens for is the functionality of both vocal registers: head voice, which is a cricothyroid (CT)–dominant muscular action, and chest voice, a thyroarytenoid (TA)–dominant muscular action. When speaking about registers, he uses the terms head voice and CT-dominant interchangeably, as with chest voice and TA-dominant.

One of the first facets of CCM singing that Eli brings attention to is the fortification of the head and chest registers. Often, he shares, a singer will have one register that is stronger or more comfortable. For many singers of pop or folk repertoire, the chest register is often stronger, and he will work to strengthen cricothyroid muscular action. Likewise, if a singer comes from a soprano choral experience and has a strong head voice, for example, they might need assistance in heightening functionality in the chest voice. By isolating and separating the registers, Eli then works with the singer to mix in the middle range. In CCM, he explains, "we often source vocal issues to registration imbalances and the constriction that can come from having too much pure chest register above middle C." The goal is a seamless alignment of both registers. Once a singer has effective use of both registers, Eli works on aligning and balancing them.

Vowel and volume also feature conspicuously in registration work. When accessing head voice, he may ask a student to sing softly on a closed vowel, such as [i] or [u]. Eli is a proponent of semi-occluded exercises, such as rolled forward [r] or lip trill, or singing on [ŋ] hum for unlocking head voice. When working to strengthen chest voice, he might have a singer produce a louder sound on an open vowel. Similarly, if working to coordinate a mixed sound in middle range, he might use [æ] or [ɛ] at *mezzo piano* or *mezzo forte*. Unless the exercise is long or slow, he has the student sing all exercises twice through without a pause for two reasons: (1) it provides an opportunity to evaluate if they have consistency in the exercise and (2) it mimics the length of song phrases. Though the vocal ranges of exercises will be dependent on each student, he has identified specific exercises that are dependable toward obtaining specific goals in vocal training.

As a teacher of many TGQ students, Eli has garnered considerable experience in teaching this population. As a trans man himself, he has a personal experience, alongside pedagogical literacy, to observe commonalities in the changing voice brought on by androgen therapy. Discussing the singing voice on testosterone, Eli remarks, "I think it's really different for everybody, but also there's some common patterns that happen: range really shrinking, a lot of difficulty through the passaggio, a lot of difficulty with sustaining pitches with any volume above middle C. Vibrato can get really wonky, and people face a lot of issues with constriction because people are used to belting up higher than they can now." Rarely has he had a trans man unable to sing certain pitches for more than a month, though areas of the range might continue to be "shaky" or inconsistent for several months or even years. Most important, Eli believes it is important to keep singing, so long as the singer is not forcing or pushing. He stresses it is important to keep the voice "alive and well." He offers supportive language and reassurance that their voice will improve with continued exercise.

Many TGQ students are keen to exercise their full range, while others are reluctant to sing in a range that does not align with their sense of gender. Eli has taught trans women who have "wanted help finding access to a higher range, and also trans feminine folks who proudly identify as baritones." For a trans woman who wants to belt like a female rock star, the technique requires slowly building the singer's strength, flexibility, and stamina to make a TA-dominant sound through the passaggio without heaviness. For a student who wants to sound like Tina Turner or Demi Lovato, he might also suggest changing the key to a lower range. Eli listens carefully to the aspirations of his singers and balances them against realistic expectations to find equilibrium between a singer's wishes and their abilities. Part of Eli's teaching is in providing vocal exercises and technical concepts to beget optimal singing while serving as an emotional support and adviser on what is possible in terms of each student's vocal growth.

Discussing the role all teachers have in supporting their TGQ students, Eli recommends that teachers read Leslie Feinberg's *Trans Liberation: Beyond Pink or Blue* and Janet Mock's *Redefining Realness* to understand the trans experience "within a broader political context." Eli suggests cisgender teachers need to do their homework by reading books and articles, attending ally trainings, supporting TGQ performers, and seeking out the perspectives of TGQ teachers and speech-language pathologists. He says, "I think the biggest thing about how to be a good teacher of transgender and gender nonconforming students is (1) opening up your worldview much more broadly, (2) letting go of the binary ideas you have that are based in heteropatriarchy that we were all raised with, [and] (3) doing your own personal work around this stuff and interrogating what being cisgender means to you." Eli is mindful that we all have limitations based on our limited experiences, and thus, as teachers, we should stay open to new possibilities and discoveries.

Voice Lessons

Located on the second floor of his home, Eli's studio has a separate entrance from the street. Immediately upon entering the room, there is a wooden desk to the left and an electric keyboard to the right. A large, floor-to-ceiling bookshelf sits on the right wall next to a mirror for the singer to view themselves. There is also a full-length mirror to the right of the singer. A water pitcher and drinking glasses are available on the desk, and a music stand is located next to the keyboard. A large window provides natural light to the welcoming space.

The lesson begins with Eli asking B about their week. Since both teacher and student are active musicians, they discuss auditions and upcoming performances. Eli enquires about B's ongoing neck pain, and B reports it has subsided slightly. In one lesson, B is recovering from a head cold, and the two discuss the vocal issues associated with head and chest congestion. This initial check-in lasts for a few minutes before Eli begins vocal exercises.

When B and Eli first started working together, more time was spent on strengthening the head and chest registers separately. In recent lessons, the focus has been on aligning and adjoining the registers. In the figures below, exercises that begin in chest voice, or in a chest-dominant sound, are shown in bass clef. This also indicates the starting key of each exercise. Similarly, exercises initiated in head voice are shown in treble clef. All exercises move up or down by half steps. Eli speaks explicitly about the intended volume, vowel, and registration of each exercise. As exercises move above C4, B is often asked to "mix" more head voice into the timbre, though at times Eli will request more (or less) chest voice depending on the intent of the exercise.

Vocal exercises occupy more than half the lesson time. Eli explains that through this approach the voice is brought into optimal use before encountering the technical needs of the repertoire. He explains, "Doing a full thirty to forty-five minutes of exercises gives you a lot more time to hear where the voice is and then design exercises to help them move and grow and shift. Eventually, the idea is when we get to song work, all the stuff we're working on in the exercises is going to start to apply itself." In the lessons I observed, the vocal exercises lasted between forty-five and fifty minutes. This ratio of vocal exercises to repertoire coaching seems to fit B's wishes for the lessons. Having explained their primary purpose for voice lessons is to work on technique, they have also confessed at being "kind of terrible about having a piece to work on." Thus, the design of the lesson meets the student's needs.

Due to the nature of these lessons, there are several more exercises to describe than in the previous portraits. Figure 5.6 shows an ascending and descending five-tone scale on a rolled [r]. The intention is to release the tongue and activate breath starting in the middle lower range. B begins in chest voice but moves into head voice as needed. Eli prompts B to let their voice move between registers as is easiest for them at the start of the lesson.

The next exercise initiates forward resonance through gliding on a hum from low Do to Sol. B is asked to move slowly between the two pitches, allowing for all the pitches between the perfect fifth to feel resonant. Like the previous exercise, this sequence begins low, starting at F3 (below middle C) and moves into head voice as it ascends. Eli encourages B to move in and out of chest register as needed to promote free singing. Encouraging a more robust sound, Figure 5.7 demonstrates an arpeggio sequence on "glei" [glɛI], which fosters abdominal support and movement of the tongue. Eli is explicit about keeping the top note in chest-mix as a way of stretching and opening the higher range of the chest register. The bottom-up sequence promotes

Figure 5.6. Rolled [r] on five-tone scale in middle-low range.

Figure 5.7. Octave arpeggio on different vowels for registration management.

a lifting of the larynx to cultivate chest registration in a higher range. Afterward, [ju] and [nu] are employed on the same pattern to promote a softer dynamic and lighter singing in head voice. While [glɛI] brought the chest voice higher, [ju] and [nu] restore balance to the mechanism by fostering head registration.

In the same way [ju] in the previous exercise encouraged head voice singing, the five-tone scale exercise in figure 5.8 also promotes breath release and rounded lips. When the tone is "wobbly and weak" on the bottom notes, Eli encourages B to keep singing, because they are purposefully bringing the head voice lower.

The next exercise, shown in figure 5.9, begins near the bottom of B's range. Singing an "ng" [ŋ] nurtures forward resonance without pushing or singing too loudly through the lower range. Eli invites B to have greater presence on the bottom note to stabilize the sound and engage the abdominals and side ribs. He also encourages them to release the lips but keep the face animated.

During the next exercise, Eli has B hold a straw horizontally beneath their tongue, supporting it with their hand so the tongue can relax over the straw. This forces the tongue forward and slightly over the bottom teeth to promote release of the base of the tongue. The exercise is built on two ascending and descending five-tone scales from low Do to Sol on [i]. Eli requests a dark [i] sound, instead of a brighter vowel. The musical design of this exercise resembles the exercise in figure 5.8, but the vowel, volume,

Figure 5.8. Five-tone scale on [u] for upper range development.

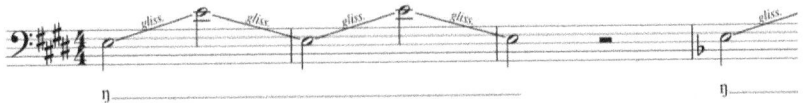

Figure 5.9. Octave glide on [ŋ] in lower range for aligning lower and upper range.

and registration are opposite, where B is singing with a full-bodied low sound. Eli has B rotate their head from left to right, as if saying "no," to keep the muscles of the throat and neck soft. Later in the lesson Eli repeats this exercise with slight modifications. Instead of a darker [i] vowel, the first scale in the sequence is sung on [a], followed by [i] on the second scale. During this iteration of the exercise, Eli asks B to place their thumb vertically in their mouth to create more space between their top and bottom teeth. The thumb also ascertains if B is singing with unnecessary jaw tension by the presence of teeth imprints on the skin of the thumb.

Returning to an octave slide, the next exercise is an octave slide on [i], promoting forward tongue placement and resonance. This exercise begins in chest voice, but as they ascend, Eli encourages B to roll into head voice. The purpose is to hear no "break" or flip of passaggio in negotiating the octave displacement and registration shift. Eli addresses larynx position during this exercise, encouraging B to "let the lower [larynx] position hold strong" when ascending. Issues related to posture, including a collapsing of the chest and ribs, are also addressed at this point in the exercise.

Figure 5.10 illustrates an arpeggio on "nyoi" [njoi] and then [a]. Performed staccato, the arpeggio facilitates a balanced onset and establishes alignment between the registers. Eli is cautious during this exercise to ensure the habitual neck pain is not aggravated by the exercise.

Next, a nine-tone sixteenth-note scale on [i] represents the largest range in a single exercise. Beginning in chest voice, this

Figure 5.10. Staccato arpeggios for balanced onset and registration alignment.

sequence requires even pressure and the ability to seamlessly travel between chest and head register with ease. After several keys in a quick tempo, B mentions that the tempo might be too quick to make even adjustments during the scale. Eli suggests a slower tempo and concurs that a relaxed pace allows for a more gradual coordination of the muscles. One final exercise, shown below, demonstrates an onset in head voice followed by a descending perfect fifth into a chest voice timbre followed by a scale in chest (or mixed) voice. This challenging exercise necessitates singing the highest note first in head voice at the start of the exercise and then in chest voice on the scalar pattern. Beginning in head register fosters a lighter mixed sound in the five-tone scale. Eli remarks that the goal of the exercise is to get enough lightness in the chest voice to ascend the fifth, but not so much that it sounds like head voice. This exercise, like many preceding it, encourages a balance in head and chest sound and a mixture in the middle, so there is control from top to bottom.

The pacing and design of the exercises are determined by Eli, though he allows adequate time for student feedback. Often after having B sing an exercise a few times, he will inquire, "What is that like for you?" Depending on the response, he will redirect B through the process, adding a kinesthetic element or offering a modification to the exercise; for example, slowing down the nine-tone scale was initiated by feedback from B.

Throughout the lessons, Eli offers supportive and positive feedback. He is quick to show excitement when B makes improvement and is reassuring when an exercise reveals challenges. Eli listens deeply to B when singing, sometimes looking away, as a method of listening with specific intention. Yet he provides constructive criticism based on aural and visual stimuli. The teacher and student have exceptional rapport and the lessons are filled with laughter and smiles.

Figure 5.11. Descending perfect fifth glide and scale for register alignment.

After the exercises are complete, around ten to fifteen minutes remain in which to work on repertoire. B presents a portion of two different pieces. In the first lesson, B works on "What's Going On" by Marvin Gaye. In the second lesson, they present "All Comes Back to You," an original song by B. For both pieces, Eli addresses resonance and vowels based on speech-oriented placement, and again investigates registration to find the appropriate musical style for the chosen repertoire. The pieces are part of B's ensemble repertoire, and so only a fragment of each is represented.

As B describes themselves as masculine-of-center, it appears the range of the vocal exercises and repertoire support this identity. The numerous exercises serve as calisthenics for the voice. The singing work B and Eli do focuses on the facilitation of both registers to provide B with flexibility and freedom to make musical decisions that their vocal technique will support.

Chapter Takeaways

This chapter investigated the perspectives and experiences of two nonbinary singers. Singers Kelly and B, alongside their teachers, provide insight to gendering in the performing arts. Their teachers, Peter and Eli, respectively, both are trans men, having had their own occurrences of affirmation and dysphoria within vocal pedagogy. Their distinct yet similar teaching styles offer a model for teaching singing beyond *bel canto* technique, with Eli having a strong foundation in contemporary commercial music and Peter a deft hand in coaching musical theatre music, both classical and belt singing. Nonbinary singers like Kelly might not employ traditional vocal nomenclature to describe their vocal range, instead opting for a gender-neutral term such as "vocalist" or "soprano-tenor." Lessons with B showed a more pop-oriented style of singing with an emphasis on allowing a lower range to develop. Both singers found greater confidence with their singing and speaking voices through singing lessons.

A major takeaway from these case studies is that nonbinary singers are not monochromatic; a one-size-fits-all approach would be problematic. Peter and Eli, in their own discrete ways, display a democratic approach to teaching by enabling their students to direct lesson pacing, repertoire selection, and language used to describe their vocal development.

Both teachers recommend teachers acquire "cultural competency" in working with TGQ singers to avoid "othering" a student or making them do the emotional labor of educating the instructor about teaching TGQ singers. This suggests that while teachers should be listening to a student to learn about the perspectives and desires of that student, teachers are also encouraged to continue to learn about TGQ singing beyond the knowledge of their TGQ student(s). Drawn from the case studies and related research, here is a condensed overview of pedagogical strategies and salient knowledge in teaching trans/nonbinary singers.

Teaching Singers

- Changing the key of a song allows a singer to embody a song that might otherwise might be out of their range or tessitura.
- Student-centeredness with lesson pacing, repertoire selection, and range development might help a student feel more comfortable by giving them agency and autonomy.
- Traditional voice classification nomenclature (soprano, alto, tenor, bass, etc.) might affirm one student but cause dysphoria in another student. Listening to and using the language a student uses to describe their singing is key.
    - Some students, "soprano" or "bass" might be affirming; other singers might choose "vocalist," "bassa" or "soprane," for example.
    - Some students might wish their trans or genderqueer identity be public, and as such want to be labeled a "nonbinary soprano" or a "trans bass."
- Gender-neutral language with teaching a group of singers (such as "all," "musicians," or "artists," to name a few) is affirming.

- Teachers may guide students to strengthen different parts of their range through semi-occluded exercises on a fricative consonant, lip buzz, or straw singing.
- Singing lessons can serve a vital role in a person's vocal and gender transition.
- Teachers are responsible for listening to and learning from their students, but also in during their own "cultural competency" homework to avoid "othering" a student or putting onus on a student to teach the teacher about TGQ singers.

Vocal Expression

- Nonbinary students might seek vocal range development (higher or lower) without the aid of hormone replacement therapy.
- Some nonbinary students, though not necessarily wishing to be identified as male or female, might be engage in hormone replacement therapy.
- Some students might desire a gender-neutral timbre and range.

Notes

1. Genny Beemyn and Susan R. Rankin, *The Lives of Transgender People* (New York: Columbia University Press, 2011).

2. Ibid., 149.

3. Declan Henry, *Trans Voices: Becoming Who You Are* (London: Jessica Kingsley, 2017), 122.

4. Bianca D. M. Wilson and Ilan H. Meyer, "Nonbinary LGBTQ Adults in the United States," UCLA School of Law Williams Institute, October 28, 2021, https://williamsinstitute.law.ucla.edu/publications/nonbinary-lgbtq-adults-us/.

5. Travis M. Andrews, "The Singular, Gender-Neutral 'They' Added to the Associated Press Stylebook," *Washington Post*, March 28, 2017, http://wapo.st/2nuXMMf?tid=ss_mail&utm_term=.f9d27ba8097f%C2%A0.

6. Michelle Kim, "American Psychological Association Endorses Use of Singular 'They' Pronoun," *Them*, November 6, 2019, https://www.them.us/story/american-psychological-association-singular-they-pronoun.

7. A. W. Geiger and Nikki Graf, "About One-in-Five U.S. Adults Know Someone Who Goes by a Gender-Neutral Pronoun," Pew Research Center July 27, 2020, https://www.pewresearch.org/fact-tank/2019/09/05/gender-neutral-pronouns/.

8. Ezra Marcus, "A Guide to Neopronouns," *New York Times*, April 8, 2021, https://www.nytimes.com/2021/04/08/style/neopronouns-nonbinary-explainer.html.

9. Shelagh Davies and Joshua M. Goldberg, "Clinical Aspects of Transgender Speech Feminization and Masculinization," *International Journal of Transgenderism* 9, no. 3–4 (2006): 167–96, https://doi.org/10.1300/j485v09n03_08.

6

Pedagogical Considerations for Gender-Affirming Vocal Music Education

> "As music teachers, we have the power to create new situations, even when we may feel the pressures to conform to the dominating practices of our spaces for teaching and learning. We cannot, to quote Loraine Hansberry (1964), afford to 'stand idly by and wait for change to occur,' but instead we must develop—as a community of learners—a culture of critical reflection and action that will lead to challenging systemic forms of oppression in education."
>
> —Brent C. Talbot in
> *Marginalized Voices in Music Education*

In the three previous chapters, portraits of six singers and their teachers illustrate models of vocal pedagogy for trans and genderqueer singers. Through portraiture analysis, I have endeavored to present an insider's view to the nature of one-on-one singing instruction with the hope of cultivating "a deeper level of understanding and empathy."[1] As a method of analysis, portraiture calls on an investigator to seek and construct an authentic account of a participant's experiences, perceptions, and practices.[2] It has been my utmost aim to serve as a clear conduit for the singers and teachers who I interviewed and observed.

In this chapter, I will discuss five pedagogical considerations for a gender-affirming vocal pedagogy. These considerations are rooted in the perspectives and lived experiences of the students and teachers who contributed to this book. Where a traditional vocal pedagogy text might focus on vocal technique, this chapter will discuss vocal technique alongside other paradigms of teaching. The five considerations include:

1. *Recognizing gender implications in musical spaces:* Gender stereotypes affirm some students, while others experience marginalization and adversity. Pedagogical language, repertoire, and performance attire will be discussed.
2. *Teaching vocal technique:* Technical know-how is an essential to promote efficient and expressive singing habits.
3. *Embodying professional responsibility:* It is incumbent on instructors to conduct their own continuing education and reflect on their own understanding and biases about gender, so as to be as welcoming and affirming as possible in the studio context.
4. *Nurturing self-advocacy:* Self-advocacy is modeled in TGQ students and teachers to instigate changes in policies, practices, and performances to be more open and affirming.
5. *Providing socioemotional support:* Teaching is more than technique teaching; providing socioemotional support was present in the applied studios observed for this study, which I consider an important aspect of gender-affirming teaching.

The image in figure 6.1 illustrates the integration and iteration of these considerations. In queering vocal pedagogy, the role of the vocal music educator extends beyond the teaching of vocal technique and explores the greater role we play in the lives of our singing students. Throughout the discussions below, refer to the table 2.1, which provides the names of the participants and how they relate to each other.

Pedagogical Considerations for Gender-Affirming Vocal Music / 187

Figure 6.1. Five considerations for gender affirming vocal music education. Source: Author

Gender in Musical Spaces

Gender in musical spaces positively and negatively impacts the experiences of TGQ individuals. Dependent on a person's identity and sense of self, gendered expectations can afford a positive opportunity for a singer to explore their gender identity through music. In other situations, singers found the gendering of musical spaces to be oppressive. The act of "gendering"—that is, the expectations, stereotypes, and labels we place on each other—is widespread and instinctive. Peter offered, "There are all these ways that we are treated by others in a gendered way that are so pervasive and so subtle." Music spaces are gendered constantly without cognizance through language, repertoire, and performance practices.

The teachers who contributed to this book demonstrated sensitivity to gendered language and repertoire in their teaching practices. The removal of all gender implications from teaching is challenging, if not impossible, but the awareness and elimination of some gendered conventions cultivates the most open and welcoming practice. Some singers feel affirmed when specific gendered repertoire or labels, such as falsetto or tenor, are assigned to them. Other singers desire more gender-neutral language. A mindful approach to language, repertoire, and performing attire with an understanding of the potential impact on student comfort is recommended.

Positive Experiences

In reflecting on earlier life experiences, Forest indicated that music and theater in his teens fortuitously enabled him to explore his masculinity. By being provided the opportunity to sing in the tenor section of his church choir and perform roles traditionally cast for male actors in school plays, Forest was given space to safely enter a masculine identity in public view, even before realizing his authentic maleness in daily life. Forest also found a safe space in group voice instruction, which provided a way for him to develop his lower range before and after the onset of androgen therapy.

B shared that musical theatre provided an opening to inhabit a male character. In preparation for the role of Tony in *West Side Story*, B found a new perspective of their vocal identity when a voice teacher described their higher range as "falsetto." This gendered language, along with the opportunity to perform this well-known male role, affirmed B's lived self-identity as masculine-of-center.

Emmett, the former professional mezzo-soprano, took delight in performing operatic trouser roles. Although trouser roles are traditionally sung by female-identifying singers, these roles provided Emmett with an opening to be masculine on stage as aligned with his offstage identity. As a concert singer, after appearing on stage in female attire for years, Emmett received acceptance when he substituted his evening dress with a tuxedo.

Isabella talked about having never *not* been affirmed by the music in her applied lessons. She has explored various ways of being feminine through musical performances. In learning, an aria for the role of a Cherubino—a trouser role from Mozart's Le Nozze di Figaro—she took delight in the very queerness that the role (also one that Emmett sang many times in his professional career) was intended to be performed by a female mezzo-soprano portraying a man on stage.

Negative Experiences

The embedded gender construct in musical or educational settings might go unnoticed by cisgender individuals, but my research found that the imprint of gender in these spaces is ubiquitous. Many times, the participants shared how the gendering of these spaces was oppressive or marginalizing. Peter, Kelly, Emmett, and B spoke plainly about the detrimental impact of gender coercion in the performing arts.

Peter discussed the dysphoria felt when made to perform female roles in musical productions in college. He disclosed that the experience was "uncomfortable," "humiliating," and "awful." Kelly also talked about being pushed into soprano roles in high school and receiving no encouragement to try other kinds of repertoire. As an enthusiast of musical theater, Kelly discussed the issue of gender stereotyping in the oeuvre. Often the audition process for musical theater in Kelly's experience is defined by gender, and at times, Kelly has been forced to dress as their assigned gender and name at birth to uphold audition requirements. Even in describing their own voice, Kelly has difficulty. They shared, "On my résumé, I write 'soprano-tenor' and then I'll put my range, but I don't know. I'm still figuring that out because a lot of the language is super gendered." Though musical theater repertoire often reinforces gender roles, Kelly wishes directors would see an auditionee solely for their vocal range, personality, and abilities, removing gender from the casting consideration. Both Kelly and Peter would like to see new material be written of TGQ characters for TGQ performers.

Emmett also discussed gender issues in staged works through his experience in opera. As a principal artist, he would frequently perform trouser roles and older female roles. Though the embodiment of a female character on stage was dysphoric, the cross-dressing was tolerable, as it felt like an adult version of playing dress-up. His sense of dysphoria intensified on the concert stage, where he would appear as "himself," but in female attire to meet audience expectations. He explained, "I always regretted it because it was so . . . uncomfortable for me." This discomfort, alongside his maturing voice, led him to start androgen therapy.

Peter, Kelly, and B talked about negative experiences in prior voice training. Peter recalled that in college, he did not connect with his voice teacher. Though he could not recollect the specific constraints of their relationship, he remembers never feeling comfortable to discuss his personal life or the gender dysphoria he was facing during that time. He believes that the way he was treated and being trained was in opposition to his authentic masculine identity. He described the repertoire assigned to him as being overly "feminine." Ultimately, Peter dropped out of the conservatory because he felt so out of place.

B experienced a similar situation. During college, they recall leaving many voice lessons emotionally distraught. "I think there were more gender pieces than I understood at the time," B explained. "I was just thinking this isn't the right fit." B spoke about "how not fitting [in] leads to feeling like, 'I'm not good.'" Later, they stated, "I have wondered what we [as TGQ individuals] internalize as our worth as performers or our capabilities or our value in musical spaces." Peter and B described a lack of self-worth brought on by their voice teachers. Kelly also experienced low self-esteem when they did not connect with their music teacher in high school. "I was always made to feel I wasn't good enough," Kelly professed, "especially when it came to the types of music they wanted me to sing because it was always very hyperfeminine." This led them to self-blame and temporarily dropping out of musical activities.

All student participants shared a similar narrative where expectations of their perceived gender were a component of feeling marginalized or dysphoric. Emmett, who disclosed that concert dresses made him feel "dysphoric," and Peter, who was cast in female roles that felt "humiliating," were forced to dismiss their own sense of identity to uphold hegemonic customs. Forest, who spoke the most positively about his gender affirmation in the performing arts, explained that the opportunity for him to explore his masculinity was not born from a forward-thinking music educator. He and B commented that the ability to enter male spaces in the performing arts derived from a shortage of performers assigned male at birth. In the need to cast a show or balance a choir, individuals assigned female at birth were invited to fill the unoccupied space, which, for Forest and B, provided an opportunity to explore their authentic masculine identity.

Discussion

This study indicates that gender conformity occurs in musical spaces in multiple ways. Asserting a need for teachers to use a "gender-complex approach,"[3] educators should examine "the micro level ways in which gender is constantly being socially constructed in the classroom as well as macro-level influences on this process."[4] Teachers need to purposefully dismantle traditions or practices that reinforce gender expectations, affirming that educational experiences can "reproduce the gender oppression . . . or they can challenge it."[5] Applied lesson teachers and choir directors should reconsider the ways in which they may unintentionally reinforce gender roles. One prevalent form of gendering in music comes in the labelling of voice classifications. Another example is illustrated in assigned repertoire and roles of opera and musical theater. A third discussion point centers around the expectations of performance attire for concerts, recitals, and auditions.

Voice Classification

Teachers should be aware that traditional voice classifications (soprano, alto, tenor, bass, etc.) are laden with gender implications. Though the Italian words *soprano* and *alto* are nouns with a masculine ending, in modern usage, these words have become associated with female singers. While our current musical lexicon has not adopted widespread alternatives for the traditional voice classifications, voice teachers and choral directors should understand that many people have a specific notion, for example, of what a soprano or a bass looks and sounds like. A trans man who sings in the soprano range might not fit that notion, and therefore might not wish to use that label for his vocal range. Alternatively, he might take delight in referring to himself as a soprano. Likewise, if a trans women sings baritone, her baritone range is feminine, even if traditional pedagogy deems it a "male" vocal range. As there is no-one-size-fits-all model, teachers should speak with their students to discover the vernacular that best fits their identity.

In addition to voice classifications, some pedagogical language, such as "falsetto" or the way vocal timbre can be described (such as "sweet," "light," "heavy," "strong") might imply gender. Interestingly, falsetto, as a function of the voice enabling treble range singing, has been regularly viewed as a feminine sound produced by a singer assigned male at birth. In the context of trans masculinity, the gender implication of falsetto is repositioned as upholding a masculine voice. Singing teachers might want to be sensitive in how they discuss timbre and range with TGQ singers. They might also allow a student to choose a label for their voice that aligns with their identity, no matter their performable or physiological range. "There's this ritual of listing people's voice types [in recital programs]," Peter explained, "but they're gendered words, so if we're identifying voice type, we can't forget that there's a gender implication." Peter suggests giving students latitude to decide their voice type assignment for printed programs. Students might also want to circumvent custom altogether and label themselves as a "vocalist" or create a new voice classification ("bassa" or

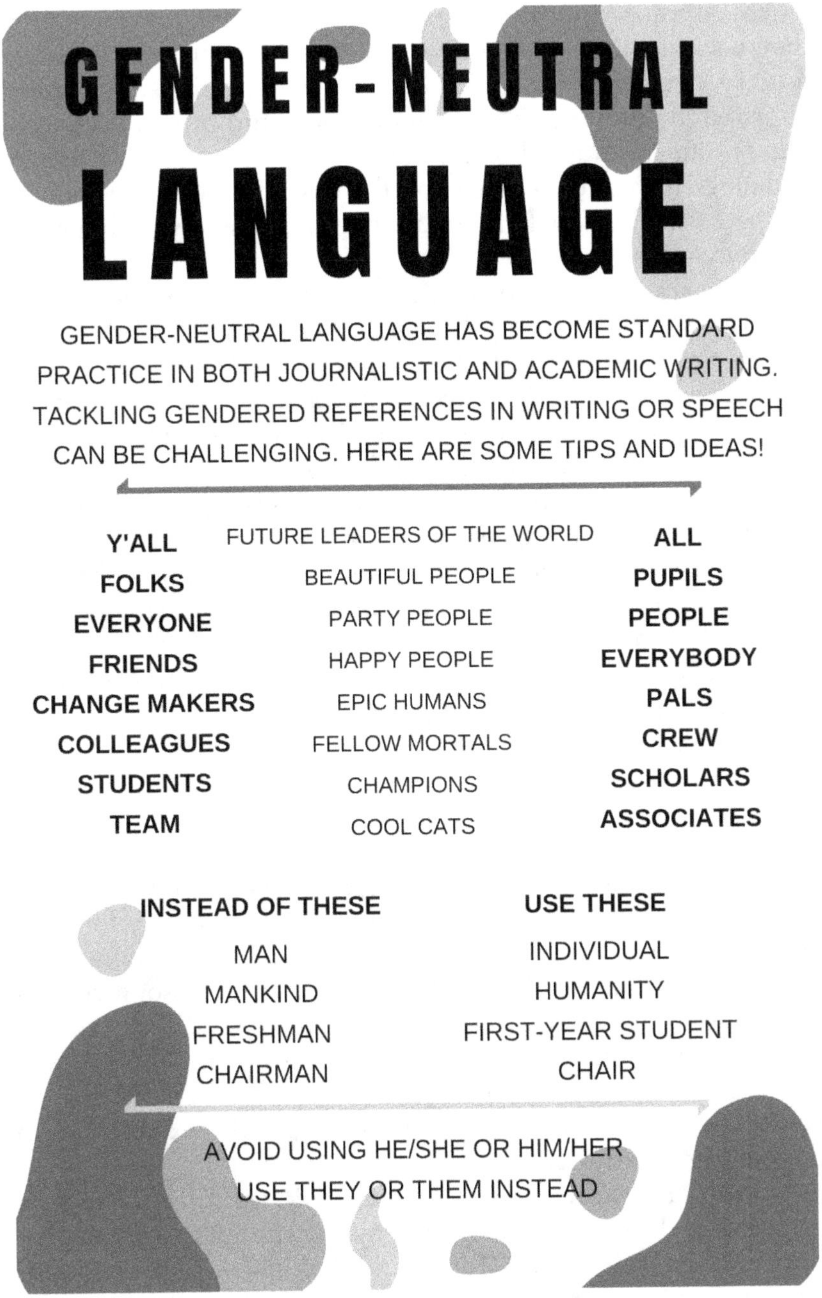

GENDER-NEUTRAL LANGUAGE

GENDER-NEUTRAL LANGUAGE HAS BECOME STANDARD PRACTICE IN BOTH JOURNALISTIC AND ACADEMIC WRITING. TACKLING GENDERED REFERENCES IN WRITING OR SPEECH CAN BE CHALLENGING. HERE ARE SOME TIPS AND IDEAS!

Y'ALL	FUTURE LEADERS OF THE WORLD	ALL
FOLKS	BEAUTIFUL PEOPLE	PUPILS
EVERYONE	PARTY PEOPLE	PEOPLE
FRIENDS	HAPPY PEOPLE	EVERYBODY
CHANGE MAKERS	EPIC HUMANS	PALS
COLLEAGUES	FELLOW MORTALS	CREW
STUDENTS	CHAMPIONS	SCHOLARS
TEAM	COOL CATS	ASSOCIATES

INSTEAD OF THESE	USE THESE
MAN	INDIVIDUAL
MANKIND	HUMANITY
FRESHMAN	FIRST-YEAR STUDENT
CHAIRMAN	CHAIR

AVOID USING HE/SHE OR HIM/HER
USE THEY OR THEM INSTEAD

Figure 6.2. Gender-neutral language. Created by Jordan Sanderson.

"masc-soprano"). In the TGQ choir of which Kelly is a member, they use the labels voice one, voice two, voice three, and voice four to circumvent traditional voice classifications. A similar approach might be employed in the voice studio. While a queering of our traditional voice labels might seem implausible, allowing singers to label (or not) their vocal ranges and timbres is a necessary ingress to rebuilding vocal pedagogy with gender diversity at its core.

More traditional choirs might not be ready to reject SATB labels, but directors can still avoid other gendered phrases like "ladies and gentlemen" or "boys and girls." Calling the sopranos and altos "ladies" or the tenors and basses "gentlemen" not only marginalizes TGQ singers, it is also unwelcoming for countertenors, women singing in the tenor section, and anyone who does not wish to be considered a "lady" or "gentleman." Additionally, using "guys" as a catchall for everyone might seem gender neutral as it is so commonplace, but this phrase is actually steeped in patriarchy. Fortunately, there are many ways to refer to a group of people without gendering, though it might take practice to be consistent. A music teacher might use any of the following: musicians, singers, learners, choristers, or even folx. Figure 6.2 provides some additional examples.

Repertoire

Previous literature on trans and genderqueer singing makes little mention of solo vocal repertoire written expressly for TGQ singers. "Choosing repertoire can be a challenge," Loraine Sims offers, "so an open dialogue about gender-neutral song choices would be a good idea."[6] Songs that do not speak directly from a gendered perspective are excellent options for students who do not wish to portray a specific gender. Teachers should also be sensitive of romantic texts that imply a specific sexuality when suggesting repertoire.

In the case studies I share in this book, the selection of repertoire was decided upon, mostly, by the students, with teacher approval. Isabella, Forest, Kelly, and B all chose their own repertoire. Emmett, and his teacher Naomi, spent part of the lesson time choosing repertoire. While Naomi actually chose most of the pieces, she did so with a superb awareness of Emmett's musical interests. Chrys, the trans woman singer-songwriter, had the most control over her repertoire; in her case, she writes music specifically for her own voice. While her teacher had less say over her repertoire choices than the other teacher-student pairs I observed, this does not imply that Chrys's teacher was hands-off with coaching the repertoire. Indeed, she helped Chrys make musical and vocal choices to develop efficiency and self-expressivity through her songs.

This study found three factors that contribute to how repertoire should be selected: (1) student interest, (2) student vocal or musical ability, and (3) desired vocal or musical growth. Figure

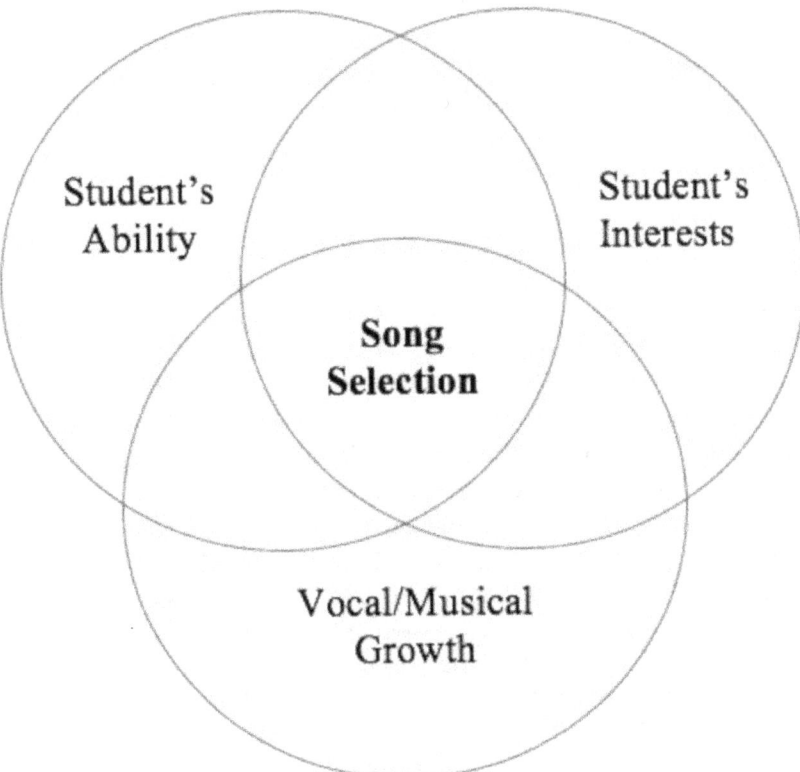

Figure 6.3. Factors of student song selection. Source: Author

6.3 provides an image of the interconnectedness of these factors involved in song selection.

Enabling students to choose their own repertoire alleviates the concern a teacher may have in assigning pieces that might cause discomfort or dysphoria for the student. For students who need more structure or help in selecting repertoire, teachers might offer a list of songs from which the student can choose. An alternative option might be to have the student write a description of the kind of song(s) they would like to sing, which provides the teacher awareness of the student's interests before assigning a piece. As evident from the voice lessons presented in chapters 3 through 5, there is no "right" or "wrong" repertoire for a TGQ singer, so long as the repertoire is appropriate for their vocal abilities and affirms their identity. In other words, if a TGQ student is interested in singing a very gendered song, let them. If they are seeking repertoire that heightens trans and genderqueer identity, there is a growing (albeit still small) compendium of repertoire written for TGQ singers. NewMusicShelf offers a new collection of twenty-first-century songs, *Anthology of New Music: Trans & Nonbinary Voices, Vol. 1*, for TGQ singers.[7] Curated by Aiden K. Feltkamp, this anthology includes pieces by Rosśa Crean, Rylan Gleave, Grey Grant, Pax Ressler, Penrose Allphin, and more. These solo pieces represent the TGQ community through a diverse range of styles from Western art song, opera, and contemporary solo pieces.

Composer and scholar Penrose Allphin's 2021 thesis draws attention to "transgender composer identity."[8] In their research, the author investigates the compositional styles of six trans and/or genderqueer composers, including Mari Esabel Valverde, whose output includes choral and solo songs, and Alex Temple, a composer of vocal, instrumental, and electronic music. Vocal music educators might also explore the music of Michael Bussewitz-Quarm, whose catalogue contains a wide range of choral pieces. The online Composer Diversity Database (http://www.composerdiversity.com) enables teachers and students to discover works by underrepresented composers of choral and solo songs, as well as instrumental music for a variety of ensembles. Appendix 2 at the end of this book provides a list of known pieces from Feltkamp's new anthology and other known solo pieces for TGQ singers or by TGQ composers.

Musicals and operas play an essential role in the lives of many of the singers in this study. Trouser roles and gender-fluidity onstage provide singers opportunity to explore their gender identity through the performing arts. There is a growing list of musicals that centralize TGQ characters. Appendix 3 provides a list of these musicals along with a short description of each. Teachers should be mindful to not assume a trans or genderqueer student will want to play an openly TGQ character. Through conversations with the student, a level of comfort and interest can be determined. Teachers may want to share appendix 3 with students who are requesting greater representation of TGQ characters in musicals and operas. The shows included in this appendix are those that contain a character who is trans, genderqueer, or nonbinary; this list does not include roles, such as Cherubino or Edna Turnblad (in the musical *Hairspray*), where the standard practice of cross-dressing is intentional for comedic impact, and does not purposefully attempt to heighten TGQ onstage representation.

Performance Attire

Teachers might want to reconsider what students are required to wear in a studio recital, voice jury, audition, or any public concert. While dressing formally is conventional, dresses and tuxedos can make some students feel dysphoric. Allowing students to select their own attire within parameters empowers each student to dress comfortably yet professionally. The convention that sopranos need to wear a dress while mezzo-sopranos can wear a pantsuit is antiquated and oppressive. Ensemble directors might want to consider a "concert black" or a matching color, while avoiding a specific gown or suit. Appendix 4 offers some "dos" and "don'ts" for performance attire that enables every singer to feel affirmed on stage.

This overall discussion on gender in musical spaces brings attention to issues of pedagogical language, repertoire, and performance attire. As Peter noted in his interview, the gendering (and misgendering) of individuals is "subtle" and "pervasive." Teachers need to practice self-reflection and critically examine how gender reification may present itself in their studio and how it may impact their students. The need for a high level of professional responsibility will be discussed later in this chapter.

Teaching Vocal Technique

The technical know-how of teaching TGQ singers will be discussed through two different lenses. First, an analysis of vocal needs and challenges will be examined to address *what* teachers are doing to teach vocal technique. Second, the foundations of instruction—including elements of modeling, scaffolding, and other processes—will be investigated to uncover *how* teachers impart vocal technique. A discussion of vocal technique opens multiple lines of inquiry, including exercises, range, and registration. While differences were found in the exercises and technical conceptions of singing among the teacher participants, they all share a common goal of helping singers find functional habitual voice use.

All teachers, as singers themselves, were initially trained in Western classical singing. Darius, Martha, Naomi, and Peter continue to subscribe to a Western classical style of vocal technique. Eli is a certified singing teacher in contemporary commercial music, and thus his teaching of B appears deliberately different from the three other teachers. Nicola teaches a variety of styles, but in her teaching of Chrys, the technical concepts match the pop musical styles of Chrys's music. While there is overlap in teacher pedagogies, the two styles of singing—*bel canto* and CCM (pop, rock, belt)—emphasize different aesthetics and methods to achieve a specific technique and sound.

Peter's teaching of Kelly resembled elements of nonclassical methods, and since he and Eli teach the two nonbinary singers, their approaches will be addressed jointly. As Naomi and Darius teach the two singers who employ androgen therapy, Emmett and Forest, respectively, their approaches will be compared.

Finally, the training of Isabella and Chrys will be discussed to address the training of trans feminine voices.

An emphasis on voice functionality is overall present in the teachers' perspectives. All teachers discuss the importance of developing healthy singing habits to promote vocal longevity. The teaching of vocal technique was constructed through a student-centered approach, in which students were given more control to define learning objectives and to suggest learning strategies. A lesson served as a joint problem-solving venture, in which a teacher and student collaborated to develop the student's capabilities. Even within a student-centered approach, singing teachers remained expert in imparting vocal and musical knowledge.

Peter and Eli

The importance of "balancing" the vocal mechanism is of high importance in teaching vocal technique for these two teachers. In lesson observations and interviews, Peter and Eli were both overt in discussing vocal registration and how it pertains to their nonbinary students. While B (Eli's student) considers themselves masculine-of-center and Kelly (Peter's student) defines themselves as genderfluid, both were working on expanding and strengthening a lower range.

The students share a similarity in registration. Both are comfortable taking their chest voices (or a chest-mix sound) up to A4. B can sing about a third lower than Kelly. B's upper range extends to F5 (maybe G5, on a good day), and they can sing in head voice to B3 or a little lower. Their middle/mixed register is approximately G3 to G4. Kelly's upper range extends much higher, to F6 as a whistle tone, and down to C4 or lower. Kelly mixes between A3 and F4. Both experience a breathy, unfocused sound in the lower part of their head voices. Both Peter and Eli are explicit with the intent of their vocal exercises as they relate to voice registration.

In discussing singing technique in contemporary commercial music, Eli explains that initial bifurcation of the head and chest registers is deliberate. He shares that a singer will usually experience one part of their range as being/feeling/sounding stronger than the other, and the goal is to bring equal strength to both parts of the voice. He asserts, "You isolate and separate the registers to get them to be as comfortable and easy and free as possible . . . then we start to work on mixing in the middle." He emphasizes three basic elements of sound: pitch, vowel, and volume. For developing head register, Eli crafts an exercise on [i] or [u] on D#4 or above, on soft singing only. To develop a mixed sound in middle range, Eli has a singer use [æ] or [ɛ] on a slide of a perfect fifth or octave at a medium dynamic. Chest voice singing is fostered through open vowels, like [æ] and [a] at a louder volume. Eli cautions, "People have a tendency to push on the bottom and then they get into big issues." Overemphasizing the lower range can cause an imbalance in the voice, which effects range, timbre, and flexibility. The purpose of the direction in dynamics is to foster a specific function or coordination of the vocal mechanism, while being mindful and intentional with volume. Using semi-occluded exercises, singing on [ŋ], slides, scales, and arpeggios keeps the voice supple. Eli also employs an exercise that draws the tongue forward. The singer holds a straw horizontally underneath the tongue while singing on [æ], to release the base of the tongue. Developing a singer's full range fosters "ease and comfort" between cricothyroid-dominant (head voice) and thyroarytenoid-dominant (chest voice) muscular action. Eli shares, "I work a lot on having the register transition be as smooth as possible and the voice be as balanced as possible." By developing one's full range, the voice is in functional order and the singer is enabled to make choices regarding voice color for different styles of music.

    Emphasizing an "holistic" method to teaching, Peter seeks vocal health and longevity with his students. A lesson is structured into four parts: physical relaxation, breath warm-up, vocalizing on exercises, and repertoire. In working with Kelly, Peter explores the upper range, followed by exercises for the low range. Peter explains, "I found earlier in my process of us working together, [the voice] was getting out of balance. There was a lot of belt singing . . . and head voice was getting tighter."

To restore balance, like Eli, Peter requests Kelly warm up their entire range, even if the upper range is never used publicly.

Although Kelly is working on repertoire designed for cisgender tenors assigned male at birth, Peter and Kelly will adjust the key signature as necessary to fit Kelly's range. Peter also contends that having Kelly sing repertoire over a wide range is not really that different than a cisgender man using falsetto in "Bring Him Home" (from the musical *Les Misérables*) while also learning a song in a baritone range. While the "tenor" repertoire Kelly sings sits in the lower part of their range, it is not substantially lower than some "female" belt repertoire in musical theatre. For example, the song "When You're Good to Mama" from the musical *Chicago* has a range of F3 to A-flat 4, similar to the range in which Kelly is singing "My Petersburg." The potential concern of Kelly singing too low too frequently is alleviated by exercises and études, which restore muscular balance in the voice.

A balance between head and chest registers and the development of a mix register maintains voice functionality in these two singers. It is useful to note that though both singers were working on their lower ranges, this development was being accomplished under the supervision of their teachers. This is especially important for B, who suffers from inconsistent throat pain. Though not exacerbated in the lessons, B's throat soreness might stem from speaking too much in the lower range when teaching or extending the lower range for too long in ensemble rehearsals.

Vocal modeling is frequently provided to demonstrate exercises and technical execution. Both Peter and Eli support the student by playing the piano on the exercises and repertoire. Frequent positive feedback is given during and between vocal exercises. Whenever constructive criticism is given, it is always delivered with a supportive tone. The teacher drives the structure and pace of the lesson, yet a relaxed atmosphere is maintained so that the student can adjust or reposition the learning. Student questions are invited and always thoroughly addressed. Strong rapport thrives in an upbeat, energetic, and positive climate.

Naomi and Darius

Like their colleagues Eli and Peter, Naomi and Darius bring heightened attention to healthy singing in their teaching. Since both teachers are working with trans men who have been on testosterone for at least three years, both students' voices have dropped in range. Forest, Darius's student, sang in high tenor range as a chorister and soloist before his transition. Now, after three years on testosterone, his range aligns closer to a baritone, extending from B2 to E4. After four years on testosterone, Emmett's range was continuing to evolve during this study. His range extends from B2 to F4, though the highest and lowest notes are not yet comfortable. It was also reported by his teacher in follow up correspondence that a lighter mechanism ("falsetto") was beginning to emerge. Forest had no falsetto, yet neither teacher nor singer found it essential to maintenance of vocal health.

Naomi's vocal pedagogy brings attention to breath support and pure vowel tone. Using exercises designed of small intervals, Naomi works on range extension by adding a pitch or two to an exercise without changing keys. The primary work is to find ease and resonance where the voice is most comfortable (E3 to B3, approximately) and extend up or down. Darius's uses semi-occluded slides of a perfect fifth or octave, bringing awareness to breath and resonance. When Naomi and Darius seek vocal balance, instead of talking about registration, they discuss a coordinated onset of muscle and breath, and having an even amount of support throughout the full vocal range.

Designing and scaffolding vocal or musical activities is evident in the similar approaches of Naomi and Darius. In working on repertoire, Darius uses several techniques to encourage better vocal use. When Forest encounters a challenging rhythm, Darius will isolate the rhythm and have Forest speak it or sing it at slower tempo. When a melodic passage is inaccurate, the teacher will slow the tempo or remove the words to enable the student to focus on fewer musical elements. Often Darius has Forest sing parts of his repertoire on a semi-occluded sound (usually [v] or [ð]) to discern consistent breath release before returning to lyrics. Other times, Forest is invited to sing a phrase on [va] or [na] to encourage legato singing. Neither Naomi nor Darius demonstrates how to sing the repertoire, but both use vocal modeling to demonstrate technique during the vocal exercises.

In working on repertoire, Darius and Naomi used different approaches based on student needs. Forest came to his lessons with his repertoire mostly learned, and time was spent on working technical needs and musical interpretation. Naomi and Emmett spent time in his lesson finding repertoire appropriate for his expanding range. She had Emmett look only at the lyrics to circumvent him reading the music and responding to high and low pitches as they present on the staff. Naomi employed several strategies to beget optimal singing. She had Emmett sing the lyrics on a vocal exercise to gain familiarity with the text. She taught the melody separately by rote, having Emmett mimic what she played. Never did she sing it for him, but rather she played the melody on the piano and had him estimate the text underlay, gently redirecting him when necessary. Eventually, when Emmett was conversant with the melody and text, they put the separate parts together, with Naomi accompanying at the piano. Darius also accompanied Forest during his lessons, so both teachers had excellent facility at the keyboard.

Both Naomi and Darius underscored the value of having trans students continue to sing during their vocal transitions. Darius, perhaps quoting Dory from *Finding Nemo,* enthusiastically exclaimed that all TGQ students need to "Just keep singing!" Naomi echoed similar sentiment in that nurturing Emmett's voice through the initial stages of his transition and onward has been an important aspect of his training. She has been able to monitor changes and redesign exercises to fit his most current vocal state.

Martha and Nicola

A safe and affirming studio environment that allows for the teaching of vocal technique is central in the studios of Martha and Nicola. In working with trans feminine singers, both teachers are encouraging and supportive, bringing about vocal change through positivity and a sense of collaboration toward a common goal. As Chrys, Nicola's student, sings in the tenor range, her pursuit of vocal efficiency is comparable to a light, pop tenor sound. There is a sought-after technique that aims for agility, clarity of tone, and evenness between vocal registers. Their lessons spend ample time developing ease and balance in the voice through vocal exercises, which are applicable to the songs Chrys writes for herself.

Martha's lessons with Isabella have a similar nature, where an uplifting and supportive spirit permeates their interactions. Vocal exercises help to develop natural, optimal singing habits of open throat, consistent breath release, and consistent tone throughout her range. Isabella shares, "One of the good parts of approaching voice with Martha is the focus on what's natural and relaxing—returning to your natural state of voice, which I think works for anyone and has really allowed me to like connect with my voice on a deeper level." Isabella's repertoire comes from well-known Western classical art song and opera composers, and as such, Martha is hands-on in coaching this repertoire. When musical mistakes are encountered, Isabella and Martha isolate these measures and work through them with a constructive approach. Never does Martha show disappointment or frustration at musical or vocal challenges, but rather they work through these incidences in an encouraging and affirming way.

Unlike with trans masculine singers who have gone through hormone replacement therapy like Emmett and Forest, there is little impact from hormones on the teaching of vocal technique with Isabella and Chrys. Isabella started hormone blockers and estrogen as an adolescent at the start of puberty, so her vocal range has been unaffected by testosterone and her range resembles a young mezzo-soprano. Her ongoing hormone regime does not seem to impact her current vocal training or vocal health, as her voice shows no signs of fatigue, jitteriness, or breathiness. When Chrys was younger, but long after puberty, she took hormones that had little to no effect on her voice. She also participated in "feminization" vocal and physical training that she has since stopped. Neither the hormones nor this specialized training seem to have had any long-term impact on her vocal habits, range, or continual development.

While Martha and Nicola never expressly describe voices as "feminine," they both affirm Isabella's and Chrys's identities, respectively, through nongendered language. For example, Nicola does not say anything like, "What a beautiful feminine sound," but she supports Chrys by being fully present, always using feminine pronouns, and supporting her vocal growth to validate Chrys's musical goals. Similarly, Martha does not overtly label Isabella's singing as feminine; she just simply sees and authenticates Isabella's femininity through exercises, repertoire, and language that encourages Isabella's intentions and ambitions. Both teachers affirm their students' gender not by attempting to outwardly (and, potentially, awkwardly) describe them as feminine; rather, their genuine presence and acceptance of their students is affirming.

Discussion

Much of the related literature deals with the specific vocal technique needs of trans men and women. Previous research provides information regarding range and registration, as well as offering vocal exercises to assist in achieving multiple technical desires, such as range development, freedom of tone, and breath support.[9] In an article on trans male voices, Alexandros Constansis encourages attention to diaphragmatic breathing because "bad habits, especially during the most challenging times in vocal transition, can easily go unnoticed."[10] The teachers in the current study all mentioned the importance of breath support and employed physical or vocal exercises designed to encourage diaphragmatic breathing and consistent exhalation during phonation. Teachers requested students to sing on voiced consonants, rolled [r], and lip trill or buzz to encourage an even release of breath.

The current study supports extant literature in how teachers understand and address range development and vocal registration. Anita Kozan indicates that "a trained singer will work on technique that allows a smooth transition across the passaggio, balancing the work of the cricothyroid muscles [and] ... the thyroarytenoid muscles."[11] Kozan's statement supports the perspectives and pedagogies of the teacher contributors in this study; however, it is prudent to note that not all students will be comfortable exploring their entire range. Offering one student's perspective, Kozan shares, "My voice teacher kept insisting that I vocalize the entire extent of my range, and it really upset me."[12] While the current study suggests singers felt no dysphoria in exercising their full range, not all TGQ students will feel this comfort. Teachers should discuss registration and range in a manner sensitive to their students.

Of the six teachers observed, all used prerecorded audio files or possessed keyboard skills to support vocal exercises and repertoire. Kozan supports accompanying students from the piano during their lessons so they might "turn away from the keyboard when vocalizing so that they do not tense up when they see they are approaching difficult places within or at the ends of the range."[13] This strategy was used by Naomi when teaching Emmett to prevent him from knowing how high or low he was singing.

Loraine Sims drew a connection between registration and specific vocal exercises. In speaking of her lower-voiced students using rounded vowels, such as [u] and [ʊ], she offers, "If they use these rounded vowels while keeping an open throat, they usually discovered an easier path into that tenor or baritone turned-over production."[14] Consistent with technical approach, teacher participant Naomi employed [o], [u], and [y] to help Emmett access the upper part of his range. Darius and Eli used a series of different vowels or semi-occluded exercises. Eli used specific vowels to foster range and registration development. Peter's exercises focused mostly on open vowels [a] and [ʌ] to promote openness in vocal production.

A commonality among the current study's participants and the related literature is the use of glissandi, also referred to as vocal slides, glides, and sirens. All teachers employed vocal sliding across intervals. Naomi preferred exercises designed on smaller intervals; other teachers showed less concern for the size of intervals within vocal exercises, permitting students to slide between fifths and octaves. Kozan suggests that exercises on thirds, fifths, and octaves are permissible, noting that "the ability to freely slide across the pitches indicates good flexibility of the larynx and freedom from 'muscling' the sound."[15] The discrepancy between exercise design may have to do with a teacher's own vocal training or stem from the needs of the student under their instruction. As this study looked at only one student per teacher, no generalizations should be drawn on how each teacher works with all their students. Indeed, based on teacher feedback, it should be acknowledged these instructors likely teach with different approaches based on student needs.

The related literature examines the importance of soft singing. In this study, Eli is the only teacher who explicitly talked about volume of sound with his student. Both Constansis and Kozan bring attention to the significance of being able to sing softly as an element of vocal functionality. In her discussion, Kozan mentions renowned singing teacher Jeannette LoVetri, regarding the importance of singing softly on a glissando. Eli studied Somatic Voicework™ The LoVetri Method, and similarities between Kozan's exercises can be seen in his approach, addressing volume and potential hyperfunctional vocal production. Naomi also encouraged Emmett to sometimes sing softer or louder, depending on the exercise. She did not speak in terms of volume but referred to dynamics intermittently, such as suggesting a decrescendo into the highest notes of a scale or melodic passage.

Vocal pedagogues Barbara Doscher and James McKinney both suggest using the falsetto register (note the gendered language) as a means of vocal development in "male" voices to access a higher range.[16] Doscher writes, "Some pedagogs favor the use of falsetto voice to develop the full head voice, contending that such an approach leads to more ring and avoids the danger of an overly dark and weighty sound."[17] According to Doscher, falsetto singing strengthens the cricothyroid muscles, which helps alleviate overtaxing the vocal muscles. Since neither Emmett nor Forest had falsetto at the time of data collection, neither teacher was using falsetto registration in exercises. Both singers had a head voice prior to transition but neither could access it after starting androgen therapy. Doscher also states that some voice teachers do not see a benefit in teaching tenors, baritones, or basses to access the falsetto register. Therefore, mentioning an inability to sing in falsetto is not commentary on the quality of their singing, but merely as aspect of their functional abilities. The concept of using falsetto as a way of lightening the sound and finding "ring" to develop head voice singing aligns with the teaching of Kelly and B, who advised it is not prudent to overpressurize in the lower range.

The nature of instruction seen in the data of this study follows the evidence reported by Kelly Parkes and Mathius Wexler.[18] In replicating a 2006 study on applied lesson teaching by Robert Duke and Amy Simmons, Parkes and Wexler found some additional elements not observed in the Duke and Simmons study. Among the differences, Parkes and Wexler witnessed that a "teacher accepts flaws in student performance."[19] While I occasionally heard issues of pitch and intonation, teachers sometimes overlooked vocal or musical mistakes. In the interviews, teachers stated they ignored musical faults either because they were focusing on a different teaching element or because they were allaying the stress of the student. Furthermore, Parkes and Wexler observed teachers speaking with their students about practice strategies, and this was seen among the teachers in the current study. Naomi underscores the importance of teaching a student how best to practice, noting that a lot of vocal progress can be made away from the teacher during a student's practice time.

The vocal exercises I observed corresponded with Vygotsky's learning theory of the zone of proximal development, in which a teacher designs exercises slightly beyond a student's current abilities while providing strategies for achieving this task or skill. The pedagogical process of scaffolding, which is closely linked to the zone of proximal development, enables a teacher to sequence and support a student in achieving a task once beyond their capabilities. Darius would slow down a song tempo or remove the text of a song to enable Forest to achieve aspects of the repertoire sequentially. Naomi taught a song to Emmett by rote, not because he is incapable of reading music (indeed, he is a highly skilled musician) but to stop him thinking about the sheet music instead of his vocal freedom. Martha would isolate specific trouble spots and help Isabella process the music using solfege or model the vocal line for her. The student-centeredness observed in these vocal lessons was not a surrendering of teacher's pedagogical wisdom or experience—indeed, each teacher was primary in guiding learning—but students were not passive, inactive, or subordinate players in the lesson. In each of their own ways, students remained in charge of overarching goals, having a hand in the repertoire they studied and the way their vocal development occurred.

In summary, the teaching of vocal technique was the primary goal in the observed lessons. While all singers were working on song repertoire, most lessons were dominated by vocal exercises used to address specific technical challenges related to breath management, range development, and registration. Teachers used modeling and scaffolded sequencing in a student-centered model to support vocal development. Often teachers would offer exercises by invitation, empowering the singers to modify them as they saw best for themselves. A combination of teacher-directed and student-centered teaching was demonstrated. Teachers gently provided constructive criticism, and technical skills were taught in a warm, supportive, and compassionate climate. Support and compassion will be discussed later in this book.

Embodying Professional Responsibility

Vocal music educators have a professional responsibility of cultural competency and lifelong learning in the teaching of TGQ singers. An individual's awareness of how gender impacts music spaces coupled with technical know-how is important to effectively teach TGQ singers. Teachers are responsible for their own learning; they should not rely on their students to teach them about being trans or genderqueer.

Eli was outspoken about the responsibility teachers have for their students. He believes it is the teacher's responsibility to do their "homework" on cultural competency. Teachers need to "attend trainings, do . . . readings about how to be an ally to trans people, show up in cultural spaces where . . . trans singers [are] performing . . . to show support," according to Eli. He also wants teachers to dismantle the gender binary component inherent in vocal pedagogy and to explore their own relationship with gender. He expounds,

> Work with the student who shows up in front of you, doing your best to let go of all gendered assumptions about that particular student, but also about yourself and every student. I think we often put trans students in this frame of feeling like we have to be really careful and tiptoe around them. Be conscious of your language with every student. Don't assume gendered things about them. I think the biggest thing about how to be a good teacher of transgender and gender-nonconforming students is opening up your worldview much more broadly; letting go of the binary ideas you have that are based in the heteropatriarchy that we were all raised in . . . [and] doing your own personal work around this stuff and interrogating what . . . gender means to you.

Eli's remarks bring awareness to the intersection of professional responsibility and personal reflection in evaluating one's assumptions and ideologies.

Peter asserts that a teacher must never "other" a student or barrage them with personal questions to learn about their experiences or perceptions. It is a teacher's responsibility to know how to create safe learning spaces for their students. "Part of being a decent person," he shares, includes creating "alternative spaces for just letting people be human." He practices a high level of professional responsibility by engaging in ongoing professional development. He shares that whenever a student brings a vocal or musical concern to his studio that he is not confident in answering, he seeks outside resources to educate himself.

Darius also talked about the importance of reaching out to experienced colleagues when working with a TGQ singer for the first time. When he first started teaching Forest, he reached out

Pedagogical Considerations for Gender-Affirming Vocal Music / 211

to a nationally known music educator-researcher with knowledge in teaching trans singers. As a gay man, Darius had been around TGQ people at community Pride events, but he knew these interactions would be insufficient to support Forest. Similarly, as a lesbian, Martha has spent time with TGQ people, but in teaching Isabella, she has spent a lot of time reflecting on her practices and checking in with colleagues to ensure she is providing Isabella a safe and supportive space for learning.

Finally, Naomi also places prominence in being a lifelong learner as a voice teacher. In working with Emmett, she collaborated with a speech-language pathologist knowledgeable in trans vocality to ensure Emmett was receiving adept knowledge. She also believes continued narrative and empirical research is paramount, commenting that the emergent research is "just the tip of the iceberg."

Discussion

Creating a safe and culturally competent learning and teaching environment is more than a secondary factor in the teaching of TGQ singers. Teachers carry a professional responsibility to not only learn the vocal technique aspects of TGQ singers but also provide them a welcoming and affirming environment. Sims supports this notion in suggesting that singing teachers "become . . . advocate[s] for your transgender students and make the studio and music classes/rehearsals safe spaces."[20] One step in fostering a safe studio space is providing all students with a gender-affirmation policy. A written policy statement of affirmation and safety creates a culture of respect within a learning environment. Provided on a teacher's website or in studio documents (e.g., syllabus, studio contract, or student expectations documents), a gender-affirmation policy statement urges all stakeholders of a studio—teachers, parents, students, or music collaborators—to uphold an expectation of safety and affirmation for all students and constituents. Appendix 5 shares a sample gender-affirmation policy statement to be used or modified as each teacher sees fit.

Engaging with this book and related scholarship is a valuable investment in professional responsibility. Teachers should seek additional resources beyond this text, some of which are provided in appendix 6. A thoughtful step in professional responsibility would be in completing an **allyship** or Safe Zone training, which are provided through GLSEN and local LGBTQ+ resource centers. There are several steps all teachers can implement to demonstrate acceptance of TGQ students, including:

- adding pronouns to one's e-mail signature to make their gender identity public and to empower others to do the same;
- display a safe space sign on their office door or in a conspicuous place; and
- revise studio documents to be welcoming of all genders, which might include modifying assumptive language and inviting students to share their pronouns.

Professional responsibility is discussed by Kozan, who says that vocal clinicians "must have sufficient knowledge not only to 'do no harm' but also to know how to 'do good,' to skillfully judge and shape vocal behaviors."[21] The singing teachers I observed provided skillful vocal knowledge alongside emotional, mental, and social support. In recognizing that teachers cannot know everything, Kozan offers a model in collaborating with a student to avoid "othering" by allowing them to guide and position the direction of learning. When speaking with a voice client, she shares, "I also work from the philosophy that you are the teacher and I am the student. . . . I ask you to bring up your observations about your voice and your experiences concerning anything and everything that could possibly have an effect on your voice . . . as if we were putting a giant puzzle together. Each piece of information could provide another piece to the puzzle."[22] In this framework, teacher and student co-construct knowledge without the need for the teacher to ask personal or probing questions. The teacher is designing a space to learn through critical and empathetic listening, instead of overloading the student with their learned know-how.

Research on independent music teachers indicates that studio teachers are already engaging in professional development.[23]

In a study looking at the characteristics of independent studio teachers, data indicate teachers regularly engage in professional development activities to improve their pedagogical skills, noting that singing teachers "appeared to be continually reflecting on their pedagogy while building their pedagogical knowledge."[24] To this end, singing teachers are encouraged to include gender inclusivity and diversity training in their ongoing development. Teacher-researchers might also continue empirical research on TGQ singing to further develop our collective knowledge. As both Eli and Naomi noted, the emerging research on TGQ singing is only the beginning; teachers and vocal pedagogues have a professional responsibility to update and construct new knowledge.

Nurturing Self-Advocacy

All students in this study were "out" in their daily lives as trans or nonbinary, and many of them spoke about being advocates and/or activists for TGQ rights. Kelly, B, Peter, Eli, and Forest are all intentionally working to modify policies and practices that marginalize TGQ performers in their communities. The efforts and attitudes regarding this form of activism are being framed as **self-advocacy**, defined specifically as speaking up for one's own beliefs, interests, or rights. While some examples of activism might also be perceived as self-agency, self-efficacy, or self-determination, self-advocacy seems the most appropriate term for this analysis, as advocacy efforts have long been a part of the LGBTQ+ community. Either through the creation of their music or in the outspokenness of their gender identity, the participants facilitate change in their local communities or further afield to create greater awareness of TGQ singers.

Based on their experiences in musical theater auditions, Kelly partnered with the organizing company of a citywide audition to modify the gender options on the audition profile form. When Kelly first auditioned, the form listed two options: male or female. Now, at Kelly's recommendation, the form enables an auditionee to write in their gender. Commenting further on gender issues in musical theater, Kelly says, "The biggest [issue] is how they phrase their audition calls.... That is the first thing that will turn people away from [auditioning for] a role; trans and nonbinary people aren't even going to walk in the room." While Kelly has as yet been unable to make any changes in how theater companies advertise auditions, the updated language on the audition form is a start toward enacting further policy changes. Kelly is also trying to be an agent of change at their online school. They explained, "The school I go to online won't let me use my [chosen] name on my ID.... I'm fighting with the administration right now." Despite requests to instructors and classmates, Kelly frequently gets called by their **deadname**, that is, the name they were assigned at birth. In some locations, such as California, deadnaming is legally considered a form of harassment after the person has identified themselves by their chosen name.

Both Kelly and B are activists as music makers. Kelly sings in a trans and nonbinary choir that actively repudiates traditions in choral music. In addition to removing traditional voice parts (soprano, alto, tenor, bass) from the choir, the members are given the opportunity to provide input on song selection, which Kelly loves. The members are also given agency from the chorus leadership to modify lyrics (if legally possible) or to cut a song from a program if it "doesn't really align with what we stand for," Kelly said. B is also highly involved in music making as a form of activism. As a founding member of a band made up of nonbinary, masculine-of-center musicians, their mission is to perform original and cover songs that address genderqueerness and the experiences of trans people of color. B explained that one purpose of the ensemble is to communicate through song the experiences of queer, trans, and people of color to audiences who do not have a window into those narratives. The group performs locally but has a growing presence with more and more national touring.

Eli and Peter practice TGQ advocacy through their teaching. Peter is open about his trans identity and purposefully cultivates a safe space for TGQ singers. His studio is made up of about one-third students who are TGQ, and he has a public presence in creating an affirming studio environment. Similarly, Eli actively works to create musical spaces for TGQ musicians and organizes group music classes specifically for this population. Eli performs throughout the United States as a singer-songwriter, and he is a blogger who has written about inclusive practices for teaching TGQ singers in the applied studio.

In addition to the teacher self-advocacy modeled by Peter and Eli, as a camp counselor-teacher, Forest talked about including queer characters in the plays he puts on with the summer camp attendees. He said, "The kids have just gotten so excited to be presented in the literature that we do." The inclusion of queer characters is important to Forest because he never saw himself represented in the shows he performed in as a youngster.

Discussion

Advocacy has long been a tool of the LGBTQ+ community seeking equality and equity. PFLAG, the well-known parents' group supporting LGBTQ+ youth, has upheld the banner of advocacy since its founding in 1973.[25] Pride flags, parades, and festivals all serve as forms of communal advocacy and activism for the LGBTQ+ community. As illustrated through the portraits in this book, TGQ students and their teachers demonstrated self-advocacy in their singing lessons and other musical endeavors.

Self-advocacy is adjacent to the theory of self-efficacy developed by psychologist Albert Bandura, who perceives that self-efficacy is rooted in the "judgments of how well one can execute courses of action required to deal with prospective situations."[26] Individuals with a high degree of self-efficacy feel able to put forth greater energy toward mastering challenges or overturning obstacles. For the TQG participants in this study, such obstacles included gender oppression, marginalization, and transphobia. "Judgments of self-efficacy," Bandura explains, "also determine how much effort people will expend and how long they will persist in the face of obstacles or aversive experiences."[27] The student contributors in this study show clear volition to incite changes in their communities and in the cultural perceptions of TGQ individuals. A person's level of support from their teachers, family, and communities might determine the endurance of their self-advocacy and self-efficacy.

The importance of **role models** was mentioned by three participants in this study. Isabella spoke at length about the importance of Martha, her singing teacher, in her life as a role model. B shared that they struggled in college having no teacher or role model to emulate. For their cisgender counterparts, B remarked, "There were models for them to fall into . . . there were teachers who looked and sounded like them for them to follow." Kelly talked about the benefit of studying with Peter, who has encountered similar experiences of gender oppression. This support enhances Kelly's ability to be outspoken about audition policies and other instances of marginalization.

Time magazine's June 2014 cover article, called "The Transgender Tipping Point," posits, "Transgender people . . . are emerging from the margins to fight for an equal place in society. This new transparency is improving the lives of a long misunderstood minority and beginning to yield new policies, as trans activists and their supporters push for changes in schools, hospitals, workplaces, prisons and the military."[28] This titular "tipping point" might be fueled by an awareness of communal self-advocacy. Bandura notes, "People who have a sense of collective efficacy will mobilize their efforts and resources to cope with external obstacles to the changes they seek."[29] B and Kelly, who participate in TGQ vocal ensembles, see themselves as participants in a larger movement of music as activism. In the last decade, several choruses for trans and nonbinary singers have been established in Atlanta, Boston, Chicago, Los Angeles, Kansas City, Manchester (NH), Portland, and San Francisco, to name a few.[30] This growing movement follows a history of gay and lesbian choruses making music as an action against social injustices.[31]

It is important to note that in this study, self-advocacy was not only modeled in changing policies or in organizing classes or concerts specifically for TGQ musicians. Self-advocacy was also exemplified by Emmett every time he appeared on the concert stage in a tuxedo, performing as a mezzo-soprano, prior to his transition. In each performance, he further loosened the constraints of concert conventions and gender conformity. Another trans opera singer asserts, "My goal as an artist and activist and transgender woman is to encourage a much bigger trans presence in classical music, and especially in opera."[32] This singer, alongside the singer participants in this study, suggests that, at least for now, trans and genderqueer artistry is a form of activism that advances a collective advocacy for the TGQ population. It is valuable for teachers of TGQ students to understand that practicing self-advocacy might be important to their students. Teachers might also nurture self-advocacy in their students by allowing them space and support to speak up for their beliefs and interests.

Providing Socioemotional Support

Students and teachers alike discussed the social and emotional support present in the applied studio. In this study, the students were effusive in discussing the compassion and affirmation experienced in their lessons. Teachers spoke about creating a conducive learning environment and developing rapport. A common pattern in the data showed that students felt emotionally supported by their teachers. There was an overlap in how the students reported feeling emotionally supported and in the description of mentorship teachers provided them. While the interviews offered testimonies of emotional support, lesson observations gave visible and discerning attestation of emotional support in the one-on-one instruction.

Students described their teachers as supportive, compassionate, and affirming. Kelly shared that lessons with Peter have helped them become more comfortable with their identity. "It's like therapy," Kelly explains, "I've gotten healthier. I've been taking better care of myself since taking lessons. It's more than just singing for an hour." After auditioning for a musical theater company that caused Kelly to feel dysphoric, they felt emotionally depleted, recounting, "The next day I had a lesson and I was just really emotional. I'd also been experiencing a lot of dysphoria, and [Peter] could tell I was upset. We spent [time] talking about all the stuff we have to go through. That was really nice to be able to talk to someone and to know I'm not alone. It felt great to talk to him about that."

Peter talked about the importance of teaching students as individuals and "to always be compassionate and respectful, to treat people as they present themselves as, or see themselves as." Peter is upfront with his studio policies to ensure all students, trans or otherwise, feel safe and protected in his studio. He shared, "It's so meaningful to me to provide a space where people can be themselves and not be made to feel differently. I think that's one of the best things about the work I do. . . . To make a human connection where they feel seen and heard is so important."

Peter strives to treat each student as an individual because his own vocal training in college was formulaic and dehumanizing. He explains, "I'm teaching a whole person, and I don't think you can really separate the person from the instrument, which is the experience I had at [college]. I was just treated like an instrument."

Though Peter is the most ebullient about compassion and support in the applied studio, other participants shared similar sentiments. The learning in singing lessons sometimes goes beyond vocal development, with Chrys commenting, "Everything about life, I learned from my voice teacher." Not only does Chrys feel supported in her vocal development, the support and accountability of lessons extends to other aspects of her everyday life, a sentiment also shared by Forest.

Emmett depicted Naomi as "compassionate" and as someone he trusts to help him develop his voice, which he compares to a person's "lifeblood." As a self-deprecating individual, Emmett was quick to be self-critical of his voice. With gentleness and grace, Naomi offered an optimistic posture and gave him little room to degrade himself. Darius was also cognizant of showing compassion and respect to his students. Whenever Forest, Darius's student, made a mistake, Darius would meet him in the lesson wherever the tasks led them, without shaming or judgment. In maintaining presence with each student, Darius articulated, "What I do is try to listen and learn and hear it through their language, their voice, and their body language what's going on with them." For each of these teacher-student pairs, there is a level of heightened rapport that extends beyond respect and familiarity.

Through interactions, body language, and a sense of togetherness, the teachers and students share a meaningful kinship. The data reveal that students were given emotional safety and support through anchored and authentic openness and acceptance. While not all students need emotional support continuously, they seem aware that their teacher's studio is a space where they will be seen and heard as their authentic selves. This emotional support appeared as compassion, kindness, and trust, enabling students to explore their artful expressiveness through their singing without fear of discrimination or marginalization.

Discussion

Crafting learning environments that are open, affirming, and safe has been the keystone to much of the related scholarship in music education. On applied instruction, Sims affirms, "Your job as a voice teacher is to teach singing and provide a supportive safe space for your transgender students just as you do for your cisgender students."[33] These articles, as well as literature from choral music education, suggest that gender-affirming learning spaces are sensitive to gender-neutral language, repertoire, and performance attire.[34] A major takeaway from this study indicates that teachers who craft open and safe studios offer socioemotional support to students in their applied lessons. This element of support in the applied studio is a clear departure from the traditional master-apprentice instructional model.

In the study by Duke and Simmons mentioned earlier, the researchers examined three master artist-teachers employed at prominent American music schools. From the nineteen common characteristics Duke and Simmons found in the applied studio instruction, teachers frequently gave negative feedback with clear intent. Positive feedback was infrequent yet protracted to give emphasis. In a replication of that study, Parkes and Wexler found similar characteristics of teaching with a few distinctions.

One finding of Parkes and Wexler suggests that applied studio instructors "tailored their teaching to fit the needs of their students, responding to . . . the need for instructional specificity, structure, and technical guidance as well as emotional support."[35] Parkes and Wexler discovered that studio teachers are more attuned to student emotional needs and teach differently to accommodate unique student situations.

Research in applied studio teaching has also identified rapport as a primary element in the applied music studio.[36] In a study on rapport in the applied studio, Mary Jo Clemmons suggests, "The one-to-one nature of applied instruction . . . encourages an interpersonal relationship between the applied teacher and the music student that tends to create an emotional connection between teacher and student."[37] Clemmons argues that the nature of a teacher's pedagogy and the "emotional climate" established by rapport is linked to student learning outcomes.[38] While it seems obvious, a teacher's emotional state influences student emotion and behavior. Strong teacher-student rapport and emotional connection as components of teaching in the applied studio are upheld by the current study.

Peter spoke effusively about his challenging undergraduate experience as a vocal performance major at a prestigious music conservatory in the United States. He shared that he was treated as an instrument, not as a unique human, and that he felt there was a lack of connection and care demonstrated by his voice teacher. As a teacher now, he ensures his students are emotionally supported in his studio. Peter's approach to teaching aligns with an earlier finding of Clemmons, who said, "Teachers do not treat their students as 'just a voice,' but are concerned with their personal and emotional lives."[39] Although Peter is a trans man and his student Kelly is nonbinary, they have a special bond because they have experienced similar marginalization and oppression. There is also evidence of a heightened emotional connection between Forest and Darius. Although as a gay man Darius is unable to fully understand Forest's lived experiences as trans, there is a kinship between student and teacher that sanctions an emotional support that extends beyond rapport.

While the data in this study indicate that learning moved quickly and students met learning targets, emotional support moved beyond basic encouragement, compliments, or words of confidence. It was more than mere sensitivity to gender-neutral language. It reached further than student accommodation and differential teaching styles. It was deeper than any effort to create rapport or a safe space for students to flourish. This emotional support was ineffable, yet it was seen and felt in the lessons.

Chapter Takeaways

The goal of this chapter was to offer some practical considerations for crafting a gender- affirming teaching approach. I situated the five pedagogical recommendations within context of my research and related literature. The teaching considerations that are a result of this study are applicable to applied studio teachers and ensemble conductors. Queering vocal pedagogy is rooted in the TGQ singers and teachers who participated in this study, and as such, the pedagogical considerations discussed in this chapter correlate to their experiences and perspectives.

Below are some key takeaways, but please keep in mind that these suggestions are neither conclusive nor exhaustive. One caveat to this list is that reading it out of context to the portraits and discussions above might elicit reductive or inaccurate interpretations. Likewise, this list does not mean to imply that affirmative teaching strategies for TGQ students can be reduced to a litany of actions. Not only does affirmative teaching need to be personal and intentional, like queering vocal pedagogy, it is should be an iterative, reflective, and flexible practice through lifelong engagement.

Recognizing Gender Implication in Musical Spaces

- Gendering in music spaces is subtle and pervasive. Be familiar with TGQ language and heighten your use of

gender-neutral language. (Appendix 1 offers a vocabulary list.)
- Recognize that while music has enabled some students to explore gender identity, gendering in music can incite dysphoria.
- Teachers should be sensitive to how expectations of gender may permeate their practices and cause potential adversity to students.
- Vocal types/sections (SATB) convey implied gender. Allow students to choose how their voice types are listed in concert programs, if at all.
- Repertoire and stage roles (in opera and musical theater) sometimes reify gender stereotypes. Be mindful if assigning repertoire and roles due to problematic gender expectations.
- Gender roles in repertoire might cause students to feel dysphoric. Enable students to pick or suggest their own repertoire.
- Providing repertoire options and musical theatre/opera roles that were written for TGQ performers or by TGQ composers might make a student feel seen and valued. Appendices 2 and 3 provide a list of songs and musicals.
- Gendered concert attire can be affirming for some students while causing dysphoria in others. Allowing students to wear "concert black attire" empowers each student to select an outfit appropriate for them. Appendix 4 provides student guidelines for choosing concert attire.

Teaching Vocal Technique

- Vocal exercises should be constructed to foster range development, registration, breathing, resonance, and articulation.
- Craft vocal exercises that promote efficient production and be perceptive to how vocal identity and gender are linked.
- Some nonbinary students might be seeking a lower or higher range to align with their identity without hormone replace therapy.

- Consider the balance of vocal registers important to avoid "pushing" in one area of the range.
- Repertoire should be selected with student involvement.
- Change the key of a song to match a singer's range.
- For a student on testosterone, keep them singing during the initial vocal transition, so long as singing causes no pain.
- For a singer newly on testosterone, let them know that their voice might crack or sound hoarse initially. Be mindful of vocal fatigue; use small intervals and soft, supported singing at first.
- The effects of testosterone on the voice might be longer lasting than previous research has observed. Monitor how the voice may continue to change, even after the first two years of hormone replacement therapy.
- Find the pitch zone of the student's voice that is easiest for them and work outward to increase range.
- If a student's goals are unrealistic, the teacher might need to set reasonable expectations of vocal development. If a student desires a timbre or range beyond the possible scope of their voice, sensitively address this with them. Collaboration with a therapist, speech-language pathologist, or parent might be helpful.
- As with any student, vocal development might be experienced in spurts. Be supportive and allow a student's authentic voice to emerge.
- Have no fear: Voice lessons with TGQ students follow similar patterns of teaching any singer.

Embodying Professional Responsibility

- Be aware that singing lessons may form a part of a student's vocal transition.
- Avoid "othering" students or asking for information about being TGQ.
- Teachers are responsible for doing their own "homework" to learn about student needs. There is an emerging body of research in print and at conferences.

- Engage in research and scholarly activities to promote continual learning in teaching a wider spectrum of singers.
- Find TGQ performers in your community and attend their performances to show support.
- Include a gender-affirmation and safety policy on a studio website or print materials. See appendix 5 for sample language.
- Complete an allyship or Safe Zone training through a GLSEN chapter or your local LGBTQ+ resource center.
- Additional resources and website links are provided in appendix 6.

Nurturing Self-Advocacy

- Students have demonstrated self-advocacy to decrease gender-oppressive practices and policies in their communities.
- Be proactive to establish practices and policies that affirm all students.
- Allow students to have autonomy and self-agency in their vocal development.
- Serve as a student's advocate when support is necessary.

Providing Socioemotional Support

- Practice empathetic listening; listen to learn.
- Provide emotional support as appropriate.
- Value a student's emotional and mental health as much as their vocal health.
- Treat all singers as individuals.
- Respond to student needs and interests.
- Be aware that TGQ students might confide in a music teacher more than other adults due to the bond developed during music lessons.

Notes

1. Donald G. Hackmann, "Using Portraiture in Educational Leadership Research, "*International Journal of Leadership in Education* 5, no. 1 (2002): 53.
2. Sara Lawrence-Lightfoot and Jessica Hoffmann Davis, *The Art and Science of Portraiture* (San Francisco: Jossey-Bass, 1997).
3. Kathleen E. Rands, "Considering Transgender People in Education," *Journal of Teacher Education* 60, no. 4 (2009): 419.
4. Ibid., 426.
5. Ibid., 424.
6. Loraine Sims, "Teaching Transgender Students," *Journal of Singing* 73, no. 1 (2017): 280
7. Aiden K. Feltkamp, *Anthology of New Music: Trans & Nonbinary Voices, Vol. 1*, NewMusicShelf, accessed November 23, 2021, https://newmusicshelf.com/product/trans-nonbinary-v1/.
8. Allpin Penrose, "Imagining the Trans Symphony: Integrating Transgender Composer Identity in Music Analysis," (Master's thesis, University of Massachusetts, Amherst, 2021), https://doi.org/10.7275/22227588.0.
9. Alexandros Constansis, "The Changing Female-to-Male (FTM) Voice," *Radical Musicology* 3 (2008), http://www.radical-musicology.org.uk/2008/Constansis.htm; Anita Kozan, "The Singing Voice," in *Voice and Communication Therapy for the Transgender/Transsexual Client: A Comprehensive Clinical Guide*, ed. Robert K. Adler, Sandy Hirsch, and Michelle Mordaunt, 2nd ed. (San Diego, CA: Plural, 2012); Emerald Lessley, "Teaching Transgender Singers," (DMA diss., University of Washington, 2017); Sims, "Teaching Transgender Students," 2017.
10. Constansis, "The Changing Female-to-Male (FTM) Voice," para. 34.
11. Kozan, "The Singing Voice," 420.
12. Ibid.
13. Ibid.
14. Sims, "Teaching Transgender Students," 280.
15. Kozan, "The Singing Voice," 418.
16. Barbara M. Doscher, *The Functional Unity of the Singing Voice* (Metuchen, NJ: Scarecrow Press, 1994); James C. McKinney, *The Diagnosis & Correction of Vocal Faults: A Manual for Teachers of Singing and for Choir Directors* (Nashville, TN: Genevox Music Group, 1994).
17. Doscher, *The Functional Unity of the Singing Voice*, 186.
18. Kelly A. Parkes and Mathius Wexler, "The Nature of Applied Music Teaching Expertise: Common Elements Observed in the Lessons of Three Applied Teachers," *Bulletin of the Council for Research in Music Education*, no. 193 (2012): 45–62, https://doi.org/10.5406/bulcouresmusedu.193.0045.
19. Ibid., 53.
20. Loraine Sims, "Teaching Lucas: A Transgender Student's Vocal Journey from Soprano to Tenor," *Journal of Singing* 73, no. 4 (2017): 374

21. Kozan, "The Singing Voice," 415.
22. Ibid.
23. Rena Upitis et al., "Characteristics of Independent Music Teachers," *Music Education Research* 19, no. 2 (2016): 169–94, https://doi.org/10.1080/14613808.2016.1204277.
24. Ibid., 181.
25. "Intro to Advocacy," PFLAG, last modified September 30, 2021, https://pflag.org/AdvocacyTools/IntroToAdvocacy.
26. Albert Bandura, "Self-Efficacy Mechanism in Human Agency.," *American Psychologist* 37, no. 2 (1982): 122, https://doi.org/10.1037/0003-066x.37.2.122.
27. Ibid., 123.
28. Katy Steinmetz, "The Transgender Tipping Point: America's Next Civil Rights Frontier," *Time*, June 9, 2014, 38
29. Bandura, "Self-Efficacy Mechanism," 144.
30. C. J. Janovy, "Transgender Choruses Harness the (Changing) Power of Voices," NPR, May 21, 2016, https://www.npr.org/sections/deceptivecadence/2016/05/21/478863157/transgender-choruses-harness-the-changing-power-of-voices#:~:text=More%20Podcasts%20%26%20Shows-,Transgender%20Choruses%20Harness%20The%20(Changing)%20Power%20Of%20Voices%20%3A%20Deceptive,a%20group%20about%20to%20debut.
31. Julia Balén, *A Queerly Joyful Noise: Choral Musicking for Social Justice* (New Brunswick, NJ: Rutgers University Press, 2017).
32. Brian Manternach, "Teaching Transgender Singers: Part 2," *Journal of Singing* 74, no. 2 (2017): 210.
33. Sims, "Teaching Transgender Students," 281.
34. Ari Agha, "Making Your Chorus Welcoming for Transgender Singers," *Voice* 41, no. 2 (2017): 18–23; Jane Ramseyer Miller, "Creating Choirs That Welcome Transgender Singers," *Choral Journal* 57, no. 4 (2016): 61–63; Joshua Palkki, "Inclusivity in Action: Transgender Students in the Choral Classroom," *Choral Journal* 57, no. 11 (2017): 25–33.
35. Parkes and Wexler, "The Nature of Applied Music Teaching Expertise," 55.
36. Harold F. Abeles, "Student Perceptions of Characteristics of Effective Applied Music Instructors," *Journal of Research in Music Education* 23, no. 2 (1975): 147–54; Mary Jo Clemmons, *Rapport in the Applied Voice Studio* (EdD diss., Teachers College, Columbia University, 2007); Richard T. Walls et al., "The Characteristics of Effective and Ineffective Teachers," *Teacher Education Quarterly* 29, no. 1 (2002): 39–48.
37. Clemmons, *Rapport in the Applied Voice Studio*, 9.
38. Ibid., 37.
39. Ibid., 221.

7

Queering as a Teacher's Habit of Mind

> "Change does not come easily. It requires letting go of old habits and traditions and embracing a new mental model for this century and for the students we teach now. It means preparing these students for a world that is vastly different from the world that most of us were educated in."
>
> —Bena Kallick and Allison Zmuda in *Students at the Center: Personalized Learning with Habits of Mind*

First developed in the 1980s, **habits of mind** is an academic framework for teaching learners to engage in the classroom and world with critical thinking skills, empathy, and an intellectual nature. Considered a set of dispositions, habits of mind extend beyond discipline-specific skills or knowledge. Though this might be too reductive, developing habits of mind in students is helping them interact and examine life's challenges rationally, methodically, constructively, and creatively. In a four-part book series on habits of mind, editors Arthur Costa and Bena Kallick, the cofounders of the Institute for Habits of Mind, propose the following sixteen habits of mind:

1. Persisting
2. Managing impulsivity

3. Listening with understanding and empathy
4. Thinking flexibly
5. Thinking about thinking (metacognition)
6. Striving for accuracy
7. Questioning and posing problems
8. Applying past knowledge to new situations
9. Thinking and communicating with clarity and precision
10. Gathering data through all senses
11. Creating, imagining, innovating
12. Responding with wonderment and awe
13. Taking responsible risks
14. Finding humor
15. Thinking interdependently
16. Remaining open to continuous learning[1]

Singing teachers and choral directors should hopefully see the work they do within these dispositions. The connections between teaching singers, developing skills beyond music making, and fostering these dispositions are numerous, even for teachers who might not be familiar with the concept of habits of mind or with the notion that we can develop these dispositions in our students through our teaching. As I reflect on the list above, I think of many students (or myself as a learner and teacher) learning to persist, taking risks, being flexible, and striving for accuracy through repertoire, roles, and techniques of singing and performing.

A link between habits of mind and studio art teachers has been established and discussed by Project Zero of Harvard's Graduate School of Education, offering eight habits of mind for studio teachers: (1) developing craft, (2) understanding art worlds, (3) engaging and persisting, (4) stretching and exploring, (5) envisioning, (6) reflecting, (7) expressing, and (8) observing.[2] Though developed with visual art teachers in mind, these eight dispositions apply seamlessly in the applied voice studio, offering "a shift toward a broader conception of educational outcomes."[3] We can see that within these eight habits of mind the disposition of "developing craft"—which for singing teachers might include broadening range, refining diction, balancing registers, or polishing stylistic choices—is just one aspect of studio instruction.

While habits of mind are often discussed as dispositions to be developed within students, as an educator, I use these dispositions to inform, reexamine, and modify my pedagogy and teaching approaches. The active voice of these dispositions (meaning, the "-ing" construction of the language) to me suggests a progressive, continuous, and iterative engagement with them. Calling this book *Queering Vocal Pedagogy* draws specific attention to habits of mind in the hopes of evoking a perpetual act of reenvisioning and shifting vocal pedagogy to be more welcoming and affirming of trans and genderqueer singers. If queering becomes a habit of mind for vocal pedagogy, it inspires uninterrupted querying and lifelong learning for both teachers and students. It would, after all, be un-queer to make queering stagnant or normative.

My observations at professional conferences and of online discussion forums reveal that singing teachers are already practicing lifelong learning through acquiring new music (the *what* of teaching) and differentiating approaches (the *how* of teaching). Habits of mind serves as structure to not only further support continuous learning, but to highlight the *who* of teaching, advocating for greater diversity of singers within studio vocal instruction. Queering as a habit of mind invites us to question, problematize, and assess all domains of vocal pedagogy: the who, what, how, where, and when of teaching singers.

Some discourse on teaching trans and genderqueer singers has focused solely on technique. Other scholarship has addressed the need for greater inclusivity. Thinking about vocal technique and inclusivity of TGQ singers in vocal pedagogy is valuable, but it might fall short of enacting an authentic change that is suggested in an act of queering. Inclusivity fails to be wholly welcoming and affirming if the space in which an individual is being included is one that upholds gender-oppressive traditions. Music educator/philosopher Elizabeth Gould discusses the value of queering as a movement toward a model of "companion-able species," where teachers and students, as companions, cocreate learning and teaching.

This shifting away from a master-apprentice model toward a focus on student-centeredness (or perhaps, a companionable-centeredness) is tethered to habits of mind when teachers empower students to direct their own learning for individualized and personalized learning.[4] Singing teachers might want to think beyond initial steps of student-centeredness, such as allowing students to choose their own repertoire or decide their performance attire, and into deeper levels of vocal development, including the construction of vocal exercises, lesson pacing, goal setting, and even timbre and vocal technique aspirations.

Centering students within teaching includes "listening with understanding and empathy," which means listening with our ears and hearts to validate and honor the desires, needs, and curiosities of each student. In discussing music teaching and brain science, vocologist and vocal pedagogue Lynn Helding explains that humans have a large capacity for empathy but tend to demonstrate higher levels of empathy for individuals closest to and most like themselves. Based on findings from social psychology studies, Helding expounds, "Most disturbing is our propensity to favor those most like ourselves and to withhold empathy from those we perceive to be very different from ourselves."[5] If we accept these studies as true, singing teachers, by the very nature of our biases, must strive to share authentic empathy and compassion for students whose identities, ideologies, and vocal desires are unlike our own. This empathy might be found in making what Karin Hendricks calls an "authentic connection," which she argues is not only necessary in music teaching and learning but also requires personal authenticity. She posits that if we are not wholly authentic with ourselves, it is challenging to make genuine connections with others around us, even those persons with whom we spend time and energy.

For students who are trans or genderqueer, and for the students who might still be questioning their identity or have not yet come to realize their gender identity (or lack thereof), being open and honest with a teacher is a step toward making an authentic connection. Empathy and compassion as demonstrated by a teacher fosters this possibility. According to Hendricks, scientists have observed that energy is exchanged between a person's heart and mind, but is also exchanged from person to person.[6] Thus, Hendricks articulates, "Heart waves in one person can influence brain and heart activity in another person who is nearby."[7] The need for TGQ students to be fully open and unguarded with their singing teacher is not only healthier for them, it impacts student-teacher rapport, studio climate, and the energy in teaching. If we ask a singer to take risks and be vulnerable in lessons and performances, many of us are requesting a student to have an open throat, open face, open mind, and open heart. How can we expect this of students who do not feel valued and affirmed during their vocal training?

In speaking with a fellow genderqueer teacher, I was reminded that "coming out" as LGBTQ+ is not a way of showing difference; it is essentially a process of making an authentic connection with others, of being seen, vulnerable, authentic, and true to one's self. Making an authentic connection requires time, openness, and vulnerability of all people. Students who do not feel compassion and affirmation from their teachers should not be afraid to move on and find another teacher; conversely, teachers might want to consider referring a student to another teacher with whom they might make a better connection, as this might be in the best interest of a student who is struggling in the studio for any reason. Teachers ought not blame themselves for not being able to connect authentically with each student who seeks vocal training. Indeed, if a singing teacher is unable to accept a student with empathy and compassion, it might be best to help them find an alternative teacher.

In the spirt of continual self-reflection and the "questioning and posing problems" habit of mind, here is list of scenarios that studio teachers and choral directors might encounter in their teaching lives. I encourage you to consider how you might respond in each of these situations, discuss them with friends, and problematize them to foster deeper and more critical thinking. Consider "What should I do?" for each scenario below.

- A student has recently revealed they are trans and wishes to go by another name.

- A student has shared with you their chosen name but does not want their parents to know.
- A trans male student wants to sing tenor, but his vocal range sits more naturally as an alto.
- A nonbinary student feels dysphoric in the dress their parents have purchased for an upcoming performance.
- You notice a student using transphobic language among their friends.
- A student is about to begin androgen therapy, but he is scared he won't be able to sing after his transition.
- A student informs you that they will be taking hormone blockers to stop the onset of puberty.
- A trans woman wants to be in a "women's" SSAA ensemble, but her voice is more appropriate to sing baritone or bass.
- A countertenor wants to sing in an SSAA ensemble.
- You have unintentionally misgendered someone.
- A colleague (i.e., collaborative pianist, stage director, choreographer) has misgendered one of your students more than once.
- A genderqueer student indicates their voice is hoarse and tired all the time.
- A gender-nonconforming alto wants to sing in a women's chorus.
- Many choral students want to wear traditional choral dresses and tuxedos, but you wish to steer away from gendered performance attire.
- On an overnight trip, a student feels uncomfortable rooming with a trans student.
- You want to change the name of a beloved and popular chorus to a name that is non–gender specific, but administration or chorus leadership is reluctant.
- A colleague feels your "safe space" sticker in your studio is politically inappropriate.
- A trans student is wearing the show choir performance attire that aligns with their gender identity, yet you think judges are docking your overall score for it.

- You have selected a concert of repertoire by women composers and your male students feel excluded in this concert.
- You live in a community where transphobia is pervasive.
- Your belief system tells you that LGBTQ+ students are abnormal or would be better off if they were straight and cisgender.

Final Thoughts

In a small Midwestern town of the United States, not far from my current residence, a teacher had a rainbow flag hanging in her classroom to show support of LGBTQ+ students. This flag remained on her wall for years until a parent filed a complaint with the school board. It was deemed a "controversial matter" and the school board unanimously approved a new policy stating that any symbol considered "controversial"—even the Pride flag, a global symbol of peace and acceptance—must be removed from educational spaces. The language of the policy reads, in part, "The teacher is responsible for creating a learning environment in which all students and staff are respected."[8] Not only does this policy impact symbols in the classroom, it extends to curricular choices, too. Teachers in the school district must now have any potential "controversial" topics approved by the principal before teaching them in their classes.

In the United States, teachers should be vessels for critical thinking, open-mindedness, and the exchange of discrete ideologies. As policies like the one above along with laws banning critical race theory[9] begin to stymie how teachers engage with learners, it is important we understand how to (re)interpret policies that attempt to muffle diverse voices. When queer theory is applied to policy texts, it renders new possibilities. In the "controversial matter" case above, though teachers are responsible for creating a respectful classroom, the policy further states that teachers must not advocate "a particular point of view."[10] A queer reading of these words suggests that teachers must then infuse curricula with *more* diverse perspectives. A music curriculum should amplify music of LGBTQ+, women, and composers of colors from a wide variety of styles to ensure young musicians are not "indoctrinated" in a single genre or kind of music.

Studio teachers are often guided by tradition and the policies of the competitions and professional organizations to which they subscribe. No matter the geographical location of a singing teacher, they play a role in shaping culture, thoughts, and ideas. How they interpret policies impacts not only their students' experiences but the students of their students—unless a pattern of "teaching as I was taught" is interrupted. Queering as a habit of mind cultivates a repetition of investigating and innovating teaching to rebuke a cis-normative mindset, whether that impacts educational policies or vocal pedagogy.

The LGBTQ+ community is a vast and beautiful array of diverse identities and ideologies. Even though these identities are often grouped together, it does not mean that all members from within this community accept one another. Discrimination and marginalization exists within the LGBTQ+ population.[11] Not all gay, lesbian, and bisexual singing teachers know how or even have any desire to teach TGQ singers. Sadly, I have found that even within the TGQ population there is a lack of mutual respect and understanding. As a genderqueer singer, teacher, and author of this book, I still have much to learn in teaching TGQ students—as it should be. Queering vocal pedagogy is a process of affirming TGQ singers within the vocal arts by dismantling hegemonies by means of deep listening, reflection, and connecting toward greater empathy and compassion. If queering vocal pedagogy is effective, it will unfetter multiple pathways to teach and authenticate all singers with diverse goals, potentials, and identities.

Finally, calling on the wisdom of Anita Kozan once more, the author and teacher says that in teaching trans and genderqueer singers, "Each of us feels called to do the amazing work of helping to heal the planet by touching the lives of the singers who come to us."[12] Kozan's inspirational words are a reminder of the greater good in teaching singing. Advocacy and awareness of TGQ individuals has increased enormously in recent years, and yet we know that TGQ people still suffer high levels of bullying in school, face discrimination within their communities, and are considered perverse by a great many people (even from within their own communities and the LGBTQ+ populace). Sadly and alarmingly, more than fifteen hundred trans individuals worldwide have died by murder or suicide in the five years I have been researching and writing this book.[13] I do not mean to end this book with such heart-wrenching data, but I think it is necessary to remember that our opportunity to make the planet a better, safer, and braver place through vocal music is needed, genuine, and indispensable.

Notes

1. Arthur L. Costa and Bena Kallick, *Activating & Engaging Habits of Mind* (Alexandria, VA: Association for Supervision and Curriculum Development, 2000), xiii.
2. "Eight Habits of Mind," Project Zero, accessed October 14, 2021, http://www.pz.harvard.edu/resources/eight-habits-of-mind.
3. Costa and Kallick, *Activating & Engaging Habits of Mind*, xiv.
4. Bena Kallick and Allison Zmuda, *Students at the Center: Personalized Learning with Habits of Mind* (Alexandria, VA: Association for Supervision and Curriculum Development, 2017).
5. Lynn Helding, *The Musician's Mind: Teaching, Learning, and Performance in the Age of Brain Science* (Lanham, MD: Rowman & Littlefield, 2020), 302.
6. Karin S. Hendricks, *Compassionate Music Teaching: A Framework for Motivation and Engagement in the 21st Century* (Lanham, MD: Rowman & Littlefield, 2018), 145.
7. Ibid.
8. Taylor Williams, "Bluffton-Harrison School Board Makes Changes to Policy Regarding Pride Flag," WANE 15, September 9, 2021, https://www.wane.com/top-stories/bluffton-harrison-school-board-makes-changes-to-policy-regarding-pride-flag/.
9. Jason Kao and Isabella Zou, "Texas Teachers Say GOP's New Social Studies Law Will Hinder How an Entire Generation Understands Race, History and Current Events," *Texas Tribune*, August 3, 2021, https://www.texastribune.org/2021/08/03/texas-critical-race-theory-social-studies-teachers/.
10. Williams, "Bluffton-Harrison School Board."
11. Alim Kheraj, "'I Was Given Training to De-Gay My Voice': What It's Really like to Work in TV If You're LGBTQ+," *Guardian*, December 1,

2021, https://amp.theguardian.com/tv-and-radio/2021/dec/01/i-was-given-training-to-de-gay-my-voice-what-its-really-like-to-work-in-tv-if-youre-lgbtq.

12. Anita Kozan, "The Singing Voice," in *Voice and Communication Therapy for the Transgender/Transsexual Client: A Comprehensive Clinical Guide*, ed. Robert K. Adler, Sandy Hirsch, and Michelle Mordaunt, 2nd ed. (San Diego, CA: Plural, 2012), 457.

13. "Remembering Our Dead," Transgender Day of Remembrance, accessed December 1, 2021, https://tdor.translivesmatter.info/.

Appendix 1
Glossary of LGBTQ+ Terms

Compiled by Vic Spencer (they/them) and Jordan Sanderson (he/him)
Purdue University Fort Wayne Q Center
(https://www.pfw.edu/q-center/)

Ace: Short for "asexual"; slang for an asexual person
AFAB: Assigned female at birth
Agender: A person who does not have or does not identify with a gender
Allosexual: A person who is not on the asexual spectrum
Ally: Someone who is not LGBTQIA+ but who actively confronts heterosexism, anti-LGBTQIA+ bias, and heterosexual and cisgender privilege in themselves and others
AMAB: Assigned male at birth
Androgyne: A person who identifies as neither man nor woman. Some, but not all, androgyne people may present in a gender neutral or androgynous way.
Androgynous: The combination of masculine and feminine characteristics into an "ambiguous" form
Aro: Short for "aromantic"; slang for an aromantic person
Aromantic: A person who experiences little or no romantic attraction to others; generally conceptualized as a spectrum
Asexual: A person who experiences little or no sexual attraction; generally conceptualized as a spectrum

Assigned at birth: Refers to the gender ascribed to an individual based on their external sex characteristics at birth; recognizes that gender is socially constructed and externally imposed; can be considered problematic by some trans people as it centers a gender identity that was forced upon them rather than the gender with which they identify

Bicurious: A person who is otherwise attracted to only one gender but who expresses curiosity about or interest in experiencing attraction to or sexual/romantic contact with someone of a gender they are not otherwise attracted to

Bi-erasure: The tendency to ignore, remove, or explain away evidence of bisexuality and the experiences of bisexual people in history, academia, news, and popular media; at its extreme, denies the existence of bisexuality and/or frames bisexuality as a phase, indecision, or hypersexuality

Bigender: A person whose gender identity is a combination of or alternates between two genders

Binding: The practice of compressing the breast tissue to create a more masculine silhouette

Biphobia: Bias and discrimination against bisexual people

Bisexual: A person who experiences attraction to people of their own gender as well as other genders, not necessarily at the same time, to the same degree, or in the same way

Boi: Slang for an AFAB person who expresses or presents themselves in a culturally/stereotypically masculine/boyish way

Bottom surgery: Surgery on the genitals designed to create a body that is in harmony with a person's gender identity

Butch: Slang for a person who identifies and/or presents themselves in a masculine way; may be used as a derogatory term for lesbians but may also be claimed as an affirmative identity label

Cisgender: A person whose gender identity aligns with the gender they were assigned at birth based on their external sex characteristics

CisHet: Slang for a non-LGBTQ+ person

Cisnormativity: The assumption by individuals and social institutions that everyone is cisgender and that cisgender people's identities and experiences are more normal, valid, and worthy of respect than trans people's identities and experiences

Cissexism: A pervasive and institutionalized system of beliefs, policies, and norms that "others" trans people by treating their needs, identities, and experiences as less important than those of cis people

Closeted/"in the closet": An LGBTQ+ person who is not "out"

Coming Out: The process of accepting and sharing one's own sexual orientation and/or gender identity. Coming out is a personal and lifelong process that looks different for each individual

Cross-dressing: Wearing clothing that conflicts with the traditional gender expression of one's own gender identity (e.g., a man wearing a dress) for any one of many reasons, including fun, relaxation, as an art form (as in drag), and/or sexual gratification

Drag: The artistic performance of one or multiple genders; "drag queen" refers to people who perform femininity, while "drag king" refers to those who perform masculinity

Dyke: A derogatory term for (often masculine) lesbians; sometimes reclaimed by lesbians as an affirmative identifier, but should never be used by non-lesbians to refer to lesbians

Fag/faggot: A derogatory term for gay and/or effeminate men or any individual who does not conform to their assigned gender; sometimes reclaimed by gay men as an affirmative identifier, but should never be used by non-gay men to refer to gay men

Femme: Slang for a person who identifies and/or presents themselves in a feminine way, specifically through a queer and/or politically radical or subversive context

Friend of Dorothy: An older slang term for homosexual men

FTM: "Female to male"; refers to transgender men and can be considered a problematic term by many trans people who do not wish to be defined by the gender they were assigned at birth

Gay: A term generally used to refer to men who are exclusively or primarily attracted to other men; may also be used as an umbrella term for anyone who experiences same-gender attraction and/or engages in same-gender sexual activity

Gay panic/trans panic defense: A legal strategy used in cases of assault or murder against gay and trans people, overwhelmingly by cisgender/heterosexual men, in which the defendant may claim self-defense, diminished capacity, and/or temporary insanity brought on by same-sex sexual advances or discovery that a current/potential sexual partner was trans; still allowed in thirty-five states

Gender: A complex system of roles, expressions, expectations, identities, performances, and perceptions that are ascribed to social categories assigned to individuals based on their external sex characteristics at birth; it is socially constructed and therefore the definitions and expected embodiments of gender identities vary between cultures

Gender attribution: The act of categorizing people as male, female, or other based on behavior and/or appearance

Gender binary: The idea that there are only two genders—male and female/man and woman—and that individuals must be one or the other

Gender dysphoria: Distress or discomfort caused by an incongruence between a person's gender identity and the gender they were assigned at birth

Gender essentialism: A belief that gender is fixed and binary and that men and women have distinct and immutable traits which are biologically determined (e.g., that women are naturally more nurturing or that men are naturally stronger)

Gender expression: How a person expresses/presents their gender to the world through their dress, mannerisms, hairstyle, etc.; this may or may not coincide with or be indicative of that person's gender identity

Gender identity: A person's sense of self as a man, woman, a different gender, no gender, multiple genders, etc.

Gender neutral: Nongendered, often in the context of language (e.g., "partner" or "spouse" instead of "boyfriend/girlfriend" or "husband/wife")

Gender nonconforming: A person whose gender expression does not match the expectations ascribed to their gender identity; this is not a synonym for identities under the trans umbrella and may often be used to refer to cisgender people who express/perform their gender in ways that conflict with traditional gender roles and norms

Gender normative: A person whose gender expression does match the expectations ascribed to their gender identity

Gender policing: The imposition and/or enforcement of normative gender expressions on an individual who is perceived as not adequately performing, through appearance or behavior, the gender assigned to them at birth

Gender roles: Behaviors, characteristics, and activities ascribed to a particular gender

Gender variance: Gender expression that does not conform to masculine or feminine gender norms

Gender-affirming: Activities, words, etc., that affirm a person's gender; "gender affirmation" is also generally preferred to "gender confirmation," as it centers the experience of the trans person feeling affirmed in their gender rather than their gender being confirmed for other people

Genderfluid: A nonbinary gender identity that is fluid, constantly changes, and/or switches back and forth. This term may also be used more generally as a way to articulate the changing nature of one's gender identity and/or expression

Genderqueer: A person whose gender is between, beyond, or some combination of genders; used by some individuals as an intentionally political act to challenge the gender binary and gender stereotypes and by others simply to describe a gender identity that otherwise does not fit within the confines of other gender terms; some, but not all, genderqueer people identify as trans

Hermaphrodite: An outdated term referring to people with atypical sex anatomy; considered offensive by many and commonly used as a derogatory term for intersex people

Heteroflexible/homoflexible: A person who is primarily or exclusively attracted to one gender but occasionally experiences and/or is open to attraction to a person of another gender

Heteronormativity: The assumption, by individuals and social institutions, that everyone is heterosexual and that heterosexual people's identities and experiences are more normal, valid, and worthy of respect than those of all other sexual orientations

Heterosexism: A pervasive and institutionalized system of beliefs, policies, and norms that "others" people of minority sexual orientations by treating their needs, experiences, and identities as less important than those of heterosexual people

Heterosexual: A person who is primarily/exclusively attracted to people of a gender other than their own, generally within a binary model of gender (e.g., men who are attracted to women and women who are attracted to men)

Hijra: An officially recognized third gender within the Indian subcontinent, encompassing eunuchs, intersex people, and trans people, and often used to describe a wide variety of culturally specific nonbinary genders

Homosexual: A person who is primarily or exclusively attracted to people of their own gender/sex; considered outdated by many in the LGBTQ+ community but still used within legal and research contexts

Internalized oppression: The process by which a member of an oppressed group comes to accept, believe, and live out negative messages about their identity group

Intersex: A person who is born with reproductive/sexual anatomy and/or chromosomes that do not fit the typical definitions of male or female

Kinsey scale: Also called the Heterosexual-Homosexual Rating Scale; developed by sex researcher Alfred Kinsey as a tool to describe a person's sexual orientation on a scale of 0 (exclusively heterosexual) to 6 (exclusively homosexual) based on their sexual behavior to demonstrate that sexuality does not fit within a strict heterosexual/homosexual binary

Latinx: A gender-neutral alternative to Latino/a

Lesbian: A term used to refer to women who are primarily or exclusively attracted to and/or have sex with other women

LGBTQIA+: Lesbian, gay, bisexual, transgender, queer/questioning, intersex, asexual/aromantic, plus; an umbrella acronym for minority and marginalized sexual orientations and gender identities; some variants will also include "2S" for Two-Spirit

Masc: Short for "masculine"; slang for a person who identifies and/or presents in a masculine fashion

Microlabel: Terms that describe specific variations of gender identities and sexual orientations, generally arising from online communities; often not widely used or accepted within the broader LGBTQIA+ community

Misgender: The act of attributing an incorrect gender to an individual, generally by using the wrong pronouns, gendered honorifics (ma'am/sir), or name

Monosexual: Umbrella term for orientations characterized by attraction to only one gender

MTF: "Male to female"; refers to transgender women and can be considered a problematic term by many trans people who do not wish to be defined by the gender they were assigned at birth

Multisexual: Umbrella term for orientations characterized by attraction to more than one gender

Muxe: A third gender category with the Zapotec culture of Southern Mexico; refers to a person who is assigned male at birth but whose gender identity and expression are not conventionally male

Neutrois: A nonbinary gender identity within the genderqueer umbrella; there is no one definition and each person who identifies with this term experiences their gender differently

Out: A person who is open about their sexual orientation and/or gender identity

Outing: The practice of revealing someone else's sexual orientation and/or gender identity without their consent

Pansexual: A person who is attracted to all genders and/or gender expressions, not necessarily at the same time, to the same degree, or in the same way; sometimes also called "omnisexual"

Passing: A term used by trans people to refer to being read as the gender they identify with and/or cisgender

Polyamory: The practice of being in/open to multiple romantic and/or sexual relationships at the same time (with knowledge and consent of all partners), including open relationships, polyfidelity (which involves multiple romantic relationships with sexual contact restricted within those relationships), and subrelationships (which denote distinguishing between a primary relationship or relationships and various secondary relationships)

Polysexual: A person who is attracted to multiple, but not all, genders, not necessarily at the same time, to the same degree, or in the same way

QPOC/QTBIPOC: Queer person of color/queer, trans, Black, Indigenous, and other people of color

Queer: An alternative term to "LGBTQ," used as an umbrella for anyone who is not heterosexual and/or cisgender; historically used as a slur but has been reclaimed since the 1970s by those who embrace the term's ambiguity, fluidity, and subversive connotations; not a universally accepted term and still considered offensive by some within the community

Questioning: The process of exploration and discovery of one's sexual orientation, gender identity/expression, or some combination thereof; a person who is engaged in this process

Reclaimed language/slurs: Terms that have historically been used as negative and derogatory ways to refer to specific groups of people, but which have been appropriated by those people as affirmative identifiers; terms like "dyke," "fag," and "queer" may be considered reclaimed

Sapphic: Umbrella term for women/women-aligned people who are attracted to other women/women-aligned people

Sexual orientation: Refers to who one is sexually attracted to

Sexuality: The way that people experience and express themselves sexually

Stealth: Slang used to describe a trans person who is not out as trans but is living as the gender with which they identify

Straight: Slang for a heterosexual person

Stud: A term used by people of color, particularly Black Americans, to refer to people (generally women) who are masculine or butch

TERF: Trans-exclusionary radical feminist; adhering to an explicitly transphobic ideology that is characterized by gender essentialism, opposition to trans rights, and the denial of trans identities

Top surgery: Refers to any gender-related surgical procedures performed on a person's chest; most commonly used to refer to mastectomies, but may also refer to breast augmentation

Tranny: Outdated and derogatory slang for a trans person; some trans people have reclaimed this as an affirmative identity, but should never be used by a non-trans person to refer to a trans person

Trans feminine: Refers to a person who was assigned male at birth but whose gender identity is more feminine than masculine

Transgender: A person whose gender identity does not align with the gender they were assigned at birth; frequently shortened to "trans"

Transitioning: The process of changing one's gender presentation from the gender assigned at birth to the gender one identifies with; transitioning looks different for each individual, but may include changing names/pronouns, changing wardrobes/hairstyles, and undergoing hormone therapy and/or gender-affirming surgery

Trans masculine: Refers to a person who was assigned female at birth but whose gender identity is more masculine than feminine

Trans-misogyny: Prejudice against trans women

Transphobia: Aversion toward, hatred and/or fear of, or discomfort with trans and/or gender-diverse people, often expressed as discrimination, hostility, harassment, and/or violence

Transsexual: A person whose gender identity is inconsistent with the gender they were assigned at birth and who desires to permanently transition to the gender with which they identify, often with medical assistance; the term is rejected as outdated by some trans people but is embraced by others who wish to designate that they have changed (or intend to change) their anatomical sex

Transvestite: An outdated term for a person who engages in the act of cross-dressing; also sometimes used as a derogatory term for trans people

Two-Spirit: A modern, pan-Indian umbrella term used by some indigenous North Americans to describe individuals who fulfill a traditional third ceremonial or social gender (or other gender variant) role in their cultures

Womxn/womyn: Alternative political spellings of "women" coined in the 1970s to avoid perceived sexist connotations of the traditional spelling

Appendix 2

Short List of Songs Written for TGQ Singers or by TGQ Composers

Table Appendix 2. Songs Written for TGQ Singers or by TGQ Composers

Composer (Last, First)	Lyricist (Last, First)	Song Title	Notes
Allegretti, Keith	Raker, Cecelia	Breathe	Included in *Anthology of New Music: Trans & Nonbinary Voices, Vol. 1*; from the 2019 opera *Good Country*
Allphin, Penrose	Various: Levy, A.; Bynner, W.; Housman, A. E., and Grimké, A. W.	as if you were an archer	For voice and piano; a set of four songs, including "At a Dinner Party," "At the Touch of You," "He Would Not Stay for Me," and "El Beso"
Allphin, Penrose	Ureña, Morgan	Open-Mouthed Gemini	Included in *Anthology of New Music: Trans & Nonbinary Voices, Vol. 1*; for voice and piano
Allphin, Penrose		strawberries mean nothing	For voice and piano; a set of four songs, including "Fruit," "Jam Jar," "October," and "Taxonomy"
Allphin, Penrose	Dickinson, Emily	the sun just touched the morning	For soprano or tenor and piano

(continued)

Table Appendix 2 *(Continued)*

Composer (Last, First)	Lyricist (Last, First)	Song Title	Notes
Burnette, Adam	Allmers, Hermann	Spätherbst	Included in *Anthology of New Music: Trans & Nonbinary Voices, Vol. 1*
Bussewitz-Quarm, Michael	Safarova, Lamiya	Lamiya's Song	For unison chorus (or solo voice), flute, and piano
Candey, Griffin	Pennington-Flax, Anastasia	Foxes	Included in *Anthology of New Music: Trans & Nonbinary Voices, Vol. 1*
Cohen, Nell Shaw	Deen, Mashuq Mushtaq	Fallen Start	Included in *Anthology of New Music: Trans & Nonbinary Voices, Vol. 1*
Crean, Rosśa	Lowell, Amy	Solitaire	Included in *Anthology of New Music: Trans & Nonbinary Voices, Vol. 1*
Gleave, Ryan	Elliot, Rufus Isabel	stranger, morning	For voice and piano or orchestra
Gleave, Ryan	Foster, Elizabeth	Walrus	Included in *Anthology of New Music: Trans & Nonbinary Voices, Vol. 1*
Gleave, Ryan	Foster, Elizabeth	Windows	For high, medium, or low voice and piano
Grant, Grey	Grant, Grey	Let's Gather the Dandelions in the Field and Wait for the Spring to Appear	For soprano and saxophone quartet
Grant, Grey	Grant, Grey	Prelude	Included in *Anthology of New Music: Trans & Nonbinary Voices, Vol. 1*; from *Michigan Trees: A Guide to the Trees of Michigan and the Great Lakes Region*
Grant, Grey	Grant, Grey	Short Songs to be Sung Aloud	For mezzo-soprano and piano

Short List of Songs Written for TGQ Singers or by TGQ Composers

Composer (Last, First)	Lyricist (Last, First)	Song Title	Notes
Hurley, Leo	Osborne, Charles	Chapel Hill Gets Lonely	Included in *Anthology of New Music: Trans & Nonbinary Voices, Vol. 1*; from the 2016 opera "The Body Politic" about a trans Muslim man
Kaufman, Dana	Swift, Tom	To my mother's closet	Included in *Anthology of New Music: Trans & Nonbinary Voices, Vol. 1*; Caitlyn's aria from *Cycle Kardashian*
Li, Melissa	Li, Melissa, and Yan, Kit	Loser Dumplings	Included in *Anthology of New Music: Trans & Nonbinary Voices, Vol. 1*; from the musical *Interstate*, an Asian-American pop-rock musical
Manfredonia, Tony	Feltkamp, Aiden K.	Your Heart	Included in *Anthology of New Music: Trans & Nonbinary Voices, Vol. 1*
Ressler, Pax	Ressler, Pax	Love Song for Me	Included in *Anthology of New Music: Trans & Nonbinary Voices, Vol. 1*
Salmonson, Hope	Levy, Amy	A Game of Lawn Tennis	For mezzo-soprano and piano; third song in the cycle *Three Amy Levy Songs*
Salmonson, Hope	Levy, Amy	At a Dinner Party	Included in *Anthology of New Music: Trans & Nonbinary Voices, Vol. 1*; for mezzo-soprano and piano; first song in the cycle *Three Amy Levy Songs*
Salmonson, Hope	Levy, Amy	In the Nower	For mezzo-soprano and piano; second song in the cycle *Three Amy Levy Songs*
Salmonson, Hope	Bige, Tawahum	Juniper Sky	For soprano and piano
Schankler, Isaac	Schankler, Isaac	Mouthfeel	For bass voice and electronics

(continued)

Table Appendix 2 (Continued)

Composer (Last, First)	Lyricist (Last, First)	Song Title	Notes
Schankler, Isaac	Burcar, Jillian	With Such Teeth	Included in Anthology of New Music: Trans & Nonbinary Voices, Vol. 1; for soprano and chamber ensemble; from the song cycle Sharp
Seward, Ashley	Millay, Edna St. Vincent	Let the Little Birds Sing	Included in Anthology of New Music: Trans & Nonbinary Voices, Vol. 1
solomon, brin	solomon, brin	And Still the Last Abandoned Angel Sings (Hallel)	Included in Anthology of New Music: Trans & Nonbinary Voices, Vol. 1; for mezzo-soprano
solomon, brin	Based on a recipe of the composer's mother	Instructions for Making Bread	For alto or tenor
solomon, brin	O'Neill, Chase	Sphere	For voice (any type) and prerecorded electronics
Valverde, Mari Esabel	Shakespeare, William	After Sunset	For high voice and piano
Valverde, Mari Esabel	Traditional/folk	Canciones del pasado	For high voice, piano, and optional flute, violin, and cello; a set of seven songs
Valverde, Mari Esabel	Paz, Octavio	Cuatro poemas de Octavio Paz	For high voice and piano; four song set
Valverde, Mari Esabel	Browning, Elizabeth Barrett	How Do I Love Thee?	For high voice and piano
Valverde, Mari Esabel	Shakespeare, William	Love Alters Not	For high voice and piano
Valverde, Mari Esabel	Valverde, Mari Esabel	Poet's Entreaty	For high voice, a cappella
Valverde, Mari Esabel	Rakovan, Jacob	The Lady and the Tiger	For high voice, bass clarinet, and piano

Short List of Songs Written for TGQ Singers or by TGQ Composers

Composer (Last, First)	Lyricist (Last, First)	Song Title	Notes
Valverde, Mari Esabel	Dickinson, Emily	The Soul Selects Her Own Society	For low voice and piano
Valverde, Mari Esabel	Shakespeare, William	Then of Thy Beauty	For high voice and piano
Valverde, Mari Esabel	Ditlevsen, Tove	To digte af Tove Ditlevsen	For high voice and piano
Wadsworth, Mickie	Bills, Zachary	556Hz	For tenor and piano
Wadsworth, Mickie	Rebrec, Angela	Lake Song	Included in *Anthology of New Music: Trans & Nonbinary Voices, Vol. 1*; For contralto and piano
Weinberg, Yoshi	Henley, William Ernest	Captain of My Soul	For baritone and piano
Weinberg, Yoshi	Bogert, Brennan LW	Kiwi Herring	For soprano and piano
Weinberg, Yoshi	Bukowski, Charles, and Shakespeare, William	Out of the Sickroom	For mezzo-soprano and piano; a song cycle of four movements
Weinberg, Yoshi	Eliot, T. S.	The Waste Land: Part 1	For mezzo-soprano and guitar; three song cycle
White, LJ	Choi, Franny	Shuffled 'Notes from "A Guide to Drag Kinging"'	For soprano and bassoon
White, LJ	Meitner, Erika	Labor Day	For mezzo-soprano and piano
Yee, Thomas	Feltcamp, Aiden K.	The Smoke Curls into the Sky	Included in *Anthology of New Music: Trans & Nonbinary Voices, Vol. 1*; from *Eva and the Angel of Death*

Website Sources and Additional Selections

- *Anthology of New Music: Trans & Nonbinary Voices, Vol. 1:* https://newmusicshelf.com/product/trans-nonbinary-v1/
- Keith Allegretti: http://www.keithallegretti.com/
- Penrose Allphin: https://www.penrosesmusic.com/
- Michael Bussewitz-Quarm: https://www.mbqstudio.com/
- Griffin Candey: https://www.griffincandey.com/
- Nell Shaw Cohen: https://www.nellshawcohen.com/
- Rosśa Crean: https://rossacrean.com/
- Ryan Gleave: https://www.rylangleave.com/
- Grey Grant: https://www.greygrant.com/
- Leo Hurley: http://www.hurleyandosborne.com/
- Dana Kaufman: http://www.danakaufmanmusic.com/
- Melissa Li: https://www.melissali.com/
- Tony Manfredonia: https://www.manfredoniamusic.com/
- Aiden K. Feltcamp: https://www.aidenkimfeltkamp.com/
- Pax Ressler: https://paxressler.com/
- Hope Salmonson: https://www.hopeariamusic.com/
- Isaac Schankler: https://isaacschankler.com/
- brin solomon: http://www.brinsolomon.com/
- Mari Esabel Valverde: https://marivalverde.com/
- Mickie Wadsworth: https://mickiewadsworth.weebly.com/
- Yoshi Weinberg: https://yoshiweinberg.com/
- LJ White: https://www.ljwhitemusic.com/
- Thomas Yee: http://www.thomasbyee.com/

Appendix 3

Musicals and Opera Featuring Gender-Expansive Characters

& Juliet
Music and Lyrics by Max Martin
Book by David West Read
In a reimagining of Shakespeare's *Romeo and Juliet* where Juliet does not die, this pop music musical features a nonbinary character as Juliet's best friend. For more: https://www.andjuliethemusical.co.uk/

A Strange Loop
Music, Lyrics, and Book by Michael R. Jackson
This contemporary musical tells the story of Usher, who is black and queer, struggling to find themselves as a musical theatre composer and playwright. For more: https://www.playwrightshorizons.org/shows/plays/strange-loop/

As One
Music by Laura Kaminsky
Libretto by Mark Campbell and Kimberly Reed
This opera tells the story of Hannah, a trans woman. Written for two voices—a mezzo-soprano and baritone—this opera was not for a trans singer, but the show has received more than fifty productions since its premiere in 2014, according to the American

Opera Project website. For more: https://www.aopopera.org/asone

The Civility of Albert Cashier
Music by Joe Stevens and Keaton Wooden
Lyrics by Joe Stevens, Keaton Wooden, and Jay Paul Deratany
Book by Jay Paul Deratany
This musical tells the story of a trans Civil War soldier through folk- and country-inspired music. For more: https://www.albertcashierthemusical.com/

Everybody's Talking about Jamie
Music by Dan Gillespie Sells
Book and Lyrics by Tom MacRae
This pop music score shares the story of a teenager overcoming bullying to become a drag queen. For more: https://www.everybodystalkingaboutjamie.co.uk/

Head over Heels
Music and Lyrics by the Go-Go's
Book by Jeff Whitty, adapted by James Magruder
A jukebox musical of songs by the pop group the Go-Go's, this Broadway show features the nonbinary role of Pythio, an oracle. For more: https://broadwaylicensing.com/shows/broadway/head-over-heels/#casting

Interstate: A New Musical
Music by Melissa Li
Lyrics and Book by Melissa Li and Kit Yan
This pop-rock musical tells the story of Dash, a trans spoken word performer, and their best friend, a lesbian singer-songwriter. The musical also features the role of Henry, a trans teenager, who is struggling with his identity and family belonging. For more: http://www.interstatemusical.com/

Musicals and Opera Featuring Gender-Expansive Characters

Jagged Little Pill
Music by Alanis Morissette, Glen Ballard, Michael Farrell, and Guy Sigworth
Lyrics by Alanis Morissette
Book by Diablo Cody
Despite some offstage and onstage controversy regarding the gender of the character Jo (who may or may not be nonbinary), singers might be interested in this musical for its score and story. For more: https://jaggedlittlepill.com/

Kinky Boots
Music and Lyrics: Cyndi Lauper
Book by Harvey Fierstein
Lola, the show's protagonist, is a drag queen created on Broadway by Billy Porter. While this role was not specifically written for a TGQ performer, a student might enjoy the musical score and the message of the show. For more: https://kinkybootsthemusical.com/

La Cage aux Folles
Music and Lyrics by Jerry Herman
Book by Harvey Fierstein
A groundbreaking LGTBQ musical from the 1980s, this story follows Zaza/Albin, a drag queen. While Zaza was not written for a TGQ performer, students might appreciate the shows message of identity and belonging. For more: https://www.concordtheatricals.com/

Priscilla, Queen of the Desert
Music and Lyrics by various artists
Book by Stephan Elliott and Allan Scott
Based on the movie of the same name, this musical tells the story of two drag queens and a trans character traversing the Australian outback, seeking self-acceptance and acceptance of family. These characters were not written specifically for TGQ performers, but students might find the popular music score and narrative affirming. For more: https://www.theatricalrights.com/

The Red Shades
Music by Adrienne Price, Matt Grandy, and Jeanine Adkisson
Libretto by Adrienne Price
This rock-musical theater opera tells the story of a young trans woman, Ida, who runs away from her home to join a group of trans superheroes in San Francisco. For more: http://www.zspace.org/redshades

Rent
Music, Lyrics, and Book by Jonathan Larson
This popular rock musical, a modern retelling of Puccini's *La Bohème*, features the role of Angel Schunard, a drag queen. Though his role was not written specifically for a TGQ performer, it has been performed by trans and genderqueer performers. For more: https://www.mtishows.com/rent

Southern Comfort
Music by Julianna Wick Davis
Book and Lyrics by Dan Collins
This folk and bluegrass musical tells the story of a group of trans friends living in Georgia. For more: https://www.concordtheatricals.com/

Musicals in development:

1. *Bad Queers: The Musical*, music, lyrics, and book by Ariel Hope Stump
2. *Brother*, music and lyrics by Robin Simões da Silva; book by Annabel Mutale Reed
3. *The Danish Girl*, music by Alex Parker; lyrics and book by Katie Lam
4. *Paper or Plastic*, music and lyrics by Joe Stevens and Keaton Wood; book by Hazel Jade and Jeff Brown
5. *The Phase*, music by Meg McGrady; lyrics and book by Zoe Morris
6. *Shapeshifters*, music, lyrics, and book by Truth Bachman
7. *Soft Butter*, music, lyrics, and book by É Boylan

Musicals and Opera Featuring Gender-Expansive Characters / 257

8. *Steep Themselves in Night*, music, lyrics, and book by Jude Taylor
9. *Stu for Silverton*, music and lyrics by Breedlove; book by Peter Duchan
10. *Tainted: A Musical*, music and lyrics by Marc Almond and Soft Cell; book by Michael McManus and Charlie Ross McKenzie
11. *Unicorn*, music, lyrics, and book by AJ O'Neill and Simon Lock
12. *Wonder Boy*, music, lyrics, and book by Jaime Jarrett

Please note: Roles like Peter Pan (from *Peter Pan*) or Edna Turnblad (from *Hairspray*) have not been included in this list. While they might demonstrate gender-bending casting, these characters are not expressly designed to represent a gender-expansive identity or the wider LGBTQ+ community. Roles that are typically played by a person of the opposite gender for comedic impact, like Mary Sunshine from *Chicago*, have not been included even though a TGQ performer might find such a role affirming. In all cases, a teacher should allow students to choose repertoire and roles that they want to sing. For more and updated information, see: https://www.queermusicals.com/.

Appendix 4

Gender-Neutral Performance Attire Guidelines

Decisions about performance attire should be made based on the manner, formality, and location of the concert and repertoire. The guidelines provided here are not designed to stifle fashion creativity or gender expression. Singers might consider that performance attire should enhance the vocal performance.

For Formal Performances

What to Wear
1. Do wear something comfortable, yet formal/dressy.
2. Do wear clothes that cover most of your body.
3. Do wear tights/leggings/hosiery if a skirt or dress does not extend to the ankle.
4. Do wear sleeves that are at least three-quarters length or to the wrist if wearing a blouse/shirt.
5. Do wear dress shoes that are comfortable for performance.
6. Do wear a belt or suspenders if wearing a suit or pants.

What Not to Wear

1. Don't wear something very low-cut or transparent.
2. Don't wear informal attire such as jeans, leggings, yoga pants, or tennis shoes.
3. Don't wear colors or materials that you think distract from your performance.
4. Don't wear heavy makeup or jewelry that you think distract from your performance.
5. Don't wear skirts shorter than knee-length.
6. Don't wear heavy materials that don't breathe under stage lights.

In Other Words . . .

1. A dress or gown is okay.
2. A skirt and a shirt/blouse are okay.
3. Trousers and a shirt/blouse are okay.
4. A suit and a shirt/blouse are okay.
5. A tuxedo and a shirt/blouse are okay.

For Informal Performances

Wear whatever makes you feel comfortable! The above guidelines might be useful.

Appendix 5

Sample Affirmation Policy Statement for Studio Teachers and Choral Directors

The [*Name of Studio or Ensemble*] is committed to ensuring the safety and well-being of all students and prohibits the discrimination and harassment of any person on the basis of race, religion, color, sex, age, national origin or ancestry, genetic information, marital status, parental status, sexual orientation, gender identity and expression, disability, or status as a veteran. The [*Name of Studio or Ensemble*] recognizes the important of gender inclusion and affirmation; any student who begins or completes transitioning while a student of this studio/choir will be treated with the utmost care and respect. The [*Name of Studio or Ensemble*] will work to ensure that all singers are valued and appreciated for their musical pursuits and interests. Any person associated with this studio/ensemble is expected to uphold this policy statement and maintain respect, gratitude, and kindness to all.

For more information on federal and state policies for the protection of LGBTQ+ students and educators, see: https://www.glsen.org/policy

Appendix 5

Sample Affirmation Policy Statement for Studio Teachers and Choral Directors

Appendix 6
Additional Resources

Compiled by Vic Spencer (they/them) and Jordan Sanderson (he/him)
Purdue University Fort Wayne Q Center
(https://www.pfw.edu/q-center/)

Asian & Pacific Islander Family Pride: Focused on ending stigma and isolation of LGBTQ+ family members in the AAPI community, https://apifamilypride.org/
Black Trans Advocacy Coalition: Advocacy organization working to address issues faced by black trans people, https://blacktrans.org/
Black Transmen Inc.: Empowerment and support for black trans men, https://blacktransmen.org/
Black Transwomen, Inc.: Nonprofit focused on advocacy and resources for Black trans women, https://blacktranswomen.org/
Brown Boi Project: Community of masculine of center womyn, men, Two-Spirit people, transmen and allies committed to changing the way that communities of color talk about gender, https://www.brownboiproject.org/
Digital Transgender Archives: An expansive archive of trans histories, https://www.digitaltransgenderarchive.net/
Equity Literacy Project: Provides free and lost-cost resources and training for educators working to combat inequity in education, https://www.equityliteracy.org/

gc2b: Trans-owned gender-affirming apparel company that specializes in making binders, https://www.gc2b.co/

Gender Nexus: Connections and resources for gender-diverse people, https://gendernexus.org/

Gender Spectrum: Resources for educators, parents, faith leaders, medical and mental health professionals, etc., about gender and gender inclusivity, https://www.genderspectrum.org/

GLSEN: National network of students, educators, and local chapters working to ensure safe, supportive, and LGBTQ-inclusive K–12 education; provides training and resources for educators, as well as curriculum and policy recommendations, https://www.glsen.org/

Human Rights Campaign: Fighting for LGBTQ+ equality and inclusion since 1980, https://www.hrc.org/resources/transgender

Kaleidoscope: Affirming support for LGBTQ+ young people and their families, https://www.kaleidoscopelgbtq.org/

Learning for Justice: Founded by the Southern Poverty Law Center, Learning for Justice provides free resources to K–12 educators around issues of racial justice, intersectionality, and human rights, https://www.learningforjustice.org/

Marsha P. Johnson Institute: Advocacy and community organizing group for Black trans people, https://marshap.org/

Matthew's Place: Resources, education, and stories for LGBTQ+ youth, https://medium.com/matthews-place

My Kid Is Gay: Education and resources for families of LGBTQ+ youth, https://www.mykidisgay.com/

National Center for Transgender Equality: Advocacy and support for trans people, https://transequality.org/

Paying for Gender Confirming Surgery: Developed by MoneyGeek with information to help trans people financially plan their gender confirmation surgery, https://www.moneygeek.com/financial-planning/paying-for-gender-confirmation-surgery/

PFLAG: Support, education, and advocacy for LGBTQ+ people, their parents, families, and allies, https://pflag.org/

Project THRIVE: Free webinars for educators supporting LGBTQ+ youth, https://www.hrc.org/resources/project-thrive-webinars

Safe Schools Coalition: Public-private partnership providing resources, curriculum guides, and more for educators supporting LGBTQ+ youth, http://www.safeschoolscoalition.org/

Transgender Legal Defense & Education Fund: Committed to ending discrimination based upon gender identity and expression and to achieving equality for transgender people through public education, test-case litigation, direct legal services, and public policy efforts, https://www.transgenderlegal.org/

Trans Student Educational Resources: Trans resources and provide support for creating change in your school and beyond, https://transstudent.org/

Transgender Teen Survival Guide: A blog for people of all ages who have questions concerning their gender identity, https://transgenderteensurvivalguide.com/

Transgender Visibility Guide: Coming out guide for trans people, http://assets2.hrc.org/files/assets/resources/trans_guide_april_2014.pdf

The Latinx Roundtable: Dedicated to promoting understanding, acceptance and affirmation of Latinx LGBTQ+ persons and their families by transforming Latinx faith communities and the wider Latinx community, https://fefamiliaigualdad.org/

TREES: Mobile education organization doing transgender education and resource building in small towns and rural communities, http://www.webetrees.org/

Susan's Place: Trans resources including general information, transition resources, and more, https://www.susans.org/wiki/Main_Page

University of California, San Francisco Transgender Care: Medical information on hormone therapy, transitioning, gender-affirming surgery, and more, https://transcare.ucsf.edu/

Selected Bibliography

Abramo, Joseph Michael. "Queering Informal Pedagogy: Sexuality and Popular Music in School." *Music Education Research* 13, no. 4 (2011): 465–77. https://doi.org/10.1080/14613808.2011.632084

Agha, Ari. "Making Your Chorus Welcoming for Transgender Singers." *Voice* 41, no. 2 (2017): 18–23.

Aguirre, Ryan. "Finding the Trans Voice: A Review of the Literature on Accommodating Transgender Singers." *Update: Applications of Research in Music Education* 37, no. 1 (2018): 36–41. https://doi.org/10.1177/8755123318772561

Airton, Liz. "Untangling 'Gender Diversity': Genderism and Its Discontents (i.e., Everyone)." In *Diversity and Multiculturalism: A Reader*, edited by Shirley R. Steinberg, 223–45. New York: Peter Lang, 2009.

Anderson, Jennifer A. "Pitch Elevation in Transgendered Patients: Anterior Glottic Web Formation Assisted by Temporary Injection Augmentation." *Journal of Voice* 28, no. 6 (2014): 816–21. https://doi.org/10.1016/j.jvoice.2014.05.002

Andrews, Moya L. *Voice Therapy for Children: The Elementary School Years*. London: Longman, 1986.

Bain, Candice, and Maevon Gumble. "Querying Dialogues: A Performative Editorial on Queering Music Therapy." *Voices: A World Forum for Music Therapy* 19, no. 3 (2019). https://doi.org/10.15845/voices.v19i3.2904

Balén Julia. *A Queerly Joyful Noise: Choral Musicking for Social Justice*. New Brunswick, NJ: Rutgers University Press, 2017.

Bandura, Albert. "Self-Efficacy Mechanism in Human Agency." *American Psychologist* 37, no. 2 (1982): 122–47. https://doi.org/10.1037/0003-066x.37.2.122

Bartolome, Sarah J., and Melanie E. Stapleton. "'Can't I Sing with the Girls?': A Transgender Music Educator's Journey." In *Marginalized Voices in Music Education*, edited by Brent C. Talbot, 114–36. New York: Routledge, 2018.

Beemyn, Genny, and Susan R. Rankin. *The Lives of Transgender People*. New York: Columbia University Press, 2011.

Beemyn, Genny, Billy Curtis, Masen Davis, and Nancy Jean Tubbs. "Transgender Issues on College Campuses." In *Gender Identity and Sexual Orientation: Research, Policy, and Personal Perspectives*, edited by Ronni L. Sanlo, 49–60. San Francisco: Jossey-Bass, 2005.

Bos, Nancy. "Forging a New Path: Transgender Singers in Popular Music." *Journal of Singing* 73, no. 4 (2017): 421–24.

Bradway, Tyler, and Ellen L. McCallum. "Introduction: Thinking Sideways, or an Untoward Genealogy of Queer Reading." In *After Queer Studies: Literature, Theory and Sexuality in the 21st Century*, edited by Tyler Bradway and Ellen L. McCallum, 1–17. Cambridge, UK: Cambridge University Press, 2019.

Bralley, Ralph C., Glen L. Bull, Cheryl Harris Gore, and Milton T. Edgerton. "Evaluation of Vocal Pitch in Male Transsexuals." *Journal of Communication Disorders* 11, no. 5 (1978): 443–49. https://doi.org/10.1016/0021-9924(78)90037-0

Brett, Philip, Elizabeth Wood, and Gary C. Thomas. *Queering the Pitch: The New Gay and Lesbian Musicology*. New York: Routledge, Taylor and Francis Group, 2011.

Brickell, Chris. "Performativity or Performance? Clarifications in the Sociology of Gender." *New Zealand Sociology* 18, no. 2 (2003): 158–78.

Brill, Stephanie, and Rachel Pepper. *The Transgender Child: A Handbook for Families and Professionals*. Hoboken, NJ: Cleis Press, 2008.

Brown, Christine A. "A Humane Approach to the Studio." In *Humane Music Education for the Common Good*, edited by Iris M. Yob and Estelle R. Jorgensen, 94–106. Bloomington: Indiana University Press, 2020.

Browne, Kath, and Catherine J. Nash. "Queer Methods and Methodologies: An Introduction." In *Queer Methods and Methodologies: Intersecting Queer Theories and Social Science Research*, edited by Kath Browne and Catherine J. Nash, 1–23. London: Taylor and Francis, 2016.

Burdge, Barb J. "Bending Gender, Ending Gender: Theoretical Foundations for Social Work Practice with the Transgender Community." *Social Work* 52, no. 3 (2007): 243–50. https://doi.org/10.1093/sw/52.3.243

Butler, Judith. *Bodies That Matter: On the Discursive Limits of "Sex."* London: Routledge, 1993.

———. *Gender Trouble: Feminism and the Subversion of Identity*. 2nd ed. New York: Routledge, 1999.

———. *Undoing Gender*. Boca Raton, FL: Routledge, Taylor and Francis Group, 2004.

Carew, Lisa, Georgia Dacakis, and Jennifer Oates. "The Effectiveness of Oral Resonance Therapy on the Perception of Femininity of Voice in Male-to-Female Transsexuals." *Journal of Voice* 21, no. 5 (2007): 591–603. https://doi.org/10.1016/j.jvoice.2006.05.005

Carter, Kelly A. "Transgenderism and College Students: Issues of Gender Identity and Its Role on Our Campuses." In *Toward Acceptance: Sexual Orientation Issues on Campus*, edited by Vernon A. Wall and Nancy J. Evans, 261–82. Lanham, MD: University Press of America, 2000.

Catalano, D. Chase. "'Trans Enough?' The Pressures Trans Men Negotiate in Higher Education." *TSQ: Transgender Studies Quarterly* 2, no. 3 (2015): 411–30. https://doi.org/10.1215/23289252-926399

Clemmons, Mary Jo. *Rapport in the Applied Voice Studio*. EdD diss., Teachers College, Columbia University, 2007.

Connell, Raewyn. *Gender: A Short Introduction*. Cambridge, UK: Polity Press, 2002.

Constansis, Alexandros. "The Changing Female-to-Male (FTM) Voice." *Radical Musicology* 3 (2008). http://www.radical-musicology.org.uk/2008/Constansis.htm

Costa, Arthur L., and Bena Kallick. *Activating & Engaging Habits of Mind*. Alexandria, VA: Association for Supervision and Curriculum Development, 2000.

Dacakis, Georgia. "Long-Term Maintenance of Fundamental Frequency Increases in Male-to-Female Transsexuals." *Journal of Voice* 14, no. 4 (2000): 549–56. https://doi.org/10.1016/s0892-1997(00)80010-7

Dacakis, Georgia, Shelagh Davies, Jennifer M. Oates, Jacinta M. Douglas, and Judith R. Johnston. "Development and Preliminary Evaluation of the Transsexual Voice Questionnaire for Male-to-Female Transsexuals." *Journal of Voice* 27, no. 3 (2013): 312–20. https://doi.org/10.1016/j.jvoice.2012.11.005

Davies, Shelagh, and Joshua M. Goldberg. "Clinical Aspects of Transgender Speech Feminization and Masculinization." *International*

Journal of Transgenderism 9, no. 3–4 (2006): 167–96. https://doi.org/10.1300/j485v09n03_08

Dimon, Theodore. *Your Body, Your Voice: The Key to Natural Singing and Speaking*. Berkeley, CA: North Atlantic, 2011.

Doscher, Barbara M. *The Functional Unity of the Singing Voice*. Metuchen, NJ: Scarecrow Press, 1994.

Duke, Robert A., and Amy L. Simmons. "The Nature of Expertise: Narrative Descriptions of 19 Common Elements Observed in the Lesson of Three Renowned Artist-Teachers." *Bulletin of the Council for Research in Music Education* 170 (2006): 7–19.

Elliot, Patricia. *Debates in Transgender, Queer, and Feminist Theory: Contested Sites*. Farnham, UK: Ashgate, 2010.

Feltkamp, Aiden K. *Anthology of New Music: Trans & Nonbinary Voices, Vol. 1*. NewMusicShelf. https://newmusicshelf.com/product/trans-nonbinary-v1/

Garfinkel, Harold. *Studies in Ethnomethodology*. Hoboken, NJ: Prentice Hall, 1967.

Garrett, Matthew L., and Joshua Palkki. *Honoring Trans and Gender-Expansive Students in Music Education*. New York: Oxford University Press, 2021.

Gelfer, Marylou Pausewang, and Bethany Ramsey Van Dong. "A Preliminary Study on the Use of Vocal Function Exercises to Improve Voice in Male-to-Female Transgender Clients." *Journal of Voice* 27, no. 3 (2013): 321–34. https://doi.org/10.1016/j.jvoice.2012.07.008

Gilmore, Stuart I., Angela M. Guidera, Susan L. Hutchins, and Willem van Steenbrugge. "Intra-Subject Variability and the Effect of Speech Task on Vocal Fundamental Frequency of Young Adult Australian Males and Females." *Australian Journal of Human Communication Disorders* 20, no. 2 (1992): 65–73. https://doi.org/10.3109/asl2.1992.20.issue-2.05

Good-Perkins, Emily. "Rethinking Vocal Education as a Means to Encourage Positive Identity Development in Adolescents." In *Humane Music Education for the Common Good*, edited by Iris M. Yob and Estelle R. Jorgensen, 158–71. Bloomington: Indiana University Press, 2020.

Gorton, R. Nick, Jamie Buth, and Dean Spade. *Medical Therapy and Health Maintenance for Transgender Men: A Guide for Health Care Providers*. San Francisco: Lyon-Martin Women's Health Services, 2005.

Gould, Elizabeth. "Companion-Able Species: A Queer Pedagogy for Music Education." *Bulletin of the Council for Research in Music*

Education 197 (2013): 63–75. https://doi.org/10.5406/bulcouresmusedu.197.0063

Gumble, Maevon. "Gender Affirming Voicework: An Introduction for Music Therapy." *Voices: A World Forum for Music Therapy* 19, no. 3 (2019). https://doi.org/10.15845/voices.v19i3.2661

Hackmann, Donald G. "Using Portraiture in Educational Leadership Research." *International Journal of Leadership in Education* 5, no. 1 (2002): 51–60. https://doi.org/10.1080/13603120110057109

Halberstam, Jack. "F2M: The Making of Female Masculinity." In *The Lesbian Postmodern*, edited by Laura L. Doan, 210–28. New York: Columbia University Press, 1994.

Halperin, David M. "The Normalization of Queer Theory." In *Queer Theory and Communication: From Disciplining Queers to Queering the Discipline(s)*, edited by Gust A. Yep, Karen Lovaas, and John P. Elia, 339–43. New York: Harrington Park Press, 2003.

———. *Saint Foucault: Towards a Gay Hagiography*. New York: Oxford University Press, 1995.

Hancock, Adrienne B., Julianne Krissinger, and Kelly Owen. "Voice Perceptions and Quality of Life of Transgender People." *Journal of Voice* 25, no. 5 (2011): 553–58. https://doi.org/10.1016/j.jvoice.2010.07.013

Hancock, Adrienne, Lindsey Colton, and Fiacre Douglas. "Intonation and Gender Perception: Applications for Transgender Speakers." *Journal of Voice* 28, no. 2 (2014): 203–209. https://doi.org/10.1016/j.jvoice.2013.08.009

Hardy, Teresa L., Jana M. Rieger, Kristopher Wells, and Carol A. Boliek. "Associations between Voice and Gestural Characteristics of Transgender Women and Self-Rated Femininity, Satisfaction, and Quality of Life." *American Journal of Speech-Language Pathology* 30, no. 2 (2021): 663–72. https://doi.org/10.1044/2020_ajslp-20-00118

Hearns, Liz Jackson, and Brian Kremer. *The Singing Teacher's Guide to Transgender Voices*. San Diego, CA: Plural, 2018.

Helding, Lynn. *The Musician's Mind: Teaching, Learning, and Performance in the Age of Brain Science*. Lanham, MD: Rowman & Littlefield, 2020.

Hendricks, Karin S. *Compassionate Music Teaching: A Framework for Motivation and Engagement in the 21st Century*. Lanham, MD: Rowman & Littlefield, 2018.

Henry, Declan. *Trans Voices: Becoming Who You Are*. London: Jessica Kingsley, 2017.

Isshiki, Nobuhiko, Tatsuzo Tairo, and Masahiro Tanabe. "Surgical Alteration of the Vocal Pitch." *Journal of Otolaryngology* 12, no. 5 (1983): 335–40.

Jagose, Annamarie. *Queer Theory: An Introduction*. New York: New York University Press, 2010.

Jarman-Ivens, Freya. *Queer Voices: Technologies, Vocalities, and the Musical Flaw*. London: Palgrave Macmillan, 2016.

Kallick, Bena, and Allison Zmuda. *Students at the Center: Personalized Learning with Habits of Mind*. Alexandria, VA: Association for Supervision and Curriculum Development, 2017.

Kalra, M. A. "Voice Therapy with a Transsexual." In *Progress in Sexology: Selected Papers from the Proceedings of the 1976 International Congress of Sexology*, edited by Robert Gemme and Connie Christine Wheeler, 77–84. New York: Plenum Press, 1977.

Kaye, Judith, Melissa A. Bortz, and Seppo K. Tuomi. "Evaluation of the Effectiveness of Voice Therapy with a Male-to-Female Transsexual Subject." *Scandinavian Journal of Logopedics and Phoniatrics* 18, no. 2–3 (1993): 105–109. https://doi.org/10.3109/14015439309101356

Kennell, Richard. "Toward a Theory of Applied Music Instruction." *Quarterly Journal of Music Teaching and Learning* 3, no. 2 (1992): 5–16.

Kim, Hyung-Tae. "Vocal Feminization for Transgender Women: Current Strategies and Patient Perspectives." *International Journal of General Medicine* 13 (2020): 43–52. https://doi.org/10.2147/ijgm.s205102

Kosciw, Joseph G., Emily A. Greytak, Adrian D. Zongrone, Caitlin M. Clark, and Nhan L. Truong. *The 2017 National School Climate Survey*. New York: GLSEN, 2018. https://www.glsen.org/sites/default/files/2019-10/GLSEN-2017-National-School-Climate-Survey-NSCS-Full-Report.pdf

Koza, Julia Eklund. "Listening for Whiteness: Hearing Racial Politics in Undergraduate School Music." *Philosophy of Music Education Review* 16, no. 2 (2008): 145–55. https://doi.org/10.2979/pme.2008.16.2.145

Kozan, Anita. "The Singing Voice." In *Voice and Communication Therapy for the Transgender/Transsexual Client: A Comprehensive Clinical Guide*, edited by Robert K. Adler, Sandy Hirsch, and Michelle Mordaunt. 2nd ed. San Diego, CA: Plural, 2012.

Lawrence-Lightfoot, Sara, and Jessica Hoffmann Davis. *The Art and Science of Portraiture*. San Francisco: Jossey-Bass, 1997.

Lessley, Emerald. *Teaching Transgender Singers*. DMA diss., University of Washington, 2017.

LoVetri, Jeannette L, and Edrie Means Weekly. "Contemporary Commercial Music (CCM) Survey: Who's Teaching What in Nonclassical Music." *Journal of Voice* 17, no. 2 (2003): 207–15. https://doi.org/10.1016/s0892-1997(03)00004-3

Luecke, Julie C. "Working with Transgender Children and Their Classmates in Pre-Adolescence: Just Be Supportive." *Journal of LGBT Youth* 8, no. 2 (2011): 116–56. https://doi.org/10.1080/19361653.2011.544941

Luhmann, Susanne. "Queering/Querying Pedagogy? Or, Pedagogy Is a Pretty Queer Thing." In *Queer Theory in Education*, edited by William F. Pinar. Mahwah, NJ: Erlbaum, 1998.

Mackworth-Young, Lucinda. "Pupil-Centered Learning in Piano Lessons: An Evaluated Action-Research Programme Focusing on the Psychology of the Individual." *Psychology of Music* 18, no. 1 (1990): 73–86. https://doi.org/10.1177/0305735690181006

Manternach, Brian. "Teaching Transgender Singers: Part 2." *Journal of Singing* 74, no. 2 (2017): 209–14.

Manternach, Brian, Michael Chipman, Ruth Rainero, and Caitlin Stave. "Teaching Transgender Singers: Part 1." *Journal of Singing* 74, no. 1 (2017): 83–88.

McCann, Hannah, and Whitney Monaghan. *Queer Theory Now: From Foundations to Futures*. London: Red Globe Press, 2020.

McEvoy, Carin A., and Karen Salvador. "Aligning Culturally Responsive and Trauma-Informed Pedagogies in Elementary General Music." *General Music Today* 34, no. 1 (2020): 21–28. https://doi.org/10.1177/1048371320909806

McKinney, James C. *The Diagnosis & Correction of Vocal Faults: A Manual for Teachers of Singing & for Choir Directors*. Nashville, TN: Genevox Music Group, 1994.

McNeill, Emma J. M., Janet A. Wilson, Susan Clark, and Jayne Deakin. "Perception of Voice in the Transgender Client." *Journal of Voice* 22, no. 6 (2008): 727–33. https://doi.org/10.1016/j.jvoice.2006.12.010

Meizel, Katherine. *Multivocality: Singing on the Borders of Identity*. New York: Oxford University Press, 2020.

Miller, Jane Ramseyer. "Creating Choirs That Welcome Transgender Singers." *Choral Journal* 57, no. 4 (2016): 61–63.

Miller, Richard C. *The Structure of Singing: System and Art in Vocal Technique*. Belmont, CA: Wadsworth Group, 1996.

Nagoshi, Julie L., and Stephan/ie Brzuzy. "Transgender Theory: Embodying Research and Practice." *Affilia: Journal of Women and Social Work* 25, no. 4 (2010): 431–43. https://doi.org/10.1177/0886109910384068

Neumann, Kerstin, and Cornelia Welzel. "The Importance of the Voice in Male-to-Female Transsexualism." *Journal of Voice* 18, no. 1 (2004): 153–67. https://doi.org/10.1016/s0892-1997(03)00084-5

Nichols, Jeananne. "Rie's Story, Ryan's Journey." *Journal of Research in Music Education* 61, no. 3 (2013): 262–79. https://doi.org/10.1177/0022429413498259

O'Toole, Patricia. "I Sing in a Choir but 'I Have No Voice!'" *Visions of Research in Music Education* 6 (2005).

———. "A Missing Chapter from Choral Methods Books: How Choirs Neglect Girls." *Choral Journal* 39, no. 5 (1998): 9–32.

Paechter, Carrie. "Learning Masculinities and Femininities: Power/Knowledge and Legitimate Peripheral Participation." *Women's Studies International Forum* 26, no. 6 (2003): 541–52. https://doi.org/10.1016/j.wsif.2003.09.008

———. "Masculinities and Femininities as Communities of Practice." *Women's Studies International Forum* 26, no. 1 (2003): 69–77. https://doi.org/10.1016/s0277-5395(02)00356-4.

Palkki, Joshua. "Inclusivity in Action: Transgender Students in the Choral Classroom." *Choral Journal* 57, no. 11 (2017): 25–33.

Palkki, Joshua. "'My Voice Speaks for Itself': The Experiences of Three Transgender Students in American Secondary School Choral Programs." *International Journal of Music Education* 38, no. 1 (2019): 126–46. https://doi.org/10.1177/0255761419890946

Palkki, Joshua, and Paul Caldwell. "'We Are Often Invisible': A Survey on Safe Space for LGBTQ Students in Secondary School Choral Programs." *Research Studies in Music Education* 40, no. 1 (2017): 28–49. https://doi.org/10.1177/1321103x17734973

Palkki, Joshua, and William R. Sauerland. "Considering Gender Complexity in Music Teacher Education." *Journal of Music Teacher Education* 28, no. 3 (2018): 72–84. https://doi.org/10.1177/1057083718814582

Papp, Viktoria. *The Female-to-Male Transsexual Voice: Physiology vs. Performance in Production*. PhD diss., Rice University, 2012.

Parkes, Kelly A., and Mathius Wexler. "The Nature of Applied Music Teaching Expertise: Common Elements Observed in the Lessons of Three Applied Teachers." *Bulletin of the Council for Research in Music Education*, no. 193 (2012): 45–62. https://doi.org/10.5406/bulcouresmusedu.193.0045

Payne, Elizabethe, and Melissa Smith. "The Big Freak Out: Educator Fear in Response to the Presence of Transgender Elementary School Students." *Journal of Homosexuality* 61, no. 3 (2014): 399–418. https://doi.org/10.1080/00918369.2013.842430

Penrose, Allpin. "Imagining the Trans Symphony: Integrating Transgender Composer Identity in Music Analysis." Master's thesis, University of Massachusetts, Amherst, 2021.

Rands, Kathleen E. "Considering Transgender People in Education." *Journal of Teacher Education* 60, no. 4 (2009): 419–31. https://doi.org/10.1177/0022487109341475

Rastin, Molly. "The Silenced Voice: Exploring Transgender Issues within Western Choirs." *Canadian Music Educator* 57, no. 4 (2016): 28–32.

Roen, Katrina. "'Either/Or' and 'Both/Eeither': Discursive Tensions in Transgender Politics." *Signs: Journal of Women in Culture and Society* 27, no. 2 (2002): 501–22. https://doi.org/10.1086/495695

———. "Transgender Theory and Embodiment: The Risk of Racial Marginalisation." *Journal of Gender Studies* 10, no. 3 (2001): 253–63. https://doi.org/10.1080/09589230120086467

Roll, Christianne Knauer. *Female Musical Theater Belting in the 21st Century: A Study of the Pedagogy of the Vocal Practice and Performance*. EdD diss., Teachers College, Columbia University, 2014.

Sanchez, Jennifer. "Acoustic and Perceptual Study of Female-to-Male Transgendered Voice." Master's thesis, William Paterson University of New Jersey, 2013.

Sauerland, William R. "Sound Teaching: Trauma-Informed Pedagogy in Choir." *Choral Journal* 62, no. 3 (2021): 32–43.

———. "Trans Singers Matter: Gender Inclusive Considerations for Choirs." *VOICEPrints: Journal of New York Singing Teacher Association* 15, no. 5 (2018): 95–105.

Sears, Colleen Anne Quinn. *Paving Their Own Way: Experiences of Female High School Band Directors*. EdD diss., Teachers College, Columbia University, 2010.

Sell, Karen. *The Disciplines of Vocal Pedagogy: Towards an Holistic Approach*. Burlington, VT: Ashgate, 2005.

Silveira, Jason M., and Sarah C. Goff. "Music Teachers' Attitudes toward Transgender Students and Supportive School Practices." *Journal of Research in Music Education* 64, no. 2 (2016): 138–58. https://doi.org/10.1177/0022429416647048

Sims, Loraine. "Teaching Lucas: A Transgender Student's Vocal Journey from Soprano to Tenor." *Journal of Singing* 73, no. 4 (2017): 376–75.

———. "Teaching Transgender Students." *Journal of Singing* 73, no. 3 (2017): 279–82.

Smith, W. Stephen. *The Naked Voice: A Wholistic Approach to Singing*. Oxford, UK: Oxford University Press, 2017.

Stark, James. *Bel Canto: A History of Vocal Pedagogy*. 2nd ed. Toronto: University of Toronto Press, 2003.

Steinmetz, Katy. "The Transgender Tipping Point: America's Next Civil Rights Frontier." *Time*, June 9, 2014.

Stone, Sandy. "The Empire Strikes Back: A Posttranssexual Manifesto." *Camera Obscura: Feminism, Culture, and Media Studies* 10, no. 2 (1992): 150–76. https://doi.org/10.1215/02705346-10-2_29-150

Stryker, Susan. "My Words to Victor Frankenstein above the Village of Chamounix: Performing Transgender Rage." *GLQ: A Journal of Lesbian and Gay Studies* 1, no. 3 (1994): 237–54. https://doi.org/10.1215/10642684-1-3-237

Sullivan, Nikki. *Critical Introduction to Queer Theory*. New York: New York University Press, 2003.

Talbot, Brent C. *Marginalized Voices in Music Education*. New York: Routledge, 2018.

Titze, Ingo R. *Principles of Voice Production*. Englewood Cliffs, NJ: Prentice Hall, 1994.

Upitis, Rena, Philip C. Abrami, Julia Brook, Karen Boese, and Matthew King. "Characteristics of Independent Music Teachers." *Music Education Research* 19, no. 2 (2016): 169–94. https://doi.org/10.1080/14613808.2016.1204277

Van Borsel, John, Griet De Cuypere, Robert Rubens, and B Destaerke. "Voice Problems in Female-to-Male Transsexuals." *International Journal of Language & Communication Disorders* 35, no. 3 (2000): 427–42. https://doi.org/10.1080/136828200410672

West, Candace, and Don H. Zimmerman. "Doing Gender." *Gender & Society* 1, no. 2 (1987): 125–51.

Yep, Gust A., Karen Lovaas, and John P. Elia. "Introduction: Queering Communication: Starting the Conversation." In *Queer Theory and Communication: From Disciplining Queers to Queering the Discipline(s)*, edited by Gust A. Yep, Karen Lovaas, and John P. Elia, 339–43. New York, NY: Harrington Park Press, 2003.

Zimman, Lal. *Voices in Transition: Testosterone, Transmasculinity, and the Gendered Voice Among Female-to-Male Transgender People*. PhD diss., University of Colorado, 2012.

Index

AFAB, 6
allyship, 212
AMAB, 6

Bandura, Albert, 215–16
Bartolome, Sarah, 20
Beemyn, Jenny, 10–11, 145–46
bel canto singing, 45–46, 173
Bos, Nancy, 28
Butler, Judith, xxi, 7–8

chest binding, 140, 238
cisgender, 4, 8
Clemmons, Mary Jo, 220
compassionate teaching, 47, 218, 230–31
Constansis, Alexandros, 23, 25, 105–6, 205
contemporary commercial music singing, 43, 173–74, 199–200
Cox, Laverne, 15, 59

de Lauretis, Teresa, xvi, 39
Doscher, Barbara, 207–8
Duke, Robert, 43–44, 208, 219

Garrett, Matthew, 70
Gender:
  dysphoria, xx, 11, 22, 84, 112, 148, 155, 189–90, 196, 206, 217, 240
  expression, definition of, 4, 7–9, 22, 240
  identity, definition of, 4, 7, 9, 240
  theory, 6–10
gender-complex education, 19–20, 191
gender-neutral language, 193
genderqueer, definition of, 4, 8, 241
GLSEN, 17–18, 212, 264
Gould, Elizabeth, 41–42, 229

habits of mind, 227–29
Halberstam, Jack, 10
Hearns, Liz Jackson, 29
Helding, Lynn, 230
Henry, Declan, 11, 146
Hershberger, Ionna Georgiadou, 24–25
holistic pedagogy, 47–48, 200–201

hormone replacement therapy,
    4, 8;
  estrogen, 64, 84, 204–5
  hormone blockers, 84, 95, 204
  testosterone, 104–8, 112–13,
    127–28, 132, 134, 141–42, 156
humane music teaching, 45

intersex, 3, 4, 6, 242

Jagose, Annamarie, 39–40
Jarman-Ivens, Freya, xvi, 40–42

Kozan, Anita, 23, 25, 29,
    205–6, 212
Kremer, Brian, 29

Lessley, Emerald, 28–29

Manternach, Brian, 26–29
master-apprentice model, 43,
    219–20
McKinney, James, 42, 60, 63,
    102–3, 207
melodic intonation therapy, 24
Miller, Richard, 63–64, 103

New Voices Bay Area TIGQ
    Chorus, 3
neopronouns, 146–47

onstage gender liminality, 1–2
oral resonance therapy, 68–69
othering, act of, 159, 182, 210, 212
O'Toole, Patricia, 12, 21

Palkki, Joshua, 20–22, 29, 70
Papp, Viktoria, 107–8
Parkes, Kelly, 44, 208, 219–20
performing attire, 126–27, 189–90,
    197–98, 259–60

PFLAG, 215, 264
portraiture analysis, 51–52, 185
professional responsibility,
    209–13

queer:
  definition, of, 39,
  theory, 39–40
queering:
  as a habit of mind, 229, 234
  pedagogy, definition of, 40–42

Rands, Kathleen, 18–19
Rankin, Susan, 10–11, 145–46
Rapport, 46–47, 159, 217–20
repertoire:
  for TGQ singers or by TGQ
    composers, 196–97, 247–57
  selection process, 194–97
resonance, definition of, 24–25
role models, 28, 146, 216

Sanchez, Jennifer, 106–7
scaffolding, 44, 202, 208–9
self-advocacy, 213–17
Sell, Karen, 47–48
semi-occluded vocal tract
    exercises, 69–70, 120–21, 174,
    202–3, 205
sex, definition of, 4, 6
Simmons, Amy, 43–44, 208, 219
Sims, Loraine, 25–26, 29, 194, 211,
    219, 275
socioemotional support, 217–21
source-filter theory, 60
Stapleton, Melanie, 20, 29
Stone, Sandy, 10
student-centered pedagogy, 44,
    71–72, 230
Stryker, Susan, 10
surgical procedures, 8, 65–67

Talbot, Brent, 48, 185
Title IX federal recommendations, 16–17
transgender:
  definition of, 3–5
  self-evaluation questionnaire, 71
  theory, 10–11

vocality, 29
voice:
  classification, 60–62, 192–94
  feminization, 24, 64–65
  identity, 22
  masculinization, 24, 104–8
  registration, 63–64, 102–3, 163, 199–201, 206
  range, 63, 102–3, 147, 201–2

Wexler, Mathius, 44, 208, 219–20

Zellman, Reuben, 3, 10
Zimman, Lal, 108
zone of proximal development, 123, 208

About the Author

William Sauerland (he/him/they/them) is assistant professor of music and director of choral studies at Purdue University Fort Wayne, conducting the choral ensembles, teaching classes in music education, and supervising student teachers. Sauerland was previously a lecturer in voice at San Francisco State University, and the director of choral and vocal studies at Chabot College in Hayward, California. Dr. Sauerland taught choral music at Lick-Wilmerding High School for six years and served as associate music director for the Grammy Award–winning Pacific Boychoir Academy. He also has ten years of experience in directing community choruses, including the Oakland Gay Men's Chorus and the Lesbian/Gay Chorus of San Francisco.

Praised by the *San Francisco Chronicle* for his "limpid tone and astonishing eloquence," Dr. Sauerland is a professional countertenor with recent solo appearances for the American Bach Soloists, Echoing Air, Festival Opera Company, Folger Consort, Musica Angelica Baroque Orchestra, Oakland Symphony Orchestra, and Pacific Chorale. A former member of the Grammy Award–winning vocal ensemble Chanticleer, Dr. Sauerland has sung throughout the world and recorded for Warner Classics.

Dr. Sauerland has presented at national and international conferences for the American Choral Directors Association,

Chorus America, Society for Music Teacher Education, College Music Society, National Association of Teachers of Singing, and the Royal Musical Association. Their scholarly writings appear in the *Journal of Singing, Journal of Music Teacher Education, VOICEPrints* (Journal of the New York Singing Teachers' Association), and book chapters for GIA Publications and Pavane Publishing. Dr. Sauerland received the doctor of education in music and music education from Teachers College, Columbia University. As a Marshall Scholarship recipient, he earned a master of music in advanced vocal performance from the Royal College of Music in London. Raised on a small dairy farm in Ohio, Sauerland received a bachelor of music in music education and vocal performance from Miami University in Oxford, Ohio.

www.ingramcontent.com/pod-product-compliance
Lightning Source LLC
Chambersburg PA
CBHW052152300426
44115CB00011B/1630